PRAISE FOR SURPRISED BY OXFORD

"Following in the footsteps of C.S. Lewis, another Oxonian famously surprised by joy, Weber chronicles her encounters with God and Jesus while studying at Oxford University, in an honest and earnest tale structured around the university's trimester school year. The tale of her coming to Christianity from an intellectual agnosticism is woven with poetry and song lyrics that punctuate and, at times, encapsulate key moments of her study and discovery. The metaphors and allusions don't make the text inaccessibly erudite, but instead illustrate the beauty and struggle of her conversion."

Publisher's Weekly

"Conveying the effects of unbridled inquiry and open mindedness, this memoir of obtaining a degree in literature and much more, also offers a peek inside of what many consider the world's most prestigious university, which Weber portrays as a place both steeped in great traditions yet tolerant of youthful exuberance. One of the best parts of the book is the author's self-deprecating sense of humor that she uses to transcend challenging moments. Brimming with inspiring quotes from literary giants and great artists, this book is a truly endearing work that offers great comfort and delight as it celebrates the Christian faith."

Booklist

"A touching narrative of friendship, love and faith. There, the author was just as often inspired by Keats and the Beatles as she was by the Gospel. Weaving lines of poetry, philosophy and scripture into her narrative, Weber grasps at the meaning of life in the pages of great works of literature and overcomes her own childhood cynicism. The delicately crafted moments when Weber's faith allowed her to think more clearly and walk more gracefully through her life are, much like her romance, worth the wait. Well-written, often poignant and surprisingly relatable."

Kirkus

"Surprised by Oxford *is a sprightly contribution to the genre of spiritual memoirs in the vein of C.S. Lewis's* Surprised by Joy *and Lauren F. Winner's* Girl Meets God. *Carolyn Weber is an unconventional thinker whose engagingly told faith journey will speak to folks who still believe that thoughtful people cannot be Christian.*"

Lyle W. Dorsett, Billy Graham Professor
of Evangelism, Beeson Divinity School

"Carolyn Weber is a formidable intellect and a sought-after college professor, as well as a great wife and mom. But what I love most about her is her heart, which you'll find on every page of this book. Showing us the world through her eyes, she brings readers along on her journey to Oxford, where the unexpected awaited her. This is a journey worth taking, and as our guide, Carolyn is candid, insightful, and charming."

Randy Alcorn,
Author, *Heaven* and *If God is Good*

"Carolyn Weber's memoir reads like a fast-paced novel. I loved the humor, skillful use of language and compelling account of her steps to finding God at Oxford. I was totally captivated from beginning to end. I simply loved everything about this book."

Marilyn Meberg,
Author and Women of Faith speaker

"Carolyn Weber has penned a memoir for the ages; a tale of learning, love, and life. She didn't come to Oxford University to think about God, but in the end she discovered that He was thinking about her, and this reality changed her life. This is a terrific book; compelling, well written, and deeply meaningful."

Dr Jim Belcher,
Pastor and Author, *Deep Church*

"Surprised by Oxford *is a three-dimensional love story about a young woman's romance with Oxford, with a handsome stranger, and (most of all) with a Savior she never wanted or expected to meet. This funny, well-written, heart-warming memoir will give you fresh joy for the love that only the grace of God can bring to life."*

Dr. Philip G. Ryken,
President, Wheaton College

"Vulnerable candor, romantic adventure, spirit and spires, a light so lovely that many students and lovers will be drawn to this journey into life. Into beauty. I found it too intriguing, and too much fun, to put down. It is all gift."

Kelly Monroe Kullberg, Author, *Finding God Beyond Harvard: the Quest for Veritas*

SURPRISED
BY OXFORD

OTHER BOOKS BY
CAROLYN WEBER

Romanticism and Parenting

Metempsychosis in the Early Works and

Short Stories of Mary Shelley

SURPRISED BY OXFORD

A Memoir

CAROLYN WEBER

THOMAS NELSON
Since 1798

NASHVILLE   DALLAS   MEXICO CITY   RIO DE JANEIRO

Published in Nashville, Tennessee, by Thomas Nelson. Thomas Nelson is a registered trademark of Thomas Nelson, Inc.

Thomas Nelson, Inc., titles may be purchased in bulk for educational, business, fund-raising, or sales promotional use. For information, please e-mail SpecialMarkets@ThomasNelson.com.

Unless otherwise noted, Scripture quotations are from the Holy Bible, New International Version®, NIV®. © 1973, 1978, 1984 by Biblica, Inc.™ Used by permission of Zondervan. All rights reserved worldwide. www. zondervan.com

Scripture quotations marked ESV are taken from THE ENGLISH STANDARD VERSION. © 2001 by Crossway Bibles, a division of Good News Publishers.

Page Design by Mark L. Mabry

978-0-8499-2183-4 (Repackage)

Library of Congress Cataloging-in-Publication Data

Weber, Carolyn, 1971-
  Surprised by Oxford : a memoir / Carolyn Weber.
     p. cm.
  Includes bibliographical references (p. 449–456).
  ISBN 978-0-8499-4611-0 (trade paper)
1. Weber, Carolyn, 1971- 2. Christian converts–Biography. 3. Conversion–Christianity–Biography. 4. College students–Religious life. 5. University of Oxford. I. Title.
  BV4935.W39A3 2011
  248.2'46092–dc23
  [B]

2011022126

Printed in the United States of America

12 13 14 15 16 RRD 8 7 6 5 4 3

Kent's

CONTENTS

CHRISTMASTIDE

HILARY TERM

EASTERTIDE

TRINITY TERM

SUMMER SUNRISE

PREFACE

A NOTE ON THE TEXT AND TERMS

The following story is based on events as they actually unfolded during my first year at Oxford University, the oldest surviving university in the English-speaking world. As a result of moral delicacy and pragmatic condensation (an apt phrase, since it conveys the compression and sweat behind selection) required of a memoir, most names have been changed, some features altered, and a few natures, at times, have been collapsed into one. But the re-created conversations, conflicts, crescendos, and conversion are, to the best of my feeble ability, true in spirit.

Oxford's academic year consists of three terms significantly embedded in the Christian liturgical calendar: Michaelmas derives its name from the Feast of St. Michael and All Angels (29 September) and runs from early October to Christmas; Hilary, named for St. Hilary (whose feast day is 13 or 14 January), begins in the New Year and ends just before Palm Sunday; and Trinity, or the name given to the tripartite being of God in Father-Son-Holy

Ghost, picks up after Easter and draws to a close in late June or early July, followed by Examinations. The summer break between the end of Trinity and the start of Michaelmas is referred to as the "Long Vacation," or "Vac." Each "Full Term" is composed of eight weeks, sequentially referred to as "First Week," "Second Week," and so on, during which lectures are given and tutorials are held. The week before term officially starts is called "Noughth Week" (a popular time for orientation events and the like).

Matriculation, from the Latin *matricula*, meaning "a roll," marks the passage of becoming a lifelong member of an Oxford College, and so, by extension, the University. Those who are beginning their studies at Oxford gather in the required *subfusc*, or the black-and-white formal wear donned beneath the academic regalia appropriate to their current academic status and program. Thus arrayed, incoming students proceed, according to college, to the common ceremony at the Sheldonian Theatre, where, in short, they take an age-old oath to respect one another, the institution, and the high calling of learning, along with the promise not to start fires in library holdings. Appropriately extinguished and distinguished, they return to their individual colleges to celebrate.

DOUBT WISELY

Though truth and falsehood be
Near twins, yet truth a little elder is:
Be busy to seek her; believe me this,
He's not of none, nor worst, that seeks the best.
To adore, or scorn an image, or protest,
May all be bad; doubt wisely; in strange way
To stand inquiring right, is not to stray;
To sleep, or run wrong, is.[1]

—JOHN DONNE

As an undergraduate in Canada, I knew of only one "evangelical," although I did not really understand this nomenclature at the time. Categorically this person would have annoyed me, except for the fact that I respected him so much. He was my seventeenth-century poetry professor, an esteemed scholar and pillar of the university. Quite elderly, he could wax on a bit in class while he incessantly shuffled his notes, which were penciled out in longhand. His popular seminars filled to overflowing. Always the perfect gentleman, he dressed in a suit for lectures and in a button-down and cardigan for office hours. I had never heard him say a gruff word, let alone curse before, which is why what he said to me in the hallway after class one day stopped me dead in my tracks.

Typical sycophantic senior, I worked up my nerve to ask him what he thought of my presentation on the metaphysical poet John Donne. No easy task, as my assigned poem was Donne's sonnet XIV:

> Batter my heart, three-personed God; for You
> As yet but knock, breathe, shine, and seek to mend;
> That I may rise and stand, o'erthrow me and bend
> Your force to break, blow, burn and make me new.
> I, like an usurped town, to another due,
> Labor to admit You, but, oh, to no end!
> Reason, Your viceroy in me, me should defend,
> But is captived and proves weak or untrue.
> Yet dearly I love You, and would be loved fain,
> But am betrothed unto Your enemy:
> Divorce me, untie or break that knot again,
> Take me to You, imprison me, for I,
> Except You enthrall me, never shall be free,
> Nor ever chaste, except You ravish me.[2]

I gave what I thought was a brilliant analysis of the domination of rape imagery in the poem. I argued that the poem illustrated a classic subversion by the dominant patriarchy (whether it be the church, the priest, the male construction of God or Savior) of the threat posed by maternal power, or the feminine *spiritus*. I thought myself quite clever, but I wanted to hear his take before the grade was finalized.

Dr. Deveaux paused, looked thoughtful, and then resumed walking. I kept pace beside him, expectant. Without missing a step, he said quietly, "It is an interesting reading of the poem, Miss Drake. And you obviously have command of the language. But you didn't seem to get the point. To really get at the essential grappling. You didn't untie that 'subtle knot which makes us man,' so central to Donne's spiritual pilgrimage."

He quickened his stride: "The truth is in the paradox, Miss Drake. Anything not done in submission to God, anything not done to the glory of God, is doomed to failure, frailty, and futility. This is the unholy trinity we humans fear most. And we should, for we entertain it all the time at the pain and expense of not knowing the real one."

"Huh?" I managed to puff, for Dr. Deveaux was a hard person to keep up with, physically and mentally.

Dr. Deveaux stopped and looked at me hard. He leaned in and whispered, "The rest is all bullshit, Miss Drake. It's as simple as that. Your purpose here in life is to discern the real thing from the bullshit, and then to choose the non-bullshit. Think of the opportunity that God has given you to study as the means by which to attain your own personal bullshit detector. Sometimes that will be particularly difficult, because those who proclaim to know the truth, well intentioned or not, are spewing the most bullshit. But you will know when you have been properly ravished. And then you'll see, then you'll see, how the entire world is eyeball deep in it and that we choose it, and that we choose it every day. But the good news is that, although we struggle with it, there is a way out. Yes, there is a very worthy antidote and option to all the bullshit."

I stood there agape as Dr. Deveaux strode away. I had no idea what he had been talking about, or that he could even talk like *that*. I was not sure if I should be offended or not. Yet something went off far in the back of my mind, or was it my heart? I could not tell, but it sounded like—it *felt* like—the small click of a combination lock.

Gee, I thought. *I'd better go back and reread the poem.*

And then I thought, to my great dismay, *I'm sure I received an F.*

Fortunately, I did not fail the course. I worked extremely hard, harder for Dr. Deveaux than any of my other professors. I received the thrill of that final A. After grades were posted I went to see him. Christmas break was about to start, and I could not get the problem of the "bullshit detector" out of my head. Was it possible that Donne's famous maxim "Doubt wisely" lay back to back with the necessity of "believing wisely" too? Were the two interlocked in that subtle knot that defines our humanity?

I knocked on Dr. Deveaux's door, but there was no answer. I was met by the secretary's dismayed face when I asked when Dr. Deveaux might be in.

"Haven't you heard?" she asked. "Dr. Deveaux passed away just after finals week. He tallied all the grades and then fell asleep in his chair. His wife found him the next morning, poor thing. Cold, pencil in hand. The funeral is next week, if you'd like to attend."

My final memory of Dr. Deveaux was from the last day of our seminar. The class's token joker accidentally spilled his coffee all over Dr. Deveaux's meticulously handwritten notes. A flutter of confusion ensued as the young man, flustered and red faced for once, apologized profusely while several of us sprang forward with Kleenex, sheets of paper, a sock—whatever was at hand. I watched Dr. Deveaux save what was left of his ancient notes without saying a word. We all sat still, too stunned to speak. Suddenly he seemed so much older, so vulnerable. I had not noticed before that his hands shook.

Then he looked up at us, and smiling, said, "No harm done. I always thought my notes too dry for their own good. And with a little faith, nothing is irreparable. Now let's see what our dear man Herbert would have said about that. Please turn next to his poem, 'The Collar.'"

Just before going abroad on my scholarship, I came across an epigram by Alexander Pope, the eighteenth-century English poet famous for his clever wit and urbane satire. Pope engraved the verse on the collar of a dog, which he then gifted the king:

> I am his Highness' Dog at Kew:
> Pray tell me, sir, whose dog are you?

Granted, the dog image is not as elegant or politically correct as some might prefer, but it does effectively beg the question: just who is your master? For we all have one. No individual, by the very state of existence, can avoid life as a form of servitude; it only remains for us to decide, deny, or remain oblivious to, whom or what we serve.

Before I left for Oxford University, the answer was easy. I was my own . . .

SPOTS OF TIME

SUMMER SUNSET

ONE

ALL THAT YOU CAN'T
LEAVE BEHIND

I was not sleeping, you are not waking me.
No, I have been in tears for a long while
And in my restless thought walked many ways.
In all my search, I found one helpful course,
And that I have taken: I have sent Creon
To Delphi, Apollo's place of revelation,
To learn there, if he can,
What act or pledge of mine may save the city.[1]

—SOPHOCLES, *OEDIPUS REX*

My arrival in Oxford, England, that early October of 1994 came with plenty of baggage. Anyone who has tried to move a suitcase full of books before will tell you how deceptively heavy such a load becomes. Fortunately I shipped most of my books ahead of time, leaving room for other important considerations, such as fashion. Like any self-respecting girl (especially one about to relocate near the magnificent city of London), I brought many shoes. I had no idea at the time of the significance of all these *soles* accompanying me. All I knew was that the suitcases were unbelievably cumbersome and that I had to drag them (as they were the cheap kind without rollers) quite some distance before I would reach my college.

Very early that morning, after a long overnight flight, I landed amid the hustle and bustle of Heathrow Airport. The flight had been stuffy, hot, and very long, so I went into the restroom, held my head over the sink, and rinsed my hair in the cool water.

The weather was still very warm for autumn, and though tired I felt refreshed, so I headed in search of the X70—the bus that runs regularly between the airport and Oxford. Again I was directed down another mazy corridor, which wound past the train and tube options. I had no idea that getting to my destination would require such labyrinthine efforts. But then again, I had no idea.

The bus ride was pleasant enough, despite feeling as though we might smash into our death at any moment on the M25 freeway. The rest of the world drives so much faster than North Americans. Here I thought we were manic, and we *are* in our diurnal living, but on our streets we are sedate by comparison to our global neighbors.

I love buses. You ride up royally high, so you are able to look down into passing cars like an artful voyeur. You also get to people-watch on the bus itself, which is always live theater. I took numerous buses to school and even more to work. Later I drove the old rundown Buick I shared with my mom and sister, the kind of car in which you hold your breath at every stoplight. *Will it keep running? Will it start when I come out in the dark? Should it be making that queer sound when I brake?* The trunk did not open, the gas tank leaked into the backseat often, and the driver's window was stuck at a crack. Sometimes my brother loaned me his beat-up green Chevy, which we lovingly referred to as the "Tank." It was about as reliable as the Buick but with one major advantage: it was so big that no one messed with you on the road. I hung a little transistor radio from the rearview mirror, since running too many things at once, such as a turn signal, wipers, and the radio, caused everything on the dash to short out. To this day I still feel an exhilarating sense of luxury when I sit in a car built after 1975.

Our driving mantra was, "Just get me there."

Funny how you become what you think.

I dozed, jolting occasionally at the driver's loud pronouncement of upcoming stops. At this early hour the bus hummed along quietly with few passengers, so the stops were infrequent. In the hazy surrealism of predawn, there really was not much to see—what I could make out was mainly countryside, though not what I would call quaint, and certainly no Shakespearean cottages or fairy folk peeping from the trees. I kept an eye out for Oxford University, certain that I would eventually be able to see the campus on the horizon stretched out gloriously like Stanford's, which is so big it has its own shuttle system, or the famously sprawling campuses of Virginia marked by languid trees. At the very least fine towers surely would girdle the campus, like those to my own undergraduate alma mater, the University of Western Ontario. When you met those crested columns, you felt as though you were entering divine real estate indeed, the mother of all gated communities. "All those who enter here *will learn*."

So you can imagine my confusion at the driver's last call for Oxford. Last call? Only a little while back, we had come upon a pretty little bridge. At that point the architecture seemed more archaic, but this *was* England, so was everything not supposed to look old? According to instructions I should have rung the bell for the stop soon after passing Magdalen College, but I had been listening for "Magdalen," as in Mary Magdalene, not "Mawdawlynn" as the Brits crazily pronounce it. All my *soles* and I should have disembarked at the stop in front of All *Souls* College. Ironically I had missed the call.

As I continued dozing the bus whistled through a busy intersection, jolting me into the realization that I should inquire of our whereabouts. Without warning we took a sharp turn onto Worcester Street, and the next thing I knew those annoying little *beeps* were sounding, indicating that the bus was backing up. Only three passengers remained, including me. The driver came down the aisle and prodded the one passenger awake, helped the elderly lady collect herself, and shouted at me to come get my luggage. I stepped off the bus with the dawn; the station was still but slowly coming to life. A young man in a rumpled tuxedo slept on a nearby bench. *Wow*, I thought, *the homeless sure are spiffy here*. I asked the driver how far a walk it was to Oriel College. His answer did not encourage me.

"Why didnae get off at All Souls, luv?" he asked in turn.

"I didn't know we were in Oxford yet," I replied. "There was no sign. Where's the campus? Where are the gates? The rows of fraternity houses? Where are the pillars? You know, the ones with the crest?"

The driver scratched his head. "I havena idear what you're talkin' boot, miss, but everyone knows that the High Road marks the way inna Oxford."

~~~~~~

The music of the enduring Irish pop band U2 was deemed "alternative," but everyone I knew growing up liked it. Once acquainted with the power of metaphor as an English major, however, I began to see their lyrics differently. On one level they suggested *eros*, or erotic love; at another level they conveyed *agape*, or the self-giving love of God. The former beckons the latter, and yet the latter does not need any predilection. Indeed all other forms of love will be healed and function most beautifully when subsumed under *agape's* rule. However, the intertwining of sex and spirituality has always haunted literature and art, perhaps because we crave the intimate and are most immediately assuaged by the sexual, and so we know of no other more appropriate language.

For their cover to the album *All That You Can't Leave Behind*, photographer Anton Corbijn photographed the band members in the Charles de Gaulle Airport in Paris. In the background the departure notices read "J33-3," a reference to chapter 33, verse 3 of Jeremiah: "Call to me and I will answer you and tell you great and hidden things which you have not known" (ESV). U2 was obviously deeper than I thought.

Before I started listening to U2, a picture framed my life. My parents stand poised on the edge of promise, steps spilling beneath them under the arch of my hometown's cathedral. They look like Grace Kelly and Cary Grant. Literally. It is a bittersweet thing, being the ruddy daughter of a Helen, the filial beloved of a Lear. The wedding was breathtakingly beautiful as though silvered and inlaid, like its frame, with mother-of-pearl.

Money grew tight, but it was not always that way. We used to live in a large home in a comfortable neighborhood with luxury cars. We enjoyed a sailboat and a cabin cruiser and a lakefront summer retreat. My father played Santa Claus to the neighborhood children, bought them all gifts, took entire Little League teams regularly out to dinner. My earliest memories involve his extreme generosity and indulgence. I breezily did the sort of things normally denied children, like sitting on my father's lap while driving golf carts or eating lobster dinners in darkened restaurants with fussy waiters. Dolls from all parts of the world decorated my room. As a challenging toddler I liked to throw things away, such as my father's expensive items, and then pronounce them "all gone." A fishing rod over the side of our boat, or a putter through a sewer slot. My father would just chuckle and buy replacements—another for himself and usually a smaller version for me. He winced a bit when I flushed his Rolex watch down the toilet, but still laughed good-heartedly at my mother's admonitions. He was handsome and tanned and smelled wonderful, like a mix of the ocean and fresh-cut grass, except when he smoked his pipe, which also smelled wonderful, as how I thought wisdom must smell, when it curls about your head.

Winters enveloped us in a fun flurry of sledding, skating, and coming home to hot cocoa. We huddled together, watching old movies in quilted succession by the fire. My mother sang all the show tunes. I would bury my face in her apron, resting against the bump of my sister and soaking in her scent of all things comforting and good. Often at night I would creep into bed next to her, just to be encircled by it. *Anyam aug* in Hungarian, my mother's first language, conveys the nuances of a "mother's bed."

Summers gleamed alive in sunshiny memories filled with splashing in the pool or lake and eating ice cream at the park. Tepid evenings relieved muggy days; black velvet nights were filled with points of light, either boundless fireflies or, on long weekends, fireworks and sparklers. After dinner, my father and I picked still-sunwarm cherries from the tree in the backyard, popping them into our mouths and spitting out the pits while sprawled together in our lawn chairs.

At age six I took my first piano lesson. I never took my second. A week later the piano was repossessed.

A freak storm hit that winter complete with thunder and lightning. Our beloved cherry tree sat on a blanket of snow, magnificent, glazed with ice. Like Jane Eyre, one night I awoke to a violent crack. When I looked outside, the iced cherry tree had been smitten almost perfectly in half. It looked back at me, bewildered, broken, smoking from its lightning hit, frost hissing. I never forgot the paradox.

Shortly afterward, we lost our first house.

These were the early days of the Great Fear, to be followed shortly after by the Confusion Era. My mom became efficient at packing and unpacking. We learned not to answer the door, to ignore the strange questions. My little sister cowered, and my big brother clenched his fists. Holding hands tightly, we walked home quickly from school, ignoring the cars that followed us or the phone calls late at night that made my mother's hands shake when she came in to check on us and we feigned sleep. Whenever it came time to move again, Mom kept us busy. Eating fried chicken and singing songs, I would sit on the counter, swinging my legs to her singing as the men went by with our things. Mom always filled the house with music, poetry, and books. Regardless of what poured out, she poured beauty back in. Somehow she managed dance and skating lessons for us and the occasional magical treat of a ballet or opera. My dad now remained absent, but no one spoke of wheres or whys. Of such things no one spoke at all.

I learned that things did not matter. Nor did homes. Things came and went. Houses changed. Stuff was just stuff. It was yours one minute and not yours the next.

"Are you sure you donnae want a cab, miss?" the driver asked, looking concerned.

"No, thank you, I'll manage," I smiled. Besides I did not have enough British currency on me for purchasing the cab fare. While I knew that Oxford consisted of thirty-eight self-governing colleges and six permanent private halls, I did not fully understand how these comprised the campus, which was thereby embedded within the city of Oxford itself. You could walk the city streets and admire, of course, the magnificent architecture of the more public common buildings, such as libraries, museums, and churches. But a college could easily be passed by undetected. Only once you entered through its deceptively humble portal did the college reveal itself in its entire serendipitous splendor.

Then it was as though you had entered another world in another time, and yet one that remained timeless, evocative of castles, palazzos, columned walkways—magical places of learning, some dating at least as far back as the eleventh century. Fountains danced in the midst of pristine lawns; rosy arbors offered peep-holes into luxurious grounds; worn wooden benches nestled in miniature English country gardens. And the color! Lush green ivy embraced ashen stone; lavender blew against tea-stained brick; copper reddened in the sun against true blue sky. Gargoyles. Angels. Grottoes. Secret gardens and yellowed paths. The effect evoked my childhood haunts, like Narnia after the thaw.

Behind the urban commotion the sanctuary of each college sprawled inconspicuously toward the next.

My scholarship had assigned me to Oriel College, established in 1324 and owning the distinction of being the oldest royal foundation in Oxford. It also sits almost exactly across the city from the bus station. Without a ride and beleaguered by shoes for every occasion, let's just say I was in for a long haul.

At the interview for my first formal job, I lied about my age so as to dodge the work hour limitations for minors. I easily looked older when I dressed older. From my early teens throughout my undergraduate degree, I followed the same pattern almost every weekday. Got up early and went to school, attended practice or some student council event, then left straight for my job, getting home shortly before midnight, usually to my mom sitting alone with a drink in the dark. After she was safely in bed, I would reheat dinner and then study late into the early morning, catching a few hours of sleep before getting up for class all over again.

While I worked various jobs after school, I most consistently worked at a ballet school, a jewelry store, and a lingerie shop. For anyone who has worked retail, you know that Sundays are not sacred, nor are holidays, so I worked those, too, gift-wrapping like a madwoman for people in more of a foul than festive mood. When I did have the occasional free evening, I usually spent it cloistered in the college library wrapped in the distinctly comforting scent of old books. I spent every moment between classes studying and countless late nights at the computer lab until my senior year, when my mom surprised me with a used laptop that weighed, oh, about five hundred pounds.

My full undergraduate scholarship depended upon keeping straight As across all courses, every year, for all four years. Without that scholarship there would have been little or no chance of getting my first degree. As it was I could barely scrape together enough for supplies and books. I learned that the coffee-and-cookie combo at the kiosk in the college common room could last you most of the day. Any spare cent went toward buying books. I snuck these "friends" along with me to my jobs, clandestinely reading Aristotle, Dickens, and Tolstoy behind the counter. I wonder what Jane Austen would say, herself used to hiding her own writing beneath table blotters whenever someone entered the room, to having had her pages read secretively behind racks of black lace teddies? Or the Brontë sisters to having been smuggled in and enjoyed among silk leopard-print knickers? Romeo's comparison of Juliet's beauty to a jewel hanging in an Ethiope's ear fills your vision when you arrange diamonds on black velvet with the night pressing against the glass of the shop windows.

For as long as I could remember, I wanted to teach. I used to make my little sister play school, bribing her with stickers and candy, so that I could play the teacher, complete with coffee cup in hand. By grade ten I knew I wanted to teach literature because, as Philip Sidney argues in the apologetic tradition for poetry, literature is the great "architectonike." It encompasses all, brings all together. For instance, you can write a poem about doing a math problem, but you cannot make a math problem convey a poem. A poet can write about law, but being a lawyer does not make one a poet. Poetry is the summit, the castle on the hill, the greatest of buildings.

Totally idealistic, I was the quintessential student. One of those inspiring or irritating students—depending on how you look at it—who reads everything assigned and then the footnotes too. And the prefaces, and the references, and the epigraphs, and the marginalia. And the wacky, unrelated stuff on the next anthology page. I devoured everything I came across. I loved it all. Even the annoying parts I enjoyed, precisely because they annoyed me and so, often, made me stop and really think. With college, my life opened up more than I could have ever imagined: into art, and history, and philosophy, and argumentation, and statistics, and postcolonial theory. I began to understand my own spot of existence in relation to the history of ideas. I began to see, both scarily and comfortingly, that all I thought had been thought before. I began to see how studying the humanities illuminates *humanitas* or "what it means to be human." What it means to become human. The decisions and the responsibilities of becoming truly humane.

After that first visit of the sheriff to our door, my father disappeared and reappeared, but he never seemed to hold a job for long, and each new scheme came with promises but no deliveries. For long stretches my father was nowhere to be seen. Randomly he would show up with his wallet full of bills and peel them off gallantly as he took us on a shopping spree— some school clothes here or a new bike there. But it was not often. And it was not consistent. Then it trickled off completely. We certainly did not know anything even resembling child support. We moved in with my maternal grandmother. My older brother went to school during the day and delivered pizzas at night, sleeping a few hours on the couch or on a mattress in the basement, never with one complaint. He assumed the mantle of father, standing there helplessly with his thumb in my parents' leaking dam.

After the arrest my brother could not get the picture of my father's face from the newspaper out of his mind; it loomed up before him as he tried to write his exams. He did not talk to his teachers; he did not say anything. After failing he was held back a year. My brother made it sound like a lucky break, rationalizing how he would get to play football and hockey for an extra season.

Once my younger sister entered school, my mom went back to full-time work. She owned secretarial skills but had been out of the workforce. A proud daughter of immigrant parents, she wanted to pay back the welfare we were forced to take and to make our own way. She dove in, took a typing test, and even out of practice beat the words-per-minute average and began a low-wage job at the local university. Over the years she diligently worked her way up, eventually becoming the senior administrative assistant to the provost. I grew up playing in provosts' offices, waiting for my mom to close up after being given piles of photocopying at the last minute. Education was particularly important to my mother, not only because of the ardent respect unique to an immigrant of the Depression era, but also, I think, because she worked so hard in its antechamber.

During my adrenaline years in high school, my grandmother lived and died with us, my brother married, and my mom, sister, and I moved into co-op housing. In theory that meant everyone living there would pitch in around the complex to earn his or her subsidy. In reality, however, it meant a handful of us cleaned and repaired around those who drank or did drugs on their back steps. It was the kind of neighborhood from which police take their time responding to calls. Mom made everything as beautiful as she could, hanging her Rembrandt and Gainsborough prints over the cracks in the walls. She continued to play her classical music, blasting it on the antique record player. Each composer signified a different household chore: dust to Rachmaninoff, tidy to Tchaikovsky, dishes to Liszt, vacuum to Beethoven. You can always hear Beethoven over the vacuum. Maybe that is one of the advantages to going deaf as a composer.

We eventually saved enough to buy a small semi-detached house in a better neighborhood, closer to campus. I signed on the mortgage with my mother just before taking my Canadian literature exam. A man is nothing without land. A woman must have a house of her own. I suddenly saw Mordecai Richler's troubling hero Duddy Kravitz through different eyes as I wrote my exam.

Throughout my undergraduate studies, there were times I could not breathe or swallow. I had trouble shaking numerous strange ailments and sometimes threw up at night for no reason.

I would obsessively check the locks on our doors and chastise myself for doing so.

But otherwise I was fine.

We were all fine.

That's the power of refrain.

"Goodness gracious, luv, whatdya have in these bags?" the driver puffed as he pulled my luggage out from the hold. "Gold bullion?" he grinned, as I gave him his tip.

"Books," I lied.

TWO

THE FATHER (W)HOLE

One can always be certain of one's mother, but one can never be certain of one's father.

—SIGMUND FREUD

As what we would now term a "directionally challenged" person, I have grown accustomed to getting lost, and I often make the most of it. But getting lost with heavy luggage takes things to a whole new level.

Sans map, I optimistically turned out of the bus station early that first morning in Oxford with the street sweepers and the delivery trucks and threaded my way back toward Carfax, the city center. The journey was not easy on cobbled streets with awkward bags in tow, and I was grateful for the anonymity of early day. The fewer spectators to my debacle, the better. By now I was streaming sweat, and every step was labored, my hands reddened by the handles and the bags flopping pitilessly onto their sides at the advent of every bump and curb. I continued down Cornmarket onto St. Aldate's, again somehow managing to miss that main street, what the natives call the "High." It was not until I hit Folly Bridge—and no, I'm not kidding; that's what it's called—that I realized I was heading away from the bustle rather than toward it, and something seemed *off*. I asked a jogger, but he was a visiting American and did not know where Oriel College was either (I would learn later never to ask joggers, as chances are they are visiting Americans—Brits do not jog, or at least they do not jog, nor sweat, on busy public streets). No shops were open yet, and I was too embarrassed to yell across the street at someone for directions, and too nervous about being accused of IRA connections to leave my luggage momentarily. I could not get out of my mind the repeated threats playing through the audio at Heathrow that your abandoned luggage will be destroyed on site, and I just could not expose such painstakingly chosen shoes to such a fate. So, utterly spent, with back aching and hands numb from gripping, I sat and rested on my luggage just outside a large meadow and did what I always do in such dire circumstances. I ate some chocolate.

Fashion comes with pain, I reminded myself as I headed back up toward Carfax, made the right turn this time, stayed on the High road, and lo and behold, spotted across from St. Mary's Church the unassuming blink-and-miss-it Magpie Lane leading to Oriel's main portal, its gate marked by a discreet German badge with three feathers: *Ich dien*, or "I serve." I jounced and bounced over the cobblestones, and toppled, sweat-and-chocolate-smeared luggage and all, into the college's front lodge. Toppled was quite literal, as for some reason all Oxford colleges insist on having a broad beam across the base of their lodge doors, perhaps to keep those who enter on their toes or to further trip up the drunk undergrads. It all makes for good sport.

What a disappointing arrival. Here I was at the greatest university in the world, and there had been no indication I was even entering a campus anywhere. The walk to the college had been long, hot, and difficult. I traveled far in the wrong direction before even realizing it. (Eventually I would find out that C. S. Lewis had done a similar thing after coming out of the train station upon his first visit to Oxford, walking toward Botley before realizing his mistake.) Later, this comforted me somewhat, but at the time I was still stunned that there were no banners, no pillars, no signs, no stadium shining with colors and letters, no—how shall I say?—American campus hoopla, not one bit. And now here I was, having tumbled quite literally head over heels, so that I sat on the cold flagstone ground of the Oriel College lodge, blinking as my eyes adjusted to the shadows of the Gothic entrance.

And then I saw it: my own name. Truly. Actually what was even more amazing was that it was my own nickname: Caro.

It stood out in front of me across a lawn of perfectly manicured grass along the east range of the college's first quad. There in large, handsome letters carved into the ornate portico of one of the most magnificent buildings I had ever seen were the words in capital letters: *REGNANTE CAROLO* to commemorate Charles I, in whose reign the quad was completed. The *CARO* was foregrounded like the printed caption of a T-shirt stretched across a well-endowed woman's chest. The beautiful and bold inscription in stone bore the name I had gone by since childhood. *Carolyn* is a feminine form of the name Charles. I had been named for my father.

This first glimpse of Oriel extended formal salutations

accompanied by what I can only describe as that cosmic chuckling. I had flown from one London (Canada) to another London (England) only to leave one Caro for another Caro. This old architecture seemed to call out to me intimately. I could hear something beyond and yet closer than family, saying it in my ear: *Caro*. Dear one. Listen. Look here.

I shook off the shudder of coincidence. I reasoned that God most likely did not exist because we could not see Him, or if He did exist, He did not interact with us in any tangible way. I had dabbled in the Bible for various course requirements, these forays mixed with a few hazy images from childhood. Reason, not faith, however, helped me build the emotional boundaries I needed to survive. I did not flounder in school or lose my focus because I did not let my father get under my skin. I did not date many men because the distraction came at too high a price. I rested assured that research provided the only reliable answers. As the old maxim went in academia, "Verify one's references." Well, you had to live life that way too.

And yet I also knew that from the very first of firsts I felt a beam deep inside of me that was connected to and recognized a beautiful source, the utmost of all "reference" points, but that the world made it a dangerous place to open up this light, to shine it, to function from it. So I packed up that feeling like a cherished outfit that was now out of style (a robe, perhaps, of too many colors) and put it away.

My father once solved a problem in a school mathematics textbook of mine that claimed the problem could not be solved.

When I mentioned my father's discovery, my teacher did not believe me at first. But after I explained the solution to him, he sat there rubbing his eyes and then told me to take a seat. Later the textbook, a staple in the curriculum, mysteriously disappeared from the course reading. I myself was terrible at math, but my once tyrannical teacher now seemed gentler with me. I labored at my homework and, thus, stumbled along. But secretly I relished the knowledge that my father could access solutions and truths that others could not.

My high school sat proudly at the center of a wealthy, established neighborhood. I went to classes with kids who received brand new sports cars with personalized license plates for their birthdays. They took elaborate family vacations and lived on tree-lined streets in beautiful old homes with spiraling staircases and dark wood furniture. They wore expensive clothing, and after school they ate packaged snacks and drank bottled water while they played video games. As a chameleon, I ended up having a wonderful, heady experience there, within those hallowed walls covered in war heroes and bright faces from the past.

It was a bit of a coup how I got in. The school earned an experimental year for a potential gifted-student program; regional student scores had been submitted for consideration. One of the teachers on the selection committee, a Native American with sparkling dark eyes and a wry, all-knowing smile, insisted, for some reason, on including me. When they interviewed the qualifying grade-schoolers and asked us what we most wanted in life, I replied with all earnestness, "A doctorate." I did not see why the committee found my dream so amusing.

Later this teacher would influence me beyond words with his infectious spirit for reaching people through literature. But for now I had my heart set on attending the larger though less academic high school where my bigger-than-life older brother had attended and was still worshipped as a god. I planned to ride quite comfortably on his coattails, thank you, wearing his athletic jerseys and basking in the respect that would surely trickle down to me from his admirers. So when the opportunity presented itself to attend the preppy, small, prestigious collegiate school centered in an old, ivy-covered, esteemed neighborhood, I naturally recoiled. Interestingly my father had gone there as a teenager. He was from a rough, other-side-of-the-tracks fringe that bordered on the wealthy neighborhood, so it was barely his high school by district division. He had been a famous athlete and promising student before he left just prior to graduating in order to help his mother with the family business.

I had to make the decision quickly; with summer approaching, the program needed to establish its members. Again my mother, with her love of what was best for us, gently counseled me into going. I did not care at the time that this program would swing doors to my future wide open. I did not notice the plaques in the entranceway listing the many national and international scholarship recipients who had emerged from the school. I was not impressed by the churning out of achievers, disproportionately high compared to any other school in the province.

Rather, I became intrigued by my father's ghost in those halls and his bright face beaming charismatically from the yearbook. No hint of self-pity, frustration, despair, or anger—just pure youthful jubilance in a World War II–era football uniform. Ultimately, I decided to go there to be, in some way, closer to him. Closer to *that* him.

The summer was a particularly hot one, full of thunderstorms and funnel clouds. My father led me through the cool, stony annals of the old school, narrating on everything from personal former glory days to actual historical anecdotes as we walked together along the worn, uneven floors. I loved my father with a certain breathlessness when he was in these rare moods. He charmed the superintendent into opening the school vault and showed me his name on a banner dating from the forties. There on a cushion lay his retired jersey. I was taken aback at how knowledgeable my father seemed, now gentle and amiable. He carried himself so tall through the halls! He seemed so different from the man who oscillated between bouts of terrifying bellowing and afternoons spread on the living room couch in the dark.

It never occurred to me how bittersweet the tour must have been for him. Returning life-tossed to a place where he had been a celebrated giant, but from which he had never been permitted to cross the finish line.

Except for a small, distinctive crest in its corner, the envelope arrived unobtrusively, like any other piece of mail. I went to my room, where I could open it alone. The words blurred in front of me: I stood there blinking at the news that I had won a full scholarship to study at Oxford University. The Commonwealth Scholarship awarded the most money I certainly had ever seen in one sum in my life. It occurred to me that I could send money home *and* still have plenty to live on. I wondered what it would be like to study without that familiar stomach-grumbling. I thought of Virginia Woolf's maxim: "One cannot think well, love well, sleep well, if one has not dined well." But would one be able to concentrate when so full? After all, hunger kept one conveniently awake.

Surviving together knits a family together. As a result, it becomes increasingly difficult to separate those threads. Whether this is a good or a bad thing, I don't know. But I do know I threw myself on my bed and wept with surprise, relief, trepidation, excitement, sadness. My heart ached at leaving home, even for my dream. What I did not see at the time was that my heart was being laid open. I had been so focused on the head that I did not see what was coming for my heart or, perhaps, for all of me.

Without my knowledge a professor of mine had submitted a nomination on my behalf. Shocked at the discovery, my mom and I completed the subsequent and seemingly endless paperwork together. The admissions application required that I check the period of literature on which I wished to concentrate for the masters of philosophy, or "MPhil," degree in literature. After much deliberation I chose the Romantic writers, dating from approximately 1780 to 1850. Partly it was because I remembered one of them, Samuel Taylor Coleridge, who noted selection as the most difficult process in creation. And partly it was because I identified with the "infinite longing" characterizing this group of writers, their grappling with and desire for the ineffable, from Johann Wolfgang von Goethe and George Sand to William Blake, John Keats, Percy Bysshe and Mary Shelley, William Wordsworth, and Lord Byron. And partly it was because they were so entertaining, if shocking. Recalling this, I put an X in black ink through the empty box with gusto.

A few months later I arrived at Oxford with newly minted BA in hand, the first person in my family to go to college, let alone graduate school. Exhilarated. Exhausted. And engaged, albeit without a ring . . . yet . . . to my college sweetheart, Ben. Initially I was drawn to him because he could quote Henry David Thoreau *and* Thomas Hobbes, and tried to live as they did too. I found the combination of living life according to the maxim that it is nasty, brutish, and short while you also wished to suck the marrow out of it while communing with nature, well, very intriguing. Blond, attractive, and tanned from working on the farm in the summer, he looked more like a movie star than a political science major. I think my father met him once or twice.

I equated keeping my head down with commitment to both my intentioned fiancé and to my studies. Magnificently self-sufficient, like William Wordsworth on his deathbed, I would have said I had no need of a redeemer. Unlike Jane Austen, I did not believe the only power afforded women was that of refusal. I had no real need of believing in men, God incarnate or otherwise.

Fathers especially were not to be trusted. They did not even seem relevant really. That much I had learned. That much I brought with me.

MICHAELMAS TERM

THREE

SIGNS, SIGNS,
EVERYWHERE ARE SIGNS

> *Some of the Pharisees in the crowd said to Jesus,*
> *"Teacher, rebuke your disciples!"*
> *"I tell you," he replied, "if they keep quiet, the stones*
> *will cry out."*
>
> —LUKE 19:39–40

One of the welcome events for new graduate students at Oriel College included a day trip to Stonehenge, the famous circular arrangement of prehistoric monoliths on Salisbury Plain. For a North American, who can feel, in cultural contrast to Europe (or the rest of the world, for that matter), as shiny and new as a freshly minted copper penny (and sadly, worth as much at times too), a place such as Stonehenge marked all that was truly *old* and thus mystical. Everyone knows Britain is full of magic; of fairies and elves; of Midsummer dreams; of witches' moons, enchanted wardrobes, and nursery rhymes—all the things North Americans supposedly do not have. Or perhaps we do have them, but we are not aware of them.

We gathered excitedly in the porter's lodge to be divvied up into car pools. I was assigned to ride with a British girl named Hannah. She extended her hand boldly, announcing that it would only be the two of us since she owned a Mini Coop. I learned she had spent much of her childhood in India. I imagined her as ivory skinned and ginger maned in crowded saffron-scented cities of raven-haired people. She then attended an American university in the South, returning to the United Kingdom to pursue the same graduate program as I. She spoke things plainly in her pretty Princess Diana accent, which undercut any harshness while creating an attractive but unsettling effect. I liked her right away.

As we drove along I could just taste the grandeur of discovering Stonehenge. With poetic muster I likened myself to that quintessential Romantic poet, Wordsworth, setting out to "find the sublime" among the Alps. I could not wait to touch the old stones, to have them "speak" to me, to have the vibrations of the ages run through my fingers, to feel the force of the cosmos surge through me as I stood at their vortex. So you can imagine my surprise and my utter disappointment when we finally asked the toothless farmer standing among the lowing and disgruntled cows, once our car ran out of gas, where Stonehenge *was*.

"Why, it's at least twenty kilometers back, love." He coughed as he pulled a pipe from his pocket. "Didn't you see the signs?" Then he added with a wink, "The countryside's covered in them. It's an easy turn off the last ring road."

"Well, bollocks," I heard Hannah hiss through her teeth.

At that moment I did indeed feel like Wordsworth, but not the triumphant, older Wordsworth upon returning to experience the magnificent Alpine Sublime. No, rather, the identification was more akin to the younger, dismayed Wordsworth when he first traveled to the famous range in search of that feeling of infinite longing mingled with wonder, fear, and awe that so captivated the Romantics, only to find out he had already passed through the mountains and missed their glory entirely. Poor Wordsworth and me. All that anticipation, all that effort, and yet, in the end, denied the cigarette.

Sensing that same cosmic chuckling, I can still remember the song "Signs, Signs, Everywhere Are Signs" blaring on the car radio as we sputtered toward the farmhouse, surrounded aptly by ha-has (or *trenches* in British gardening). But we had missed the signs. As a result, we spun on endless ring roads all morning, accompanied by the Five Man Electrical Band belting out: "If God was here he'd tell you to your face: man you're some kind of sinner!"[1] On one hand, ring roads are a highly sympathetic form of infrastructure. It's a pity we don't have more of them in North America; they accommodate the most indecisive driver quite graciously by allowing for multiple chances to get off at the right (or wrong) point. On the other hand, you can just keep going in maddening circles.

> And the sign said, "Everybody welcome, come in,
>   kneel down and pray."
> But when they passed around the plate at the end
>   of it all, I didn't have a penny to pay.
> So I got me a pen and a paper and I made up my
>   own little sign.
> I said, "Thank you Lord for thinking of me, I'm
>   alive and doing fine."[2]

"There is nothing as pitiful as a young cynic," Maya Angelou famously wrote, "because he has gone from knowing nothing to believing nothing." I realized that I was still caught on the ring road—on that, thank goodness, forgiving ring road—but that eventually, at some point, everyone needs to get off, including me. It is easy to coast and even easier to mock the signs, but reading them, *really reading them*, and then making the largest decision there is, the greatest decision to which all others defer and are tied back to—to know who we are, what we stand for, and for what we are responsible—to read the signs and then choose the right way . . . well, that's *hard*.

Rolled to a stop and destitute amid angry cows, I wondered just what I signified. As I teetered on the beginning of a new life at Oxford, I wondered what my own "sign" or my note-of-self might read.

And then there was that word, strung out from the song: *sinner*.

It is up there (or perhaps I should say down there) with the Book of Common Prayer's synonym for man as a "lowly worm." Such Christianese. I'd be damned, literally, if I was a sinner. I had never maimed or killed anyone, nor pushed elderly ladies or small children into the traffic. I had never stolen large amounts of money or someone else's spouse, for that matter. I did not really even curse that much, and drinking gave me a headache. I had not inhaled, and I was a really nice person—I am Canadian, after all. Sinner? Yeah, right. I was a *good person*. Isn't that all it takes to be a Christian? To not be some kind of sinner?

Shaking his head at women drivers, the farmer brought us some gas and refused payment. After the impersonal terseness of American construction signs that say only Bump or that illustrate with simple lines how a road is about to change course, British signs seem positively loquacious, a little quirky but far more cordial. As we finally entered the parking lot to Stonehenge and approached an impending pothole that stretched like a moat in front of our car, the first sign cautioned us to Mind the Gap. When we left, the exiting sign warned us of Changed Priorities Ahead.

Later that week, we huddled on the floor for the orientation movie night, crammed into the small room of the Graduate Tutor, a mass of graduate students from around the world passing around beer and cigarettes to each other as though lifelong friends. A handwritten Welcome Orielenses sign hung over the door. An old television, the kind with rabbit-ear antennae, sat glumly in the corner, hooked up to a VCR from the eighties. Back then they were cutting-edge technology for Oxford. The American students began complaining at the audio quality as soon as the picture started. Rustling. Coughing. Chatting. A tall German student stood up and boomed, "Shut up!" from the back of the room. In the ensuing silence, you could hear the lip smacking of newly connected drunk couples "snogging" (or "making out," as Americans would say—neither term quite captures the romance) in the dark corners.

The university's crest with its Latin motto stared out from the podium on which the television was precariously perched: *Dominus Illuminatio Mea*: "The Lord is my light."

The motto appeared on letterhead when I picked up my book lists. On the china, staring up at me in the dining hall. Lurking inside my teacup. On sweatshirts bobbing throughout the sea of tourists flooding the streets. It hung directly over my head, a massive writing on the wall, in the Bodleian Library reading room. The Oxford University crest peered out at me from everywhere. There was no escaping it.

Beautiful to look at, I thought. It was something one might see on a knight's shield as he slew a dragon in one of those medieval illuminated books. But now? In this stuffy, restless world of a room? It seemed so archaic and immaterial.

The orientation movie was *Chariots of Fire*, which tells the story of two young British sprinters competing for fame in the 1924 Olympics. I was struck by the line spoken by the character Eric, a Scottish missionary, saying that when he runs, he feels "God's pleasure."

What does it mean to feel God's presence, let alone pleasure, in something you do?

"If you do what you love, you will never work a day in your life," my mom used to say to us. For me that love entailed studying and discussing literature. These also became the means by which I was yanked from one existence into another, and by which my "training" would prepare me for my most fundamentally challenging reading of all. And for the mother (or father) of all metaphors. Soon I would see that for everyone, everything is training for the great race.

To that point I had not realized that in doing something I love, and at which at times I may even excel, I felt something I could only define as akin to an electric volt deep in my core. From where did this *power* come? Was it the presence—extension or workings or shadow—of something else in me? Or was it something else encouraging me to love through what I love?

Whoa.

Someone near me in the dark belched, and then I felt someone grope me from behind. "Jerk," I hissed as I turned around.
It was my new friend Linnea, raised in Los Angeles, and part
Ukrainian, part Lebanese. We met soon after I arrived since we
would be sharing the same academic supervisor. She had long,
luxurious dark hair and big, wild eyes. I had already learned that
her personality was the same: wild, sensuous, at times dark. She
was Romanticism personified to me. Nothing wallflower about
her. Heart-stoppingly gorgeous, she was also tempestuous and
sharp. She leaned in next to me, and immediately I was enveloped in the smell of sage and incense. I whispered to her about
my love epiphany.

"What if everything operates by love?" I said to her. "I mean,
what if this God presence that this runner guy feels is God moving through us and through everything we do? If so, why do we
resist it? What if everything horrible that happens, from drive-by
shootings to illness, is because we have broken this chain of love,
and we don't know how to put everything *right* again?"

"You sound like John Lennon," Linnea stated blankly.

"No, really."

"Yes, you do. Or like Lincoln. Or Kennedy. Or Jesus, for that
matter. Be careful you don't get shot. Or crucified. It doesn't pay
to be too optimistic." She tossed her mane of hair.

"Were you a goth in high school?" I whipped back. "I'm talking about something more than optimism, even more than hope,
though hope foreshadows it. Those are lovely but intangible. This
is very tangible. I *feel* it at work. I *see* it in things. I see when it's
not in things."

"You aren't making any sense," Linnea sighed.

If I'm not making sense to Linnea, I worried, *I really must not be making sense. She constantly operates in an alternative reality. That's her home. She rarely makes sense, and now I've confused* her.

"Hey, don't worry about it," she laughed. "The crucifixion was ultimately not such a bad thing."

I tried to discern her face, but the room was too dark. I took a swig from my tiny Euro-sized Diet Coke can and settled back into the sweaty room, unable to hear the runners on the small screen over the couple snogging right behind me.

FOUR

THE STORM
BEFORE THE CALM

Few people have the imagination for reality.
—JOHANN WOLFGANG VON GOETHE

In 1879 the first twenty-one female students arrived at Oxford. Women were not afforded degrees until 1920, and then five women's colleges eventually formed. All colleges are now coed but only after a slow process. Oriel, the last of the Oxford men's colleges to go coed, did so in 1985. That means by the time I arrived, Oriel had been admitting women for just short of a decade. One can imagine the odds: literally a sea of men per every woman.

It was a feminist's nightmare. It was a debutante's dream.

Men came out of the mahogany-paneled woodwork in a steady stream. What a glorious place to be a young, straight woman! In the Middle Common Room (MCR), as the graduate social area is called, people from every race gathered. I had never seen so much cosmopolitanism in one place. But everyone was bound by what I came to recognize only as that infamous Oxbridge wit. Sure, there were the usual self-important people that one may find anywhere, but I was surprised to find that they were the minority. For the most part I continually found my new peers to be delightful company: clever, humorous, dedicated, interesting. Conversation in the MCR was never dull. And the line of courtly lovers for any woman was never short. Unexpectedly, it was Oxford that taught me it was okay to be both feminine *and* smart, that intelligence was, as a friend put it, a "woman's best cosmetic."

For all the practical jokes, for all the gregariousness and bad puns, for all the stealing from the fridge, swing dancing, and mocking of our professors, it was this room that signified our commonality, we who were joined by a shared and deep belief in the ability of intellectual inquiry to ameliorate our world. It was in this room that we all made our introductions, and for many, lasting relationships. And it was in this room where I first met the man who would, quite literally, change my life for eternity.

"Orielenses" henceforth, following our matriculation ceremonies at the grand circular Sheldonian Theatre, everyone gathered back in the college MCR for a social. It was the first time I drank "Buck's Fizz," a delightful concoction of orange juice and champagne. I counted the other female students. Eight of us, in a room of, oh, at least eighty or so men. What terrific odds!

How sad, then, that I was not interested romantically in these adorably flushed men with crisp bow ties drawn debonairly under their chins. My girlfriends back home would have been terribly disappointed in me. But two things kept me from jumping too quickly into the freshman dating game. Ben, for one. I missed him and loved him, and I thought marrying him a good next step. I assumed this came from keeping my head about it all. It paid to be pragmatic and appropriately restrained about life plans.

The other reason that the high number of fascinating, attractive, and accomplished young men in the room did not cause me to completely hyperventilate was my homesickness. The telephone bill was already sky-high, and I had only been there a few days. As the proverbial saying goes, I felt "lonely in a crowd," making polite conversation with a heavy heart.

The next thing I knew, the loud American whose voice I recognized from our group photograph earlier that morning was standing next to me. "I overheard you say you missed your mother," he said, softly this time, to my surprise.

I don't know if it was all of the Buck's Fizz or the jet lag or both, but as we moved away from the crowd, I found myself telling him how close my family was, how we had survived so much together, how supportive my mom was of my dream, but how her face looked at the airport. I explained how I finally had enough to live on, but not with much of a margin to entertain such bills, especially if I was to afford plane tickets at Christmas. I told him that I knew I should be excited and grateful to be here, and a large part of me was, but another part of me barely got out of bed in time for the photo this morning.

The tall, dark, and I now noticed, very handsome American

smiled, "I understand, at least a little. I miss my family, too, and I grew up basically on peas."

I almost choked on my Buck's Fizz. Did he just say *peas*? I assumed this striking stranger who carried himself with such grace had either a title or Roman numerals after his name, or both. Almost every other person in the room did, or so it seemed.

I guess I did not mask my surprise quickly enough (a hard thing to do since the fizz backed up in my nose made me sneeze) because he "God blessed" me and then added, "My parents dedicated their lives to a very important cause, starting at the grass roots. They put all they had into it, emotionally and financially, and as a result there were a lot of sacrifices."

"I'm sorry to hear that their investment was such a failure," I offered. I hate peas.

"Failure?" The American looked genuinely startled. "No, my goodness, not at all. Quite the opposite."

"So they are wealthy now?" I assumed again.

"Yes, in the most important sense. But no, not in the way the world usually measures things. In that sense we have always lived hand to mouth. We've owned next to nothing most of our lives. And yet all our needs were miraculously met. And I can say with confidence that my parents are together and determinedly love each other, and they raised us very happily in that love, and . . ." He looked about to say something else, but we were interrupted by a waiter offering a plate of shrimp.

I was grateful for the diversion, which allowed me to indulge—undetected—in a wistful smile. After eating a few shrimp as politely but as hungrily as I did (a pained restraint detectable to those who understand deprivation amid abundance), the American conceded, "I had scholarships, too, some athletic, some academic, some totally random, but always enough to patch things together nicely. And then I worked in a steel mill during the summers to save up my book money."

"Wow. Were you ever hurt?" I asked. Suddenly folding leopard-print knickers didn't seem that bad.

"A few times, but only once really badly, when the crane knocked me out the window," he replied calmly, taking a sip of his Buck's Fizz. "But enough about me." He offered me a napkin. "We need to solve your dilemma on missing the home front. I don't have phone money or much time for long letters, either, but as a professional cheapskate and a bit of a tech-geek, I do know how you could talk to your mom every day for free."

He had my complete attention. I leaned in.

He leaned in too. I felt as if we were about to share a very important secret.

"Have you heard of e-mail?" he whispered mischievously.

I essentially used my computer as an upgraded typewriter. When anything with an electrical cord even senses me coming, it shuts down and refuses to function.

"Sure, a little," I stammered, not wanting to look like a complete idiot, especially in front of someone with so much presence. With so much of *something* I could not quite put into words. Whatever it was, once you move beyond the initial and superficial jolt of physical attraction, you begin to see how it holds your attention in more profound ways.

"If your mother is a secretary on a campus, then she has it, and as a student here, you can too. It's unlimited, essentially real-time, and best of all, it's free! You just have to get a login from Computing Services, and I'll show you the rest in five minutes. Piece of cake." He finished his Buck's Fizz with a flourish.

I will refer to him as TDH, or Tall, Dark, and Handsome, for convenience's sake.

A few days later I met TDH in the small, cramped computer lab tucked away under a dorm staircase. He showed me how to create and open an e-mail account, as well as send and receive messages. That was wonderful! I could make regular contact with my mom at no cost, since she had e-mail at her campus job. As fast typists we could cover much ground that way.

Once I was all set up, TDH modeled for me how to open and reply to a message through his own account. I hunched over his shoulder, taking in how to enter a password and open a message. He showed me his in-box and scrolled to his new messages. He decided to open an unread message as an example, so he chose a note from a good friend of his back in the States. TDH clicked on the message, and it opened up before us. My eyes grew wider as I took in the screen. To TDH's dismay, I'm also a fast reader:

> Have I got the girl for you! I really think you two should meet, and I will plan for you to get together when you're back in town. She's fun, intelligent, beautiful, accomplished, and super godly. In her late twenties and, yep, still a virgin!—Alex

"What on earth?" I exclaimed, startling the other two students huddled nearby, playing computer games.

Then it all became clear, like a flash in a great pan, the kind of pan that fries to a crisp poor, sweet, and unsuspecting virgins in the hot oil of male lust.

TDH stammered, "Wait. It's not what you think. It must look strange, I know, but let me explain."

"Explain what?" I retorted. "What could there possibly be to explain? Are you and your friends part of some sort of deflowering cult? Is this about notches on your bedposts?"

I narrowed my eyes at him and hissed, "My big brother warned me about sharks like you." Suddenly I really missed my brother, a successful disc jockey who began working for the police department. His voice spoke of himself: strong and safe.

"No, wait. You have it all wrong," TDH rushed to explain. "Alex is one of my best friends, of the highest character. He's a struggling psychology student trying to make—"

"Trying to make it with 'godly virgins'?" I cried, getting angrier by the minute.

"No, no! Nothing like that. He's excited about introducing me to a woman who appears to have her spiritual priorities in place . . ." TDH swiveled around, red faced. "She must talk about it publicly or something—I don't know how he would have even known such a thing about her. He probably mentioned the virginity thing for its novelty in someone in her late twenties, but also because it's most likely very deliberate for her."

"Huh?" I cut him off. I had never heard *that* one before. *Man, this guy is good.* Crossing my arms over my chest, I pulled myself up straight.

Responding to my posture, he took a breath. "Look, I owe you an explanation. Are you free sometime this week after dinner? Can you at least come by my room for coffee?"

Sure, now, I have heard that *one before.* I inwardly rolled my eyes. *The old coffee-and-context routine.* I mean, everyone flits out of each other's rooms here on a (usually) platonic basis—that was just part of college room culture. *But does this guy really think I'm that stupid?*

I looked at TDH hard. I mean really, really hard. The kind of hard where my eyes were like man-hating lasers about to slice through his pathetic skin and incinerate, upon impact, his already shriveled heart. And then something gave me pause—exactly for what reason, I was not sure. And in that pause I made a decision. Despite hearing my protective big brother's voice warning me, "Pack heat, little girl."

"Okay," I said, calm on the surface. "When should I come by?"

FIVE

THE POISON TREE

I was angry with my friend:
I told my wrath, my wrath did end.
I was angry with my foe:
I told it not, my wrath did grow . . . [1]

—WILLIAM BLAKE

Dismayed, I looked down at my reading list for next term. Oxford professors gave the reading lists out well in advance so that students could spend the breaks between terms reading and preparing. Each term consisted of an eight-week flurry of papers, tutorials, lectures, argumentation, and oh yes, countless black-tie events. You needed to plan your workload accordingly or you would never survive.

Education was still considered a privilege in England. At

Oxford you took responsibility for your efforts and for your performance. No one coddled, and no one uproariously encouraged. British respect for the individual, both learner and teacher, reigned. If you wanted to learn, you applied yourself and did it. Grades were posted publicly by your name after exams. People failed regularly. These realities never ceased to bewilder those used to "democracy" without any of the responsibility.

For me, however, my expectations were rattled in another way. I arrived anticipating to be snubbed by a culture of privilege, but when looked at from a British angle, I actually found North American students owned a far greater sense of entitlement when it came to a college education.

I did not realize just how much expectations fetter—these "mind-forged manacles,"[2] as Blake wrote.

Oxford upholds something larger than self as a reference point, embedded in the deep respect for *all* that a community of learning entails. At my very first tutorial, for instance, an American student entered wearing a baseball cap on backward. The professor quietly asked him to remove it. The student froze, stunned. In the United States such a request would be fodder for a laundry list of wrongs done against the student, followed by threatening the teacher's job and suing the university. But Oxford sits unruffled: if you don't like it, you can simply leave. A handy formula since, of course, no one wants to leave.

"No caps in my classroom," the professor repeated, adding, "Men and women have died for your education."

Instead of being disgruntled, the student nodded thoughtfully as he removed his hat and joined us.

With its expanses of beautiful architecture, quads (or walled lawns) spilling into lush gardens, mist rising from rivers, cows lowing in meadows, spires reaching high into skies, Oxford remained unapologetically absolute.

And did I mention? Practically every college within the university has its own pub. Pubs, as I came to learn, represented far more for the Brits than merely a place where alcohol was served. They were important gathering places, overflowing with good conversation over comforting food: vital humming hubs of community in communication.

So faced with a thousand-year-old institution, I learned to pick my battles. Rather than resist, for instance, the archaic book-ordering system in the Bodleian Library with technological mortification, I discovered the treasure in embracing its seeming quirkiness. Often, when the wrong book came up from the annals after my order, I found it to be right in some way after all. Oxford often works such.

After one particularly serendipitous day of research, I asked Robert, the usual morning porter on duty at the Bodleian Library, about the lack of any kind of sophisticated security system, especially in one of the world's most famous libraries. The Bodleian was not a loaning library, though you were allowed to work freely amid priceless artifacts. Individual college libraries entrusted you to simply sign a book out and then return it when you were done.

"It's funny; Americans ask me about that all the time," Robert said as he stirred his tea. "But then again, they're not used to having *u* in *honour*," he said with a shrug.

There is nowhere to hide in an Oxford tutorial. These classes are incredibly intimate, usually two, perhaps five students at most, sitting with a professor who is a leading expert in his or her field.

And there you are. In the ring. With The Terror. It's just tiny, feeble you, another student or two smarter than you, and your professor, *far* smarter than you. Oh sure, your professor civilly serves tea or sherry, depending on the time of day, but The Terror remains.

Gradually, however, The Terror morphs into The Excitement as you begin to lose yourself in the luxurious tendrils of a stimulating argument. Time always flies, the hour (or two or three) leaving you exhausted, happy, perturbed, and yet strangely satisfied by the end. I was always grateful for the walk or bicycle ride back to college, dinner, or the pub afterward to allow things to settle or rise in my thoughts. The physical movement required to navigate winding paths home aided the mental digestion.

As a result, pursuing one's degree at Oxford becomes for most not a matter of a prerequisite for a job, or to please one's parents, or to make a minimum income bracket. Rather, the opportunity to study here seals an experience marked by intense personal growth resulting from a genuine desire to learn. A heady, hearty experience that changes you forever because it cracks you open ultimately to the humility of learning, which is where all of this wanted to take you in the first place.

❧

"Are we really expected to read all of these over the next few weeks? Especially during *Christmas* vac?" Fred, a lanky Irish student with sharp, dark eyes blurted the burning question we all wondered but feared to ask. Everyone sat waiting somewhere between relief at the question having been asked and yet dreaded expectancy. All the ideas represented by the list looked appealing yet daunting. *A terrible beauty*. I shuddered.

"Your flair for the rhetorical question, McCoy, never fails to impress me," Professor Nuttham responded with his habit of addressing us by our last names as if we were players on some sort of academic football team. "Whether that impression is favorable or not remains an item for debate."

He turned to the rest of us: "I would like to hope that you are passionate enough about your studies, convicted enough about your life journey, to read these recommendations out of your self-motivation, out of your desire to learn and pursue and enjoy. An education forced is no education at all."

I thought about how it seemed *anything* forced made it nothing at all.

Professor Nuttham started picking up momentum. "Studying alone doesn't make one wise. But neither does action." And then he was off. "Just what is wisdom?" he cried. "Just what is discernment?"

I love crazy professors. I'm beginning to think more and more that it must be a requirement for the job.

Professor Nuttham looked at each of us. Calming down, he leveled us with a quiet question: "Yeats wrote, 'The best lack all conviction, while the worst are full of passionate intensity.'[3] Which are you?"

We all sat there, staring at him.

Proud of the ensuing silence, Professor Nuttham pulled himself up. "An Irishman *would* say that." He winked at Fred.

Dr. Deveaux crossed my mind. All that reserved formality, and then suddenly the wit shone through as a sunbeam—not the tearing-down kind, but the building-up kind.

"Yes . . . I love how the Irish are so comfortable with paradox that they revel in it. In fact, if you took it away from them, I

suspect they would start gasping like fish out of water. No wonder their land's name, now removed from its Gaelic notions of
abundance in 'eire,' evokes anger, or 'ire,' and yet also the rich,
cooling green of a sea-colored jewel. A 'terrible beauty' indeed.
They understand oppression and repression and explosion, but
they remain a culture of faith—faith that creaks and groans and
pulls, but is alive and never dull. And which urges them to art, to
poetry, to song—these, too, are forms of action. Of passion. Of
conviction. Yes, of love." Professor Nuttham nodded as he leaned
back in his chair.

I remember flying from home. Her face pressed up against the
glass as my small plane began moving along its small runway.
Simultaneous desolation and exhilaration. For her. For me.

"You will save us," my mother said in her quiet way, which
was her most serious way, as I waited to board. Her demeanor
reminded me of my grandfather, the one who believed if you
looked hard enough, you could find any answer in a book. The
line struck me, but I assumed she was happy for the opportunities
my education would bring me and, thus, my family.

I did not understand what my mother really meant. What
she might not have known she meant. There was a lot I did
not understand. I did not understand why my captivating but
tumultuous father flitted in and out of our lives. Why, when he
did show up, was it dramatic and dangerous, and always led to
me exploding and then shutting down? I did not understand
how he could be so fiery intelligent and yet so unwise at the
same time.

There were no chinks in my brother's armor. Student council leader, top athlete, supersmart, and rapid-fire funny, he was my role model, our protector. So much depended on him.

Back then I only saw him cry once. It happened after the shattering of the glass pane over our screened front door. My sister hid upstairs in the closet. Too indignant and angry for fear, I huddled with him inside the tiny bathroom, trying my best to comfort him. Matt, always composed, ever upbeat, crumpled on the floor, sobbing. My father was bellowing outside, calling his only son an embarrassment, a failure. My mom was making breakfast, silent, in her housecoat and curlers in the kitchen. Detached. Shut down.

Once married, my brother decided not to have children of his own. As a child it never occurred to me he had distractions, or that the massive "dad" weight on his teenage shoulders precluded so many opportunities. How shocking it would have been to lift up that helmet and reveal his own youth—a boy-man knight with many dragons to slay, alone.

What is wisdom? What is discernment?

I could grasp (though of course never understand or condone) remote sins—overt acts of terror or hatred, atrocities flashing across the nightly news in faraway lands or happening to people I did not know. It was the immediacy of sin that was more slippery, the sins right under my nose, under my own skin.

I did not understand the pervasiveness of sin—how I simultaneously wove it and got caught in it, and just how far-reaching its effects were. We always assume that its great gnarled roots lie somewhere else; at least I know I did. I always felt certain that someone else was responsible for casting shadows on my vista.

The flinging of small pebbles. The dropping of large rocks. The pond ripples out as a result either way, and the waves bring it all back to shore.

⸻

"Well, Drake, what do you think?" I heard Professor Nuttham's voice call out my last name somewhere in the distance. I shot into hyperalert, pushing the coats of my mind aside as I stepped back through the portal into the present. Since Oxford boasted a favorite childhood author, C. S. Lewis, I decided to revisit the Narnia Chronicles for my evening reading. As a result, Aslan was on the move in my imagination.

"Isn't it obvious that he is trying to create a name for himself, trying to enter the lineage of being a great epic poet?" Linnea interrupted. Fred followed closely, arguing, "No, I think he is primarily about metaphorical strategies of faulty man-made institutions: government, the military, organized religion."

What? Who? My mind raced. John Milton. Yes, that's who. Author of the great seventeenth-century English epic *Paradise Lost.*

> Out of the fertile ground he caused to grow
> All trees of noblest kind for sight, smell, taste;
> And all amid them stood the Tree of Life,
> High eminent, blooming ambrosial fruit
> Of vegetable gold; and next to life
> Our death the Tree of Knowledge grew fast by,
> Knowledge of good bought dear by knowing ill.[4]

My friends were trying to throw me a lifeline. Sinking, I looked at them with a worldful of gratitude, and took it. But just as I started going under in an attempt to say some load of theoretical crap, something actually quite sincere leapt in front of my speech, clear and confident and in my own voice.

"I think Milton is trying to feel his way through the dark." It just came out, as I had just done from the wardrobe. Obviously it, too, within me had been grappling for the surface. I tried not to look surprised.

Professor Nuttham stared at me intently. "Go on," he said. Linnea and Fred looked at each other, and then at me, nervously. Again Dr. Deveaux's image came to mind. I realized that the answer swelling up in me came from a very real, very personal place.

"He is going blind on one level. I can only imagine how particularly horrendous that would be, especially for a writer. But does he fear going blind, being blind, on another level even more so?" I heard myself saying, "Why, exactly, is he 'justifying these ways of God to men'? For whom is he writing? God doesn't need justification. He certainly doesn't need us. God doesn't need anything."

The room stayed quiet.

"Yet, it doesn't make us superfluous or unimportant, the fact that God doesn't need us," I rushed on. "Actually, quite the opposite. It's because He loves us *in spite* of not needing us that makes His love so, well, *awesome*."

Dr. Nuttham raised his eyebrows; slang was not encouraged in tutorials.

"In the original sense of the term," I quickly clarified. He lowered his brows in acceptance.

Inside me lights began to go on, an electrical surge; though out of habit, I checked the swell in my heart.

"Yes, I see what you mean," ventured Linnea. "I tend to confuse what I desire, what I think I need, with what I love or pretend to love. Even with the best intentions, everything, at some point, gets muddled. Can anyone love perfectly?"

"For man," I replied, "the trees grow so close together! I know I can't always tell the vines apart, especially in the dark. But there is no pretense in a love that is not based on need of the giver, that is not based on consumption of the other, but only on magnification."

Everyone stared at me with that initial Yeatsian silence. I surprised everyone, including me. Where had all of that come from?

I paused, collected my nerve, and then threw caution to the wind and added, "I think Milton is trying to show us the difference between Eden and heaven. Like the rest of us, he's trying to feel his own way along that continuum."

Everything in the room stayed very, very still. I willed the clock to chime, but it didn't.

"Despair *is* the greatest sin," Dr. Nuttham finally responded slowly. "It involves forgetting that God is there. Forgetting that He is good and that all He is and does extends from and works toward this perfect goodness. That doesn't mean that He allows evil, or creates it, or perpetuates it. That's our entwinement. Rather, He uses even our evil toward His good. We all need forms of remembering this first great love . . . writing, reading, creating, *being*." He paused, looking surprised too. Then he added, "I see," and smiled at his own inadvertent wording. He continued smiling softly as he rose to make tea.

Linnea leaned in and whispered, "*Whoa*." She put her fingers to her mouth and puffed, as though to sign that I had been smoking the funny stuff before class. I made a face back at her.

But I had to admit, I did feel a little high.

SIX

SHAKEN, NOT JUST STIRRED

*A sudden bold and unexpected question doth many times
surprise a [woman] and lay [her] open.*

—SIR FRANCIS BACON

It was a dark and stormy night (truly), when I boldly knocked on the door of the virgin predator. TDH loomed in the entryway; it struck me then just how very tall he was. In the computer lab he had been seated. But against the already short medieval arch to his room, he looked massive. He welcomed me in, and I stepped inside.

I gasped at the large bow window opposite. Spacious, with a bed, sitting area, and window seat, his room boasted one of the best views from the college. It looked out over the High onto the magnificence of St. Mary's Cathedral. How very different it was from my room, I thought with dismay. Mine was small and cramped, with a slanted floor and a view of bricks. If you dropped a coin, it rolled to the far corner by the door. If you left the window open during the day, you returned to a pigeon roosting on your radiator by evening. With its low light and great view, however, TDH's was obviously a chick-magnet room. Music by the Oriel College choir played softly in the background, haunting and beautiful. His bed was made, neat and tidy. Two chairs sat across from each other in the window nook. A bottle of Bailey's with matching glasses glinted from the little table.

Humph, I thought.

Pictures of his family decorated his desk and shelves. Smiling brothers—I could tell at once, since the family resemblance was undeniable. His father stood behind them all, looking proud and kind. His mother, bravely surrounded by her brood of men, shone bright and loving.

I opened our conversation by commenting on the pictures. That's when TDH surprised me. He began to speak at length, warmly and sincerely, about his deep respect for his mother. He talked about the sacrifices she had made for them, her inspiring spirit as the hub of their family, and the strengths she owned. He spoke unprompted and un-self-consciously.

Okay, I reasoned to myself. *Ax murderers luring female victims surely don't chat about their mothers this way.* I began to feel my guard slipping a little. Well, almost, recalling *Psycho*. So when TDH stepped out to make some coffee, I wandered over to his desk. It was obvious he was studying theology. Bibles of all kinds and commentaries were lined up within easy reach. Augustine and Aquinas were irreverently but impressively spread out in a mess of eager consumption. *Okay*, I thought again, *surely a serial virgin marauder doesn't think so highly of his mother and study the church fathers.* I felt my guard slipping again. Again, almost.

TDH returned with our coffee and motioned for me to sit. The classical music stopped, so he started the next disc. He handed me my mug. "Glad our last exchange was not, in fact, our last." He smiled; then, clearing his throat, he launched right in, "Well, no doubt you were curious and probably horrified when you saw that e-mail."

I didn't say anything, enjoying the sight of him twisting in the wind. Sinking into the comfortable chair, I took a sip of caffeine and braced myself. U2's hit "Pride (In the Name of Love)" entered the silence. Bono's voice arched over the line "one man betrayed by a kiss."

This is gonna be good, I thought.

Like all savvy orators, thinkers, teachers, and conversationalists, TDH began with a question. I should have expected that, but it caught me off guard. Served me right for teetering so precariously on "almost."

"Well, as I strap on my protective gear for this potentially very risky ride"—he settled into his chair—"I wondered, for context, what kind of a religious background, if any, you grew up with?"

"What do you mean?" I responded, not sure where he was headed.

TDH looked at me with genuine interest. "Who is God to you? I'd really like to know."

No one had actually asked me such pointed questions on the topic before. No friends or family. Certainly none of my teachers, even in class discussion.

I felt like a hummingbird that had hit the glass. Hard.

"Well," I stammered, "are you sure you'd really like to know?"

"Yes," TDH answered without hesitation.

Yes.

~~~~~~

TDH turned down the CD player. Now only my voice mingled with the shadows in the room. I explained how I grew up in a loosely European Catholic household. Although my boyfriend ardently called himself an atheist, I held firmly to agnostic, since I could not really disprove God. While I owned a distant respect for the sanctity of sacraments, the quiet reverence when entering a church, all the guardrails for living a "safe" life, I did not understand the reason for any of these rituals. As I gave it some thought, I had to admit why my father, too, might feel conflicted about "fathers." A drunk who beat my young immigrant grandmother, my paternal grandfather left his family before my father was walking. Over the years my father caught fleeting glimpses of my grandfather watching him through the schoolyard fence, or at the back of the church during my parents' wedding. I met my grandfather for the first time when I was twelve. My father tracked him down, only to find him dying. He spent their short reunion handling my grandfather's affairs and awkwardly bringing us children in tow to see him.

God, I supposed, existed somewhere on the periphery and in the abstract. Knowing him any more intimately than this seemed entirely alien to me.

"What's your take on Jesus?" TDH asked simply. "Do you know much about Him?"

"Of course I know Jesus," I practically guffawed. "Everyone knows Jesus."

This guy is *a wacko*, I thought. *I mean, does he think just because I'm from Canada I've lived under a rock my entire life?*

"Well then, what do you know about Him?" TDH looked at me intently, kindly.

I opened my mouth but then stopped. Images of cows and sheep huddled in a manger came to mind, followed by a thin, sickly man hanging on the great cross at the front of my grandmother's church. I remembered how my sister and I washed our sticky fingers in the holy water after sneaking treats into our pew. I saw a man gentle-eyed, bearded, robed, and sandaled, suspended in the pages of time on my grandmother's kitchen wall. My idea of Jesus remained bound to the plastic baby from my public school nativity plays, which were eventually banned, along with the Lord's Prayer and anything resembling a hymn, by the public school board. Faith was not a familiar concept, let alone a way of life.

My mom prayed fervently every night in whispers. I admired her constancy although I wished I knew her heart better. She trusted in various saints and believed in a heavenly, if somewhat clockwork, Father, yet Mom became uncomfortable when faced with what Jesus claims. She's a Libra, so she's naturally indecisive. Like her earthly father, she enjoyed shocking people by declaring Jesus the first communist. Jesus was a poor, perhaps confused, itinerant hippie to be pitied—someone who got in over His head when He was really just a well-intentioned guy. I would smile when she said these things.

What is faith? How does one have faith? I could not have given any kind of answer to such questions. If God existed at all, He seemed, perhaps, interested at times, though just barely.

But *Jesus*? He seemed tougher to place. It suddenly

occurred to me that apart from the clichéd images or flat memories, I did not know who this Jesus was in 3-D. Random images and pieces of stories. This body—born, dead, risen, or otherwise. I had no clue why He had come, and why He had to die, and if He really was raised from the dead. Or if any of it really mattered.

Repentance. Resurrection. Redemption. Grace? Such words meant nothing to me.

Talking to TDH I suspected my background resembled countless others nowadays in North American culture. Lots of astrology, but little theology.

TDH listened without interrupting.

"Did you know any Christians growing up?" TDH asked when I had finished.

"Sure. Aren't most good people 'Christian'?" I tossed out my rote response.

TDH did not say anything, so I gave it some more thought and added slowly, "Well . . . there was one girl in public school and another in high school who talked about knowing Jesus, but the former dressed in homemade plaid clothing, and the latter was pregnant by her senior year and had to drop out before graduation." *Besides*, I thought, *I was far too busy with more important matters, such as my studies and bills and student council. Such as deciding whether to eat lunch or take the bus, since I couldn't afford both. And keeping everyone around me happy so that I could be happy too.* "A Savior, a Holy Ghost, and 'hearing the voice of God'?" I added instead, "*Creepy!*"

TDH laughed in agreement. "Well then, what's your take on this Jesus?" he prodded.

I explained how in my hometown of London, Ontario, Canada—a colonial miniature of London, England, with its own Thames River and a Wellington Square interspersed among Native American archaeological sites—we have no polite need of a Savior. I certainly had no memory of anyone espousing any real relationship with Jesus, how that is achieved, or *why* or even *if* it mattered.

Or maybe I had?

Dr. Deveaux and his polite profanity crossed my mind. I started to open my mouth but then closed it again.

"What is it?" TDH prompted gently.

I remained silent. How to tell him? What words were there to say? I certainly did not think God lurked among families like mine—loving enough to get by without Him, but broken enough not to deserve His attention.

❧

Something else occurred to me as I sat there, embraced by the shadowed light of the bay window. I felt like a sleeper on the brink of waking, trying to grasp a fleeting dream.

Hesitantly I stammered, "Well, when I really think back on it all, I guess I have always felt some sort of presence—I don't know what exactly. I mean, for instance, if we're going to return to the whole virginity thing, I have always felt as though we are all made for deep relationship. I don't mean this in a prudish, judgmental way, but in the sense that whenever we do give up easily on people, or have one-night stands, or divorce, especially on a whim, it's no wonder we feel empty inside, even if we don't want to admit it. We seem 'wired' for so much more." But then I caught myself. I sipped my coffee to prevent my saying to TDH that I certainly was not going to trust in any multiply translated book or human preacher or random set of doctrines. I pursed my lips as the cream and sugar rolled over with the spite.

TDH sat there quietly across from me. The streetlights cast strange shadows across the little table between our two chairs. His silence made me nervous. I was starting to fear that I had tipped my hand too much. Before he could ask another question, I decided it was my turn to raise the racket.

"Well then, what's your take on it all? What's your background, and why do you have virgin hunters for friends?" I ventured.

"Hmmm." TDH emerged from his own thoughts. "Well, if you're even loosely Euro-Catholic by background, then you can at least appreciate that virginity is linked to many people's notion of faith, and not just for Mary."

I nodded. I could see that. I did not understand it completely, but I could see it.

Seeing my acknowledgment, he shrugged. "Well, that's what it is to me."

I looked at him bug-eyed.

Amazingly unruffled, he continued, "For many, the label 'Christian' conjures up mostly unfortunate and inaccurate (if often deserved) images of cultural misfits who are strange, out of step, unthinking inhabitants of the fringe who live stiff, joyless lives, speak through rote, jargon-based scripts, and have swirls for eyes."

You bet it does! I yelled inwardly. I must have flinched involuntarily, however, because TDH gave me a knowing smile. A handsome, lopsided smile.

"For me," he explained, "at least in good faith, I hope, being a committed 'Christian' is a label that is not really cultural at all. It is theological."

I listened carefully; I figured I owed him the return of the favor.

"This might totally shock you," he continued, "but I am one of those people who believe that Jesus Christ was, indeed, everything He said He was."

Wow! I thought but said nothing, instead studying TDH carefully. *Do these freaky Jesus people actually live among us, undetected?*

As if he were reading my thoughts, TDH continued. "If I'm honest, many of today's Christians are freakier than Jesus ever was. It's funny how life often seems the greatest barrier to faith, even for those who claim to have it." TDH sighed. "I cringe at these stereotypes too. A lot of Christians really do sound like complete weirdos. The bigger buffoons, however, I think, might be those who seem to glory in flogging this stereotype, instead of being curious, or maybe courageous, enough to look behind it."

I sat perfectly still. He shrugged. "Especially since it raises, much of the time, their own issues."

Humph. I shifted in my seat, curious without conviction.

"*You* are no doubt enlightened," he inserted in a gracious tone, "but contrary to urban legend, there is actually an entire underworld of Christians who are normal, alert, engaged, even a good time. Many are very smart, well educated, even leaders in their fields. These are people who participate in real life and the open-minded discussions about it. I have met some of them in reading and in person." He grinned. "But I digress."

Grinning, too, I could not help but think of Lord Byron's

pronouncement that in life there exists no such thing as a digression.

"According to the Bible," TDH continued, "Jesus said some pretty crazy stuff, which most people who at least recognize the guy's name have never actually engaged and dealt with."

True, I conceded internally. *I mean, I'm sitting here judging, I guess, and I have never really read the Bible or done much informed exploring. Especially sad for a student of literature*, I realized weightily.

"I would be happy to explain more about what I believe, to the degree you are interested," TDH offered. "But for now, here's the one-minute version, and you may know all this."

I settled back, growing more intrigued but trying not to show it too much.

To his credit TDH did not speak through a rote, jargon-based script; nor did his eyes swirl as he began. "The human condition is *sin*, that nasty three-letter word no one likes to talk about. The original sin was, of course, Adam's and Eve's in the garden of Eden, disobeying God and choosing their own way. And all human beings have inherited the disease, so to speak. *Sin* is essentially 'separation from God,' the consequence of serving ourselves over everyone else—in a word, *hell*. Hell is a very real place, the default destination (after death) for all human beings who remain separated from God."

"Okay," I said, to ensure that I was tracking. "So what is heaven?" I asked.

"Well, distilled again, the Bible says that heaven is like an ideal world, the perfect place, a restored world without sin or death or decay, where human beings are reunited with God and enjoy the ultimate and eternal experience of joy, peace, and fulfillment beyond words," TDH answered. "Think of your perfect day, your perfect life, and multiply that by something big, and maybe you're glimpsing the outer gates of heaven."

Cool, I thought. "But if I'm always, or eventually, going to prefer myself—my own needs and wants—then how do I get from A to B? I mean, how do I shift from being 'separated' to being 'reunited'?"

"Good question," TDH nodded. "That's precisely where Jesus comes in. Christians believe that Jesus was who He said He was. That is, He was the Messiah, the perfect Son of God, who became man and died in our place to save us from sin so that our relationship with God could be restored."

"Whoa," I whispered. Even if too crazy to be true, I had to admit this, too, was a very cool idea.

TDH smiled so genuinely I had to smile as well. "Put another way, this Messiah is the fulfillment of prophecy. The One sent by God to a sin-stained world to defeat death and save His people, who, incidentally, turn out to be anyone who wants a relationship with God." TDH took a sip of his coffee.

"What of the 'chosen people'?" I asked, certain that this must be an elitist God. A picky, prickly God.

"Well, in some ways, I think it's also a '*choosing* people.'" TDH smiled again.

I threw him a confused look.

"You may have heard the old argument, just which one is this Jesus: liar, lunatic or Lord?" TDH asked.

Well, that sure encapsulates things, I thought to myself.

TDH continued, "It all comes down to Jesus Christ, and what you *choose* to believe about Him. Jesus claims He is the Son of God. Jesus claims He died for you and rose from the dead. He claims that the only way to cancel out your sin and spend eternity in heaven is to believe that He is who He said He was. These are the claims on the table. Bold claims. It will make you wince, won't it?" he sort of asked.

I definitely winced.

"Personally, I think the boldness of the claims makes the choosing a lot easier," TDH ventured on. "Most people who have never actually read the menu probably assume they can order à la carte at the Jesus table or customize their own recipe of faith. But you can't say yes to the historical figure and a few parables but pass on miracles, the resurrection, and the Son-of-God thing. That is not the offering. Christ is a fixed meal. It is all or nothing with His claims. Everyone is invited, but only you can decide if you actually want to eat at His table. For those who do believe in Christ, it means getting real, being honest about your sin, and living your life as if you really mean it."

I looked down at my half-empty cup.

"And what about the Bible?" I asked, bracing myself with more caffeine.

TDH gave it some thought, then replied, "Well, in a nutshell, a Christian believes that the Bible is actually the revealed Word of God, true, inerrant, and thus 'holy.' God gave us the Scriptures because He wants us to know Him. The Bible is powerful—there's no other way to put it, though I admit that sounds freaky too. Technically the Old Testament spells out the prophecy of redemption. Then the fulfillment of that prophecy, and its application to our real lives, happens in the New Testament through Jesus Christ."

"I see." I mulled it over. Prior to that image, the Bible had simply seemed one big, holy, confusing mess. And somewhat of a killjoy, if you asked me, rather than a joy maker. Impressionistically speaking, of course. Like most folks I knew, I had never *really* read it.

I sipped my coffee in silence.

"Things sort of come full circle, I guess," TDH said gently, "like the birth, death, and resurrection of Christ that Christians believe in. With honest introspection comes repentance. And with repentance, the heart is laid open for real relationship. And with real relationship comes restoration and truth. You can't experience real relationship without at least attempting self-awareness."

True, I thought.

"Or authentic apology."

Very true, I thought again, tracing the rim of my now-empty cup. *Perhaps God sets us in families to learn this firsthand?*

"But other than sincere introspection, which leads to repentance and to the open hand and heart required for faith, the really neat thing," TDH added so joyfully it made me look up, "is that there isn't anything you can *do* or *be* to earn or deserve God's love."

I studied him, uncertain. I had worked so hard for everything I had achieved. Surely this could not be true.

"So what is faith?" I asked, hesitantly, not sure if I wanted to know the answer.

TDH leaned forward so that his face was now entirely lit by the streetlamp glow. "Faith is simply belief in the gift of eternal life, made possible by Christ's death and resurrection," TDH offered. "This gift of grace is ours for the taking. We just have to accept it. And then living your life according to this love is the other present, if you pardon the pun," he smiled.

I smiled back, in spite of myself. I love puns.

"This is the 'gospel,' or what you might have heard referred to, and appropriately, as 'the good news,'" he concluded very simply.

I nodded slowly. No one had ever explained it to me like that before.

"Wow! There is no doubt that believing real Christianity requires some ginormous intellectual leaps of faith. God-became-Man. Resurrection. Life eternal. Heaven and hell. It's not exactly a neat and tidy math equation, is it?" I asked, exhaling.

"Definitely not. The leap is huge." TDH sighed with agreement. "There is one small comfort I lean on, however, which helps my head meet up with my heart and soul," he said sincerely. "The Christian faith can be accused of lots of things, but incoherence is not really one of them, I don't think. It seems to me that it is a *bona fide* worldview. It at least has an answer for the universe, an intelligible plan behind life, and a God big enough to handle it. If one has to choose (for *not* choosing is also a choice), that's more than any other available alternative can offer. But that is a pretty big can of worms I just opened!" He coughed jokingly.

I smiled and worried. I liked to connect with everyone, while not being defined by anyone, I reminded myself. Christianity, as I knew of it, seemed far too incompatible with having gay friends or going to a rock concert. And now this Jesus required I make a conscious decision? It seemed to me you could not possibly have your communion wafer and eat it too.

"So, if you want a good summary of what real Christians believe . . ." He paused.

I shrugged in agreement. Why not?

"As a well-rounded literature student, you might actually enjoy looking up and dissecting something like the Apostles'

Creed. Think of it as a group of professor types in the fourth century trying to agree on what's important to the faith. You may well have seen it in the Catholic catechism. It is also generally accepted by a dozen or more of the biggest Protestant denominations. Every one of its twelve lines is carefully constructed and wrought with huge questions for the inquiring mind to explore and fight with," TDH smirked. "It's not iambic pentameter, mind you, but it does pack quite a punch."

I looked over at his desk, remembering his own studies.

"A punch," he said simply, "that every fighter must either take or dodge."

All good food for thought, but I was not going to let him off that easily. I decided, instead, to take a leaf from my mom's book and change the subject. Or, rather, change the subject *back*.

"What about that e-mail?" I cringed.

"Look," he addressed me honestly. "It's not as if being a virgin before marriage dominates everything for Christians. It's not an interview question or some sort of prerequisite for real relationship, or heaven, or otherwise. Rather, I like to think of it as a special gift related to a joy that only a fulfilled promise can bring. Whatever it is, it's the ideal for marriage and a commandment, as God has put it to us. So as a real Christian, I have to take it seriously and trust that there must be some important element in the design." But then he took a deep breath, "Granted, as a single man, my red-blooded male flesh sometimes wants to scream at God for this 'guide.' But if I'm honest, it's not actually that difficult for me to understand why I am way better off if I just stick with His plan on this one," he said, finishing with an audible exhale.

Stunned silence from me.

Oh, I thought, harking back to my almost-fiancé. Something rang painfully true, or at least relevant, inside me. Something brilliant and shining lost from my childhood and deemed irretrievable, like sea glass at my feet—there one moment, gone the next as the tide swept in.

"So, what was your background?" I managed to pose politely, all the while burning to ask instead, "Do you think women are therefore secondary, submissive citizens? Will you make love to your wife through a hole in a sheet? Or make her feel guilty if she works outside the home and doesn't have a dozen kids? Do you hate gays? What do you do with all that pent-up sexual tension? Is your family like that girl's from *Footloose*? Do you look the other way when the guy in church cheats on his wife or abuses his kid? Do you read the smutty part of novels? Do you ever have *any* fun?"

TDH answered with a sincerity that halted the stream of questions rising up in my head, at least for the moment. "I feel lucky that I grew up in a home that taught and upheld these beliefs, but I have also thought them through very carefully for myself. My dad is hip, fun, a bit of a war hero, too, I guess. He is a pastor of all things, but he's also a real person—a person who understands what it is like to long for things, to suffer, to be at odds with the world. And by enduring example he has shown me, along with my mom, that while it's not often easy living a life committed to Christ, it is the only life that makes sense and the only life that matters." He sat back. "So that is what I believe."

I thought of my brother's jokes about coiffed television pastors. I squinted past TDH's shoulder, trying to get another look at his dad's hair in the photo.

"Caro . . ." I looked back at him. "It's all good." He winked.

I sat there, empty cup in hand. Changed. Somehow.

"Well, all this may sound totally wacked to you." He grinned infectiously. "And hopefully I'm not as disgusting as you must have first thought." He stretched in his chair. "So shall I walk you to the door, and you can just politely smile from afar when we bump into each other in the porter's lodge? Or shall I get you another cup of coffee?"

TDH stood up, waiting.

Just who was this Jesus? And, to be fair, was I even qualified to judge? I did not have a relationship with Him; I barely even knew Him. I certainly didn't know Him as TDH seemed to know Him.

Fill my cup or leave the table?

I continued to think. *Could Christians actually be "normal"?* And yet there was something about TDH that was decidedly *not* normal, and yet decidedly not freaky either. For that something I was strangely grateful—curious about, drawn to, and intrigued by. *Something* set him apart, but I could not quite put my finger on it.

A car suddenly backfired on the street below, shattering the expectant silence like a starting pistol. I held out my mug with the Oxford University crest on it.

"The way you made it the first time was perfect," I confessed, unnerved.

SEVEN

SWEET-TALKIN' SON
OF A PREACHER MAN

*Even in the valley of the shadow of death, two and two
do not make six.*

—LEO TOLSTOY

So there it was, that stormy night. I finally heard the gospel. Plain and clear. From a guy who looked like the traditional James Bond, but who could not be further from the sexual conquest caricature. That is the bizarre thing about the good news: who knows how you will really hear it one day, but once you have heard it, I mean really *heard* it, you can never *unhear* it. Once you have read it, or spoken it, or thought it, even if it irritates you, even if you hate hearing it or cannot find it feasible, or try to dismiss it, you cannot *unread* it, or *unspeak* it, or *unthink* it.

It is like a great big elephant in a tiny room. Its obvious presence begins to squeeze out everything else, including your own little measly self. Some accept it easily, some accept it quickly, and some are struck with the mystical reality of it right away. These people have no trouble bringing the *unseen* into the realm of the *seen*. But others of us fight the elephant; we push back on it, we try to ignore it, get it to leave the room, or attempt to leave the room ourselves. But it does not help. The trunk keeps curling around the doorknob. The hook is there. It may snooze or loom or rise and recede, but regardless of the time passed or the vanity endured, the idea keeps coming back, like a cosmic boomerang you just cannot throw away. I did not realize this was part of the grace of it all—such relentless truthfulness.

From that night forward I began nailing TDH incessantly with questions—all the oldies but goodies, such as how could a loving God, who is omniscient, set up such a trap in Eden for his own children to surely fall like that? How could a supposedly all-loving God allow pain and suffering? Why do children die? Isn't it hard enough to believe in one God, especially without any actual proof, let alone a Trinity? How can I be a sinner if I have never really done anything all *that* bad? Is hell really fire and brimstone? Are Christians actually naive enough to take the Bible as truth, to believe all those madcap stories?

And, of course, the whammy: why doesn't this God, here and now, *do something*? Or put another way, just where *is* He?

I slung them at TDH like arrows of outrageous fortune, one after the other. Certainly he would stumble. Surely at any point a shaft would break in his heart, and he would bleed to death.

The onslaught continued for months after this first conversation. I now understand why the words *conversation* and *conversion* are evocative of each other, turning toward each other, yet separated merely by where you are "at."

All being said, it was probably TDH's unwavering tone of patience, respect, and kindness that spoke more to me than all the syllogisms or intellectual arguments put together. All of this, of course, infuriated me.

"I would hope a God that I believe in is bigger than I am," he said one night. I argued that I could not appreciate something if I did not understand it. He held that his appreciation for something only grew if he could not comprehend it fully.

After one particularly intense conversation, we both finally realized the time. Where had it gone? It was so late as to almost be early. I stood up to go, irritated and ill at ease. At the doorway I shot one last arrow over my shoulder. I couldn't resist.

"This God, your Jesus," I said, "for all of His so-called love and sacrifice, sounds awfully exclusive. Even harsh. And besides, how do we even really know He is who He claims to be?"

"That's your decision," TDH said. It was now his turn to look at me hard. "Jesus was crucified among common criminals, a thief to His left and to His right. One denied Him and ridiculed Him; the other recognized the consequences of his sin, proclaimed Jesus' innocence, then asked Him to 'remember me when you come into your kingdom' [Luke 23:42]. Do you know what Jesus said to Him?"

"No," I replied, but then added cynically, "Yeah, He probably told him, 'You bet I won't remember you. You live a life of sin and then you expect to be forgiven? And at the very last minute, in the face of fear and death and possible judgment? How hypocritical is that?!'"

TDH continued to look at me, answering simply, "Jesus said to him, 'Today you will be with me in paradise' [v. 43]. Only God knows our hearts, the innermost workings of our souls.

Ultimately, that is for Him to judge. And thank God I am not God. But in the case of both the thief on the cross and other stories like it from the Bible, there isn't a single one of us on this earth not like them in some way, shape, or form."

Seeing my hesitation, TDH moved to the edge of his seat with a look of resolve. "Caro, the thief in his hour of need was pinned to a cross, helpless to act and utterly vulnerable. Like the prodigal son, in many ways we are each ruined, hungry, and destitute—driven, literally, a slave to our ways. All that's left at times is the raw awareness of our need. Humility, or the ending point of being lost, can become the starting point of righteousness."

Rather than feeling bulldozed, as I would have expected to feel (especially by a man), I felt steered away from the edge of a cliff. Boldly. Carefully. Lovingly.

"The Father, whether as all-powerful landlord or lowly companion in our hour of crucifixion, rejoices in that open heart and responds with one equally open, one that has always been open. So if you really think about it," he said softly, "thank God these stories end as they do. Quite literally, *thank God*."

I stood puzzled at the doorway. Somehow the shaft had ended up in *my* heart.

I shuddered at the sudden apprehension that grace trumps karma.

TDH winked at me. "To paraphrase a prophet, Caro, the Lord has plans for you, and they are not for calamity" (Jer. 29:11). Then he opened the door for me to go.

It was those morphing hours when night is almost becoming day, when you are not sure whether to refer to it as "late" or "early"—the "darkling" hours, as poets such as John Keats or Thomas Hardy would say—when I left TDH's room. The elephant came with me. Together we watched the dried leaves swirl in a minifunnel cloud in the corner of the quad. Together we walked back to my room with the approaching dawn. I still remember the birdsong. Despite the walled gardens, the magnificent castlelike buildings, the cobblestone streets, there is always birdsong in Oxford.

My room was more cramped than ever with the elephant in tow. I turned on the radio by my bed and then went into the nook of a bathroom and turned on the shower. The weather report: storms throughout the week, fog, intermittent showers, and some sun. In short, we could expect a bit of everything and nothing predictable. *Ancient Mariner weather*, I thought. *Rainbow weather too.*

I stepped out of my typhoon bathroom into my robe and wrapped a towel as a turban around my head, feeling now quite shamanic. It was then that I noticed how Dusty Springfield's voice filled the room:

> *The only one who could ever reach me*
> *Was the son of a preacher man.*[1]

You've got to be kidding me, I thought wryly as I sat on my bed. Irked, I reached over and turned off the radio as I pulled the towel from my damp head and threw it across my only chair. I lay back on my slim, lumpy army cot. Thinking again of TDH's room, I savored my dissatisfaction as an ill-tempered child and struck my pillow, trying to fluff it up to the impossibility of my liking.

The windowpanes in the soft morning light cast a shadowy cross on the ceiling directly above my bed. I turned defiantly on my side, my back to the window. But I could not get comfortable. I tossed and turned beneath the paradoxical weight of the silhouetted cross. I could not help but see it, so rudely overt for a subtleist like me. I squeezed my eyes shut. But when I opened them again, there it was, looming, literally, over me.

"Okay, okay, I get the hint," I said out loud.

Very funny.

It ticked me off.

EIGHT

JESUS, THE GREAT POLARIZER

You have enemies? Good. That means you stood up for something, sometime in your life.

—WINSTON CHURCHILL

A nyone wish to join me in blessing the Irish?" Edward stood up in search of his usual Guinness. At most British pubs you place your own order at the bar; sometimes hot food was brought to you, but usually you picked up your own drinks. The implicit statement (a British trait in general) behind the absence of waiters was that you took responsibility for your own drunkenness.

"If you want to really tick people off, just bring up the word *Jesus*." Rachel looked at each of us around the table, mischievously. Edward sat back down, intrigued in spite of himself.

Hannah leaned in. She savored tripping up inattentive or

87

inconsiderate people. At her American college she inserted an obscenity in her thesis, just to see if anyone would catch it. She was prepared to dismiss it as a typing mistake if anyone reacted, but no one did. She remained proud of herself for that one.

"I know what Rachel's saying," Mark grinned. "Years after my conversion, I still get a kick out of the inevitable reaction. Say *Jesus* and people either get happy, or they get mad. They either smile, or a cloud comes over their faces. They are either elated or irritated. Embarrassed, they try to change the subject or walk away. Or engaged, they pursue deeper conversation and connection. No other name has such potency. Not Clinton, not Gandhi, not Thatcher, not Lennon." Mark paused, and then added, "Contrary to what he thought."

The entire table, regardless of spiritual position, let out a communal laugh.

"Whenever things are getting a little boring at a cocktail party, for instance, or in the cashier's line, it's sure to spice things up. Try it. Speak *Jesus* and see what people do." Rachel sipped her lager.

"I'd probably dismiss myself from the conversation and make my way to the bar," Linnea giggled.

"Seriously," agreed Hannah, "I bet most would shake Jesus off like a guy with a bad pickup line."

But not without being a little permanently unsettled by it, I thought. *It's hard to shake off an elephant perched on your soul.*

Rachel shrugged. "Some people are saved by statements or by secrets. Others by arguments or exclamations, echoes or resonations."

Edward *humph*ed.

Dorian picked up the shaker and started pouring salt out onto the table. He smoothed the white pile into a glimmering page.

Then he drew a line in it. "Not sure where you stand, Edward?" he asked pointedly.

Edward *humph*ed again as he rubbed his face hard with his hands. "I'm getting a pint," he announced as he stood up and walked to the bar.

Gathered in the college pub, this eclectic group of friends was unique. Although we each held different marks on the God-o-meter, I felt entirely safe with all of them. As we grew to know each other well, I had been providing regular installments about my conversations with TDH. Unfortunately TDH could not join us often. Enrolled in the most compressed degree program of all of us, he curbed more of his social time to study. We owned little pity for TDH, however, since he enjoyed the exclusive Christ Church college by proxy through his renowned supervisor. Arguably the most famous of the Oxford colleges, Christ Church boasts, among countless other elaborate things, extensive grounds and a dining hall so beautiful you can barely focus on the food before you. The college even employs "beadles" (security guards wearing little black hats) to patrol the premises and scold wayward tourists for touching the grass.

I looked at the women. Linnea and Hannah were openly searching and deeply kind. Linnea saw the metaphorical in everything, while Hannah was all about pragmatics. Raised a Christian by missionary parents in various third-world countries, Rachel's cosmopolitism wore a deep compassion. She spoke almost a dozen languages, including some minor tribal dialects. All three women were loyal and strong; they were there for me in a heartbeat, quick to remind me that I was amazing, competent, and loved.

I considered the men. There stood Edward, leaning maverick-like against the bar. Attractive in that unshaven, bohemian writer kind of way, he used his British accent as a weapon on American women, quoting from *Moby-Dick*, his favorite book (need I say more?). Dorian's father ranked as one of the wealthiest men in the Middle East before they immigrated to the U.S. He looked just like JFK Jr., except for the fact that he had lost his hand as a child in a street bombing while visiting relatives. He also had a deeper tan. After he became a Christian, his parents threatened to disown him, but his father loved him too much to carry out any such act. Now his mother and all of his siblings were Christians too. His father, proud and fierce, forbade saying grace at dinner. Yet this patriarch remained perplexed by his strange, new family who continued to adore and respect him.

Then there were the two older students, returning for their graduate degrees in theology: we often jokingly referred to them as M&M. One was an Irish priest, Michael, attractive and jovial. *How can he be a priest?* I thought when I first met him. I reserved the same politically incorrect judgment for him that I did for most of my male gay friends, who usually tended to be disproportionately attractive as well: *what a waste!* I slowly grew to respect Michael's articulate and then living definition of "calling," however—a concept I had never truly considered before.

Mark was born in Vietnam to an American father and then came to New York, eventually making a lot of money and doing a lot of drugs. After getting sober he attended college, where he became a Christian. He considered becoming a professor, but his inaugural experience irritated him. "Everyone assumed I would teach Asian American literature," he told us. "They are shocked when I insist my specialty is Hebrew and the Old Testament." Realizing, too, that academia does not leave much margin to minister to others, he decided to go to seminary in England.

Atheist, believer, and everywhere in between, we would often go to Evensong, or the Anglican liturgy of prayer that is sung in the evening. Bound by a common liturgy, each college offers a different experience of the service. A motley crew, we would travel together, dropping into services first on a whim, then eventually as a custom of common enjoyment. With its candlelit and melodic beauty, the evening ritual brings peace at the close of day. The increasingly familiar words, sung low and meditatively, linger and then drift off with you into your dreams.

"Have you tried talking to Ben about any of this?" Hannah asked. "I mean, you'll be *marrying* the guy, Caro. Shouldn't he know about the spiritual questions you are facing?"

"I've tried," I stammered, thinking of how tricky it seemed to bring up Jesus to someone whose opinion of me mattered greatly, but who once compared believing in God to holding firmly that the world was flat.

"No one gets their knickers in a knot about anyone except Jesus," Mark said plainly. "If you were telling your fiancé you were considering Buddhism, or Islam, or Wicca, you wouldn't be so clearly anxious. And he would likely have taken it all in stride, because you would be tolerated, even celebrated, for your open-mindedness, your multiculturalism, your hipness. But Jesus? *Whoa.* That's a whole other gig."

Michael nodded; he was one of those sneaky, undetectable priests because he did not conform to wearing the clerical collar usually required. "Better get used to people thinking you've sold out to a mindless culture, which is really ironic," he said more wistfully than judgmentally, "given that although our culture, at least in the North American and European sense, might primarily identify itself as 'Christian,' most don't appear to really live a life in intimate relationship with Christ."

"Yeah," Mark continued, "believe me, I know. Tell your friends you 'found Jesus' or that He found you, and they'll start avoiding you, assuming that you sit up at night condemning everyone on every little thing. Better prepare yourself. Folks didn't even understand Jesus in His own time, even in His own hometown. So if it were like that for the God of all creation, why would it be any better for you? All your former professors, all your peers, in fact, everyone who doesn't, well, 'get it,' will think you are . . ."

"A freak," Dorian stated. Several people sitting around us turned to look at me accusingly.

"Or nutters," commented Hannah.

"Or more precisely, a nutty freak," Edward muttered as he lit the cigarette between his lips.

"Boy, you're making it sound all the more attractive," I retorted.

"Cynicism is the last refuge of petty minds," Linnea said with her usual flair.

"You don't believe either," I shot back at her.

"Unlike you, however, my dear, I'm not looking for reasons not to believe," she shrugged.

I heeded Confucius on that one and stayed quiet for once.

"Caro, I can see the conversion happening on your face," Michael said gently. Such a presumptive statement normally would have affronted me, except that Michael lilted it in his beautiful Irish accent.

"I can hear it in your multileveled homesickness." His words struck my first Achilles' heel.

"I can too. You're a smart girl, Caro," Rachel interjected. "Why don't you look into this Jesus thing for yourself? Why don't you start by reading the Bible, plain and simple? I'm amazed that those who are quickest to defame it are usually the ones least acquainted with it."

There. That struck my other Achilles' heel. *Ouch.*

Pinned now, I listened in spite of myself.

"Do you know what the word *conversion* means?" Michael asked. "Sorry, I'm an etymology nut. I love the source of words, their origins and evolutions. Thanks for indulging me."

Gee, he has me there too, I thought. *For all of my shoes, I'm running out of heels.*

"It's from the Latin *convertere*, 'to turn around, transform,'" Michael explained. "'To turn together.' Also connected to the Old English *cierran*, which meant both 'to turn' and 'to return.' As in 'turning back on something to see it again anew.' Or, to put it another way, it's 'returning to something from which you turned earlier,' but understanding it now, returning to it with a new way of seeing it."

"Hey, hold on," I cried, trying to rein them in. "I haven't actually *become* a Christian, remember?"

"Oh, it's just a matter of time now," Rachel said, patting my hand. "Once you start asking the questions that really matter, it's pretty inevitable."

"Now, now," Dorian said, "don't go freaking her out. That never does anyone any good."

"You're sure freaking *me* out," Edward chimed in as he returned to the table and sat back down. He crossed his legs and pulled his knees up to his chest, making his James Dean demeanor only look more wounded. Then he made a cross over his pint like a bishop presiding over communion before taking a long drink. "Aren't all *evangelicals*"—Edward shivered at using the word—"crazy people with billboards, shouting from the street corner? Surely anyone with any intelligence can't subscribe to something as vague and insular as faith, let alone 'organized religion.'"

"Oh, that's so demeaning." Rachel took the bait. I could see Edward start to grin. She saw it, too, and threw her cardboard coaster at him.

"But really," Rachel insisted, "so unfair. Just as Christians automatically cannot be folks who give serious thought to what they are doing. As though millions of people for hundreds of years across hundreds of cultures have simply had it *wrong*. Chesterton was right when he claimed that 'the Christian ideal has not been tried and found wanting; it has been found difficult and left untried.'"

"You have yet to try me, Caro." Edward smirked as he licked the foam from his glass rim.

"So, what to trust then?" I ignored Edward and addressed Dorian.

"Who," Dorian replied.

"What?" I asked, confused.

"Not *what*, but *whom*," Dorian said in his precise, textbook English, which, spoken with the trace of a childhood Arabic accent, reminded me of an exotic bird—familiar in species but with the flourish of a colorful, unspeakably beautiful tail.

"Okay, now you sound like a *Laurel and Hardy* replay," I huffed, frustrated.

Edward reached over me to steal a sip from Rachel's glass, but she slapped his hand away.

"Uh-oh, here we go," groaned Hannah. "Can't we all just get along now, children?"

U2's famous front man, Bono (born Paul Hewson), shared the gospel with author Michka Assayas during an interview. "There's nothing hippie about my picture of Christ. The Gospels paint a picture of a very demanding, sometimes divisive love, but love it is." Assayas responded that he wished he could believe in such wonderful hope, but he found it implausible, even lunatic. "Christ has His rank among the world's great thinkers," he told Bono, "but Son of God, isn't that far-fetched?"

Bono, arguably the world's current most famous rock star, replied:

No, it's not far-fetched to me. Look, the secular response to the Christ story always goes like this: he was a great prophet, obviously a very interesting guy, had a lot to say along the lines of other great prophets, be they Elijah, Muhammad, Buddha, or Confucius. But actually Christ doesn't allow you that. He doesn't let you off that hook. Christ says: *No. I'm not saying I'm a teacher, don't call me teacher. I'm not saying I'm a prophet. I'm saying: "I'm the Messiah." I'm saying: "I am God incarnate."* And people say: *No, no, please, just be a prophet. A prophet, we can take. You're a bit eccentric.*

We've had John the Baptist eating locusts and wild honey, we can handle that. But don't mention the "M" word! Because, you know, we're gonna have to crucify you. And He goes: *No, no. I know you're expecting me to come back with an army, and set you free from these creeps, but actually I am the Messiah.* At this point, everyone starts staring at their shoes, and says: *Oh my God, he's gonna keep saying this.* So what you're left with is: either Christ was who He said He was—the Messiah—or a complete nutcase. I mean, we're talking nutcase on the level of Charles Manson . . . This man was strapping himself to a bomb, and had "King of the Jews" on his head, and, as they were putting him up on the Cross, was going: *OK, martyrdom, here we go. Bring on the pain! I can take it.* I'm not joking here. The idea that the entire course of civilization for over half of the globe could have its fate changed and turned upside-down by a nutcase, for me, *that's* far-fetched . . . [1]

Bono is self-admittedly no scholar. But learning and wisdom are not the same thing. Besides, Bono sure is nice to listen to when you are studying, when you are making out, when you are driving. His voice, calling . . .

"You better get used to seeing things differently from most, to being able to see properly at all," Michael said, reaching across the table to lay a hand on my arm. "It comes initially as a shock, but then you'll eventually get more used to it. And then it comes with an array of emotions, a depth of consciousness you are humbled and exalted by. Conversion. *Everything*, including yourself, gets turned around. Transformed."

"What happens if you turn *from* one, but can't fully turn *to* the other?" I cried. "Tell me, Michael, is there a word for being eternally, pathetically, insurmountably 'stuck'?" I paused, searching for the right words, the words that would convey exactly how my soul ached but could not quite leap. They were evading me.

The entire table sat still.

"Tell me," I finally got out, grappling for a light switch in the dark. "Is there a word for wanting to forget this God and Jesus and the whole mess? For wanting to forget it *all*?" I pinned him with my eyes.

"*Despair*," he reminded me, draining his glass.

NINE

THE CONUNDRUM OF TIME

We returned to our places, these Kingdoms,
But no longer at ease here, in the old dispensation,
With an alien people clutching their gods.[1]

—T. S. ELIOT

Life at Oxford University opened before me in a vastness of "firsts." Most importantly it was the first time I had *time*. My full scholarship prohibited my holding other jobs for additional income. This unfettered time to contemplate came as a tall, cool glass of water after a long, dry season of hard work, little sleep, and much responsibility.

Most mornings after tea (which usually includes some sort of scrumptious fare as well as the hot drink for the Brits), I would cross the front quad still knee-deep in mist to pick up my mail in the porter's lodge that smelled of damp stone and erudition. Curling through the ivied corridors and traveling worn steps, I would make my way to a library, lecture, or tutorial, often passing the central market alive with sights, smells, and the yells of clerks. High walls, centuries old, siphoned me off from the crowd of tourists on the main streets. After being wound around blind corners came the sudden burst of magnificent courtyard: Radcliffe Square was so dazzling your eyes could barely take it all in. On the left looms the great Bodleian Library, housing within severe, serious walls almost every book ever published. Within its box the readers sit in rows like armies of old, but engaged in intellectual battle. On the right, by contrast, the Radcliffe Camera offers a domed paradise for the bibliophile. Enwombed here books embrace the reader due to the round ambulatory behind the massive arcade. Mood rather than resources usually determined in which building I chose to read. Everywhere countless courtiers, explorers, knights, members of the monarchy and gentry, academics, saints, and various patrons looked down on me from faded paint, rich veneers, or chiseled stone. Peering into my thoughts. *Envying me or pitying me?* I wondered. Me, alive and otherwise occupied. Them, long having known the secret of death.

The morning after I heard the gospel, however, I woke up with what felt like a hangover. Little would I know it was of the spiritual kind that accompanies the inevitable dawn of realization that life is not, perhaps, what we previously thought it was. And we cannot go back to pretending. What a headache to be caught in that liminal space! Literally.

Despite every effort to bury it conveniently away, that intimate first conversation with TDH kept buoying to the surface. Like a falcon, I circled back to the room lit by shadows.

Unable to shake my headache, I ventured out in search of good, strong, American-style coffee—no easy find in tea-guzzling England.

Out on the street I strode faster and faster. *Yes, I'll set it right once and for all,* I told myself. *Then I'll get the ring of his words out of my head. I'm sure a good anticatechism will show him all the holes, all the frays, in the cloak he believes you can simply touch and be healed. Poor, provincial pastor's boy; he needs someone to enlighten him. I'd better prepare myself for his despair. Maybe he'll rip his shirt open to display his Evangelical Superhero logo, and show his true colors: that he is a wacko like all those other "born-agains," trying to save others from the "eternal enemy," from the well-meaning destruction of their own lives, all the while deaf, dumb, and blind to their own shortcomings. Or maybe he'll snap like a twig and admit it was all a fraud. The result of how his upbringing brainwashed him, guilted him, tricked him—how he wanted desperately to believe what his father believed, or needed to believe. He'll sob and admit his addiction to porn. I bet he gives to charity but yells at his mom.*

Determinedly I took my steaming coffee from the little kiosk at the market and set my sights on reading the Bible, cover to cover. I faced one hurdle, however: I did not own a Bible. And I wanted to start reading it *right then and there.* I can't explain why, except that perhaps annoyance—and a little, just a little, curiosity—led me to do it. *I will approach it as any other book,* I told myself. *I am a trained reader. I will read it thoroughly and with purpose, and then use it as fodder to support my own thesis.* It did not matter that I could not identify what that thesis actually was (what student can?). It was just a book, after all. Just an old book that's caused a lot of wars.

The sunlight, cold and clear, made everything sparkle in the crisp autumn air. The libraries and bookstores were not open yet; the entire city remained hushed and hallowed. Expectant.

I turned back to Oriel with the intent of cutting back through Magpie Lane. But as I waited to cross the High, St. Mary's Church, sitting resplendent in her shroud of architectural splendor, caught my eye. Her side door was open. *I bet I can find a Bible in there*, I reasoned, so I entered objectively.

A sea of pews greeted me, each with a Bible and a hymnal tucked neatly inside every few feet. I could sit anywhere and have my pick, easily within reach.

I thought at first that I could discreetly take one, or rather borrow one, and no one would notice. But then I thought better. Reading from a stolen Bible? Something in that seemed a little coarse, even for a cynic like me. So instead I made my way to one of the back pews and sat down, irreverently crossing my ankles on the genuflecting cushion and resting my coffee on the handy little shelf for the welcome cards. I opened a Bible and began at the beginning, a very good place to start.

Before I really knew it, stealthily entering St. Mary's by the side door with my morning coffee became something of a ritual for me. The church always owned a particular hush during the rush of a weekday. Sometimes I would return late in the evenings, too, after the Bodleian closed. I would step out of the chill into the candle glow. I enjoyed the peace, the solitude, the seeming transgression.

Purchasing my own Bible seemed too much of a commitment, like getting married. Besides, the church was right across the street from my college, so, as they say, why purchase the cow when you can get the milk for free? I began coming more and more often.

Lilies in the field, a house with many mansions, the command to love one another—familiar echoes from an unfamiliar context. Seeds planted but nothing, really, I thought, to reap.

In this back pew I read the Bible steadily on borrowed pages. I devoured it, just as a best-selling book (which, coincidentally, it always has been). Even the long, monotonous lists. Even the really weird stuff, most of it so unbelievable as to only be true. I have to say I found it the most compelling piece of creative nonfiction I had ever read. If I sat around for thousands of years, I could never come up with what it proposes, let alone with how intricately Genesis unfolds toward Revelation. That the supposed Creator of the *entire universe* became a vulnerable baby, born in straw, to a poor girl who claimed to be a virgin and who was betrothed to a guy probably scared out of his wits, but who stood by her anyway. It unwinds and recasts the world and our perception of it: that the Holy Grail is more likely to be the wooden cup of a carpenter than the golden chalice of kings.

No wonder this stuff causes war, I thought as I read, *between nations and within each of us.*

While my time for contemplation, study, and socializing increased, my interaction with "home" whittled into small points of light. Communication became necessarily efficient through notes and phone calls.

The communal telephone sat in the "tunnel"—literally a dark underground passageway connecting the main college to the graduate student living quarters. No matter the time of day or night, it was chilly and damp in the antiquated red booth etched with graffiti. And so much for privacy. Even with the door folded shut, your voice echoed through the passageway. As a result, arguments had to be whispered, which somehow diminished their effect. Gossip had to be shared in code. I half expected to meet a grumpy troll or a mischievous imp seated beneath the inside shelf, engaged in reading the dangling telephone book. I could almost see the goblin going through its disheveled pages, looking for an unsuspecting number to prank call.

One night, after the annual Christmas party in the MCR, I went to call my fiancé back in Canada. All that snogging going on around me had made me miss him. But even more, I wanted to prod his godlessness a little. I liked testing men. It was one of my little hobbies.

Because of the time difference, it was just after midnight for me but still early evening for him. He picked up on the second ring, sounding chipper. I did not even say hello but launched straight in.

"Do you really love me?" I huffed into the receiver.

"Carolyn?"

"Yes. Who else would it be? How many other women do you have calling you with the same question?" I teased in a strained way.

"Of course I do. Are you okay?" Ben sounded concerned.

Silence.

"Have you been drinking?" Now he sounded irritated.

"No. Yes. No. I'm not drunk. You know I barely drink. Yes. I'm okay. Well, no. No, I'm not. Well, actually, I'm trying to figure out if *we're* okay . . ." I stammered, wishing I could smell him over the phone, that I could nuzzle my nose into his shoulder and all these inconvenient thoughts would go away.

"What do you mean? Of course we are." His voice was calm, reassuring, rational. "This is short term, remember. If you are getting anxious again at our being separated—"

"*Why* do you love me, Ben?" I interrupted.

"Well, you are beautiful, smart, funny, for starters," Ben chuckled. "Want me to go on? Shall I list your attributes alphabetically? Let me count the ways."

I smiled into the phone, in spite of myself. But woman cannot live by flattery alone. I bucked up and prodded deeper.

"What if all those things were to disappear?" I started. "I mean, what if we were old, or sick, or poor, or bored with each other, or annoyed by each other, or sleep-deprived, or tortured, or impotent, or—"

"*Whoa!* What are you getting at, Carolyn?"

"Well, what if one or both of us weren't happy? What if one of us wasn't 'doing it' for the other anymore, or things just weren't 'working out,' whatever that means? And I'm not talking about extremes, like physical abuse or mindless adultery, of course, but what about boredom, or frustration, or just ordinary selfishness?" I took a breath, "What if things weren't, well, *perfect*?"

"Things will never be perfect, or they could never be for long," offered Ben matter-of-factly.

"Precisely. But what if they were permanently imperfect? What then?"

"Well, what about it?" I could hear Ben eating something on the other end of the line. "Of course we are thoughtful, loving adults committed to one another, and to compromise, and to a fifty-fifty relationship. Are you afraid that I won't stay home with the kids if you end up getting promoted?" Ben chuckled again.

"No. I'm worried that you will leave the kids and me, and I'll be left alone to fend emotionally as well as financially, because we've had a long time without sex after one of the kids was born, and a secretary you work with flirts with you and caters to your ego. I'm worried that you will leave me because I'm diagnosed with cancer, and you can't bear it, or you are diagnosed and assume I can't bear it. I'm worried—"

"Do you think I'm some heartless moron?" Ben cut me off. "I mean, come on, no one gets married with the idea of getting divorced. And neither of us is wealthy enough for a prenup." Ben's buoyancy was a hard nut to crack.

"I'm worried that you would leave me for a myriad of reasons," I continued. "That you would leave me physically and/or emotionally. That you would leave me for, well . . ."

"Who?" Ben prodded.

"*You.*"

There. I had said it.

You and me, at the root of the tree, I thought.

"What on earth do you mean? Why would you think that?" Ben sounded wounded.

"You don't serve anything, anyone, larger than you," I ventured.

"Well, neither do you," he retorted.

True. Hmmmm.

"So what do you want from me, then?" Ben asked, putting on his mask of calm I knew so well, even admired. "I would hope my word would be enough."

"I wish it were too," I sighed, then added quickly, "and please, I don't mean to imply that it isn't. But, well, it isn't backed up by anything really. And neither is mine when I think about it."

"It's backed up by *me*, just as yours is backed up by *you*. And I trust you implicitly," Ben stated.

"But I don't. I can't. No matter how much I want to, I just can't." I pulled my sweater close around me in the chilly booth. "Ben, I can't help but think that if things worked out, it would be lovely; it would be lucky. It would arise from convenience and perhaps a certain moral fortitude on both sides, and perhaps even long bouts of selflessness. But not of a guaranteed sort. Or with a larger reference point or perspective. Not the kind that arises out of a spiritual discipline, for instance, rather than emotional fulfillment. Yes, what about loving out of a *decision*, out of a hard commitment, even contortion at times, in which we believe, trust, and answer to . . . something larger than ourselves? It seems to me that on our own we're too fallible. We all are. Despite the best of intentions, life gets complicated."

"You are still so scarred by your parents' situation, by your father's actions in particular. I resent that so much, Carolyn. It taints *us*," Ben identified justifiably, but also with a note of accusation. "Your lack of trust and fear of intimacy robs us of so much. You should draw more healthy boundaries, as I do. If something isn't working for you, let it go."

That's precisely my point, I thought but did not say.

"Maybe so," I said instead. "I acknowledge that to some degree, but I'm also tired of everyone chalking everything up to the 'Freudian baggage,' as if I can't think or feel past it in any way. And the emphasis on mind over matter, or denial, or utility, or productivity as the only answers. A legal piece of paper, a well-intentioned promise in a pretty church—it all goes to prove how connected we all are in our fallibility. One weakness causes another . . ."

He stayed quiet, so I waded back in. "Ben, it's funny; since

I've arrived here, things are revealing themselves to be not as I thought them to be. I mean, I thought I would learn all these things, and I would be certain of more and more. But in fact, I find myself being sure of less and less. I find myself looking at others and realizing that it's not just my life that appears whole on the outside but is broken on the inside. Of course I am a functioning, and I'd like to think, even thoughtful person. But I'm a mess in so many ways, maybe not overtly in terms of how culture sees messiness, but a mess just the same."

"No, you're not. You have it all together, Carolyn. You always have, just as I do. That's why we'll make such a wonderful pair," Ben announced confidently.

"Yes, of course, the average person has it 'all together'; many folks can pull that off, at least from the outside for varying bouts of time. But everyone gets caught in the mire," I realized out loud. "Every decision you make, I believe, really does affect everyone else in some direct or indirect way."

I paused, suddenly thinking of Dr. Deveaux, thinking of how truth exists in paradox. A shudder of something welled up inside of me, a new but familiar insight.

"It's like a great diurnal and eternal paradox: nothing matters and everything does!" I almost shouted into the phone. "The present is important, but eternity is too. Wait—yes, no, yes."

"Huh?" Ben breathed. "So what are you saying? We can only marry, truthfully, if we each believe in God? That morality, commitment, contentment, goodness, can only exist with God?" Ben loved a good argument, too, God bless him.

"I don't know. There are many people who are quick to tell me that God is fictitious, that everything I yearn for but can't quite put into words is merely a short in my psychological wiring.

These are people I admire professionally, and often people I care about deeply. But when I really look at them, their lives are just as fissured by pain as mine, often more so. They don't seem to know consolation, or peace, or how to experience joy regardless of circumstance. Of course, I often see qualities in their lives I admire, but not a core essence I long to have. In fact, in many cases I sense more emptiness under scrutiny than fullness, if that makes sense. And yet most, I find, either choose to ignore this, or even worse, they discount, even patronize, those whose lives are lived deliberately—those who at least 'walk their religious talk,' and bear spiritual fruit from it, if you'll pardon the cliché. No, instead they stay stuck." I stopped, breathless. *Where did all that come from?*

"Everyone is free to live as he or she sees fit," Ben pointed out.

"Yes, yes, I know all of that," I said irritatedly.

"Then why are you bothered by it at all?" Ben asked.

I tried to put my finger on it. "I guess what really bothers me is that they expect me to ascribe to their stuckness." I heard Ben suck in his breath. Oh, I hadn't meant it to be personal! *Wait, I don't believe in anything, really*, I reminded myself. Maybe I had played the game too far? Ben seemed now to have retreated entirely on the other end. I traced the numbers on the phone pad with my finger and waited.

"Do you still want to stay stuck with me?" he finally ventured softly.

I gave a winced smile, but luckily or not, he couldn't see. I took a deep breath.

"None of this matters anyway," I sighed into the receiver.

"Rescinding your great diurnal paradox, Carolyn?"

Shoot.

"Look. It's late, Ben. Forget about it. Forget I said any of it. I'm a cheap date—I shouldn't have given you a call after a pint."

"Good night, Carolyn. I love you."

"Thanks. I know. I love you too. Good night, Ben."

More silence.

The telephone booth seemed suffocating. It was just the telephone troll and me now. I could hear his little fingers drumming on the cover of the book, impatient to make his prank call.

The tapping grew louder. Slowly I realized the sound was coming from outside the booth. From within the brightly lit interior, I could see nothing when I peered out into the darkness. As I leaned into the window, however, I could make out a face staring back at me from the other side of the glass. Alarmed, I jumped back. A voice syruped, "I love you too," and the face blurred into a set of smashed lips, pressed into a sloppy pucker against the glass.

"Very funny, Philip," I said as I whipped open the accordion door. "Be careful not to get your lips stuck."

"Wouldn't be the worst place I've had them stuck." He shrugged and then proceeded to make a puffer fish face against the window as he slid down the glass.

"Okay, okay. That's enough. Here." I helped pull him to his feet. "You look like Mick Jagger." Indeed, Philip did. With his long, dark hair usually pulled into a ponytail, his eyes constantly narrowed into cynical slits, and his scrawny legs painted into his hallmark tight black jeans, everything about Philip was taut, except his lips. They seemed to pour out excessively of his otherwise contained body. Pouty and haughty like Lord Byron's, they gave his face the air of a petulant child's, which sorely undercut his attempt at cultivating a blasé, man-of-the-world persona. Maybe it was because he didn't have a clubfoot and a cloak to counteract them.

But Philip was also regularly "tight" in the British sense of "drunk." Rather than incoherent, however, his drunken rants were quite the opposite: he would intersperse metaphysical disquisitions with entire love sonnets. His massive amount of knowledge was made all the more impressive by the fact that, when drunk, he usually spoke in perfect blank verse, or what English majors recognize as unrhymed iambic pentameter. That is, when he was not being crude.

Philip decided to stop fighting gravity again and slumped to the ground. Sitting cross-legged like a leprechaunish guru, he studied me with half-closed eyes.

"Quite the conversation you were having there, my lady Carolina." He grinned like a Cheshire cat.

"Thanks for respecting my privacy, Phil!" I snapped back.

Phil closed his eyes completely and began chanting,

> Of Man's First Disobedience, and the Fruit
> Of that Forbidden Tree, whose mortal taste
> Brought Death into the World, and all our woe,
> With loss of Eden, till one greater Man
> Restore us, and regain the blissful Seat . . .[2]

I cut him off. "Phil, give me a break."

He patted the ground beside him, signing for me to join him. "Come, my heavenly muse. Let us sit on the vast abyss and make it pregnant."

"It's late, Phil. I'm tired. I'm going to bed."

"Alone?"

"Phil. Go get some coffee."

"Alas, me too, lass. Alone."

Phil paused, sighing into his lap. Then he looked up, grinning again. "It's not good for man to be alone."

"Good night, Philip," I said over my shoulder as I turned to go.

His voice, surprisingly rich and coherent now, rose up behind me:

> Love cannot fill the thickened lung with breath
> Nor clean the blood, nor set the fractured bone;
> Yet many a man is making friends with death
> Even as I speak, for lack of love alone.[3]

"Phil, should I be alarmed that you are rhyming?" I interrupted. "Edna St. Vincent Millay. Lovely."

"Surely you could spare me 10p for the phone, luv?" he asked, awkwardly trying to pull himself up.

"Phil, it's late," I called out, adding maternally, "Shouldn't you be going straight to bed?"

"I first need to make my nightly anonymous phone call," Phil replied with an air of duty.

"You're kidding me. A prank call? Aren't you a bit too old for that now?" I stopped, looking back at him.

"Ahhh." Phil stretched, starting into his iambs. "Let us not use such misleading terms as *prank*, shall we, Caro, dear one? Who does not like a call in midst of darkest night, declaring undying love?"

"What if a man picks up?" I asked.

Philip just looked flat at me. "Does it matter?" he asked quietly.

He had me there. I turned to go again, but Phil beckoned, "Just 10p, a few pence, a tuppence a bag to feed the birds, luv."

I fingered a coin in my pocket and threw it over my shoulder to him, as I had during my high school trip to Europe when making a wish in the Trevi Fountain with the hopes of one day returning to Rome.

"*Grazie, mea Carolina*," Phil called out after me, as though he had read my thoughts. "Consider it a small contribution to mankind. One call at a time. Everyone needs a ring of love, luv."

As I continued walking away, I heard the door to the booth shuffle open and close, then the echoing silver sound of the coin dropping into the slot as I reached the end of the tunnel.

TEN

DOES LOVE
JUSTIFY ALL?

> *These dull notes we sing*
> *Discords need for helps to grace them;*
> *Only beauty purely loving*
>   *Knows no discord;*
> *But still moves delight,*
> *Like clear springs renewed by flowing,*
> *Ever perfect, ever in them-*
>   *selves eternal.*[1]
>
>   —THOMAS CAMPION

Very little exists comparable to the experience of "high table" at an Oxford college. The opulence, breathtaking; the event, a smorgasbord for the senses. It makes me think of the young heroine Cassandra Mortmain's description in *I Capture the Castle*:

> There was a wonderful atmosphere of gentle age, a smell of flowers and beeswax, sweet yet faintly sour and musty; a smell that makes you feel very tender towards the past . . . The table was a pool of candlelight—so bright that the rest of the room seemed almost black, with the faces of the family portraits floating in the darkness.[2]

Family, in this case, consisted of monarchs, patrons, and former headmasters. Fine china, silverware older than the United States, numerous crystal glasses set around your plate that chime with the music of the spheres when clinked in a toast. The meal may be interspersed with entertainment or speeches, guests ranging from actors to philanthropists to presidents. Waiters carrying silvered domes surreptitiously emerge from doors hidden in the wainscoting. It reminded me of an Agatha Christie novel, fortunately without the murder when the lights go out. I half expected *Batman*'s Bruce Wayne to emerge from a secret cellar.

The meals are always extravagant, but on a guest night (or a meal in honor of a special college visitor or event) the feast numbers several courses, ushered in with sherry and then wine pouring white, pouring red, and then dessert punctuated by coffee. But sweets mark a false end, for an array of cheese, crackers, and fruits follows, enjoyed with cordials, liquors, ports, and whiskeys, which overflow far into the evening in the adjoining comfort of the faculty lounge or Senior Common Room (SCR).

For the traditional Christmas dinner, this guest night was particularly beautiful, the room adorned with garlands of evergreen and wreaths of holly like the Ghost of Christmas Past. The air like a John Betjeman poem, all "heavy with bells / And mushroomy, pine-woody, evergreen smells."[3]

I had been invited by the provost to join him at high table in honor of my Commonwealth scholar status. Since each guest at high table was welcome to bring a date, I invited, in turn, TDH to join me, partly because I knew he would appreciate the decadent meal as much as I, but also because, even though he irritated me, I was, in fact, fond of him in some strange way. In spite of his being a Christian.

I wore an exquisite cream-colored dress that my mom mailed to me just for such a special event. It must have cost her a month of lunches and all her gas money, at least. I tucked into my purse the elegantly calligraphed menu card to mail to her since Mom loves reading menus even more than actually eating the food. This way, I felt as though she could savor every bite along with me.

Startlingly memorable in his tuxedo, TDH met me at the hall porch as the dinner bell chimed. We lined up with the crowd to enter under the frontispiece with the Virgin and Child.

The guest of honor was a brilliant scientist whose expertise lay in the intersection of time, space, speed, sound, and light. He once cracked a notoriously complicated algorithm, which won him much fame. I had the honor of being seated next to him and across from the provost's wife, a lively and incredibly informed woman who had the knack for bringing a group of seemingly disparate people into a rich conversation with ease. Within minutes of being seated and being sherried, we were all engaged in a fascinating discussion about the relationship between spirituality and science.

The scientist explained patiently, as best he could in layman's terms, his theory of black holes in the universe and the dimension of time.

Then the provost's wife leaned in and asked intently, "But Dr. Sterling, do you believe in God?"

For a moment, he seemed taken aback. A hush fell over the table.

She rephrased the question. "For all of your immense scientific knowledge and rational research, do you think that your theories, or any scientific theories, are, or can only be, at odds with the existence of God?"

"Of course these theories must be at odds with the existence of God. What rational theory would not dispel an irrational one?" Dr. Rieland, our token professor of philosophy, interrupted.

"God and state don't mix, so why should God and science?" a prominent American politician chimed in.

I took a sip of my wine, trying to swallow the increasingly familiar fear creeping up my throat. The laughable temptation to defend something I did not understand.

Suddenly I felt extremely young . . . and very little.

Then I noticed that the famous scientist remained silent too. In fact, he had not said a thing. He just kept listening and looking—it was hard to say—was it sad, or was it, well, *slightly amused*?

I broke my bread and started buttering it, trying to act nonchalant. "Dr. Sterling," I heard myself saying, "you haven't answered Mrs. Nicholby's original question. I would be very curious as to what you have to say." I ignored the irritated glares from a few senior professors, startled that a lowly student tolerated at high table would dare speak. Others, however, agreed, and the provost's wife reached over and gave my hand a squeeze.

At first I thought he might be put out at having been put back on the spot, for Dr. Sterling looked straight at me, saying nothing. Then he smiled. Something about him—I could not say exactly what—but something about him reminded me of Dr. Deveaux.

"I've been enjoying this lively conversation, this God-and-science dilemma; such a treat for a reclusive researcher like me," he winked. The table now turned on him, expectant. He paused, as though measuring his words carefully. Then he began.

"Well, I wonder if it's much like the secret of the magnet, Miss Drake."

As a Romanticist, I found his science intriguing. I smiled back.

"Do tell," Mrs. Nicholby urged him on.

"Everything I've witnessed in the natural world seems to operate in a desire to attain equilibrium. What rises, falls. What heats, cools. What freezes, thaws. The magnet both attracts and repels the thing most like it, another magnet. Yet without this force, nothing in the world would function. We are the only planet in this solar system with such delicate conditions for life. The axes of the poles would cease to spin, the tides would halt, the sun would fail to rise and set, if these forces did not exist in a relationship of attraction and repulsion, a relationship which seeks this equilibrium that allows for life," Dr. Sterling explained.

"Are you saying that these things exist in perfect relationship?" the provost asked.

"That's a difficult one to answer, as things currently stand. Perfect enough, yes, to perpetuate life on the planet. But imperfect enough to contribute, at times, to our suffering, wouldn't you say?" Dr. Sterling tried again to get the peas to stay on his fork.

At the remembrance of peas, I stole a glance at TDH, seated further down the table. Everyone was listening now, and, strangely, he seemed to wear the same look of amusement as Dr. Sterling.

I stifled my own giggle. *Here we are*, I thought, *TDH and me, poor scholarship students at high table, and still eating peas!* The peas were soaked in brandy and sprinkled with a mix of aged imported cheeses, mind you, nestled alongside tender venison wrapped in buttered white asparagus tips, with tiny roasted potatoes topped with toasted pine nuts. But they were still peas.

"What of life and death?" Dr. Rieland queried.

"Precisely," replied Dr. Sterling, finally successfully maneuvering several peas into his mouth.

"Huh?" the American politician coughed before he caught himself.

"You mention what rises, falls; what heats, cools. But what of what lives? It dies, as all must die, Dr. Sterling. And then what of this equilibrium? This great magnet?" Dr. Rieland persisted.

"Yes, true, that's where there is a momentary crack in the equilibrium," Dr. Sterling conceded. "Remember, though, I didn't say it was perfect in its current state, did I? Just perfect enough, for the moment, which seems pretty generous to me."

"A momentary crack? Surely this is a cop-out, given the nature of time," intervened Dr. Rieland's guest. A fellow philosopher from Cambridge, he was editing a volume on Nietzsche with Rieland.

"We barely scratch the surface of time!" Dr. Sterling exclaimed. "A fissure is only as broad as you perceive it to be. It may be minuscule from one perspective—barely perceptible, and yet from another, it may seem massive, even overwhelmingly uncrossable, like a black hole in space. Is it a mountaintop or an abyss? It might depend on *how* you are seeing. For instance, from which angle you are looking or with which eyes." Capturing some more peas, he added, "What lives, continues to live, forever, if the perfect equilibrium is restored, if the relationship is repaired between the two ends of the magnet, or the two sides of the chasm, so to speak."

"Oh my! What has this got to do with God and science?" asked the politician's wife with a little laugh.

"Everything," Dr. Sterling cried most seriously. *"Everything!"*

"Are all scientists mad?" she leaned in and whispered to me. I nodded, turning my head away slightly as a means of trying to escape the overpowering cloud of Tabu. Now I understood why the word *perfume* roughly evoked the French as "through smoke."

"Let's be frank, shall we?" Having finished his peas, Dr. Sterling set down his fork.

"Oh, let's!" The politician's wife clapped her hands together with glee. I braced myself as another wave of Tabu came at me.

Dr. Sterling wiped his mouth with his Christmas-red napkin, then spread it out before his plate. "The more I discovered of the scientific world, the more it convinced me of the amazing interconnectedness and brilliancy of God's design. People tend to think of science as being at odds with faith, but nothing could be further from the truth. The one only confirms the other; the one only illuminates its echo, and yet its limitations and dependence in the face of the other."

He meticulously arranged his silverware on top of his napkin as he spoke.

"While they are connected, there is a difference between fear and awe," Dr. Sterling continued, fiddling with his knife. "We shouldn't be afraid to embrace the awe. All of my work has only proven to me that the imprint of the Divine lies on the natural world. So why wouldn't the same be the case for science?"

With a quick flourish Dr. Sterling yanked the crimson napkin out from under his silverware. The cutlery remained undisturbed but was now glinting on the pristine white tablecloth.

"Oooh, well done!" The politician's wife clapped again. I held my breath.

Dr. Sterling turned to another guest, Dr. Inchbald, an eminent heart surgeon from the States.

"Dr. Inchbald," Dr. Sterling appealed to him passionately, "you see people live and die in your line of work. You literally know what it's like to hold a beating heart in your hand. In many circles, and especially among your astonished patients and their grateful families, you are a god."

Dr. Inchbald blushed. I marveled at his humility, this man who saved lives daily as I sat reading.

"What say you?" Dr. Sterling pinned him with his smile. "How do you reconcile God and science?"

Dr. Inchbald set down his fork and looked down at his hands. At first, I thought he was just trying to finish chewing, but then I realized he had stopped doing everything, his head bowed. When he raised it, he looked at all of us very sincerely.

"I admit," he said softly, so softly we all had to crane to hear, and so we all moved in closer, a disparate bunch of similarly expectant faces. "I admit that I don't know what to think about God, about death when I see it happen. When I have to inform a patient's family that he didn't pull through, or that no matter what we can try to do, it won't be enough to save him." He grew very quiet. "The hardest ones, for me, I think, are the children."

We waited amid the clinking of antique silverware on fine

china plates rising up from the other tables, like dissonant music from a nearby room. Dr. Inchbald shifted a little uncomfortably under the attention, but then he took a breath and drew himself up, speaking more loudly.

"Sometimes I want to rage against God when I see the lifeless body of a teenage boy who was running a court and shooting baskets only a short while ago. Or when I operate on a tiny new baby with a hole in its heart. Or when I see the blue lips of a grandmother who was only just kissing her grandbabies that morning." He paused, and then smiled wryly. "One of my specialties is massive coronaries, a funny kind of 'specialty' to have in life, when you think about it."

Really? I thought to myself. *Try reading dead people for a living.*

Dr. Inchbald looked at each of us. "But one heckuva alarm bell."

We looked back, quiet.

He continued, "You had better think through God if you're going to stay in one piece. I've had colleagues try to sidestep God, but that only cracks them apart even further in the long run."

I thought of my own specialty in eighteenth- and nineteenth-century literature. We all have specialties, special gifts. *Are they important,* I began to wonder, *only insofar as how they bring us to God? Is it in how they reflect His perfect love through each of us to others?* Charged with a sudden volt, I thought back to the orientation movie night. *Otherwise,* it dawned on me, *these "specialties" are nothing special.*

The surrounding darkness threatened to swallow me up, seated at the table in its midst, in my little pool of light. Without warning everything we do seemed meaningless, regardless of our lines of work. Was any way of trading my time for money, or for that matter, any expenditure of time, for nothing of any true value in the end?

But just as suddenly the darkness receded, the pool of light seemed to take me in, as I thought how anything we do—any job, act, gesture—becomes meaningful if done with a heart for God. Was this the great diurnal paradox looming up again—nothing matters and everything does? I stared at the candle flickering before me, deciphering the seeming coolness of blue and green dancing, so improbably, within the bright orange and red. Which was hotter? Which was purer?

I had to admit, to my growing concern, reading the Bible was becoming rather addictive. There did indeed seem to be something for everyone, including me.

After all, who reads the book of Ecclesiastes and identifies with not a single thing?

I blinked the flames from my eyes and turned my attention back to Dr. Sterling. He was studying Dr. Inchbald thoughtfully.

Dr. Inchbald continued, "I've seen science and medicine do much good, and I've seen it have no effect, despite the most valiant efforts. These lines on my old face are hard-won, and I'm now slowly growing proud of them," he chuckled. Then his voice grew even stronger. "After many years, and I admit after many stiff drinks after many hard days, one morning I stood suspended over one heart, scalpel in hand, about to cut in. It was a bit of a Monty Python moment, as I've liked to come to call it."

The provost raised his eyebrows and gestured with warm curiosity for the doctor to continue.

"Well, as I was standing there, all the uncertainty of my life, the absurdity of all this death, and all our attempts to ward it off, came down to a pinprick of light—like the glint off the scalpel in my hand. As I looked down I realized my hand was shaking, the ultimate downfall for any surgeon, but especially a heart surgeon. I panicked and felt as if I was being swallowed up in, well"—he looked over at Dr. Sterling—"a black hole."

Dr. Sterling chuckled.

"When all of a sudden, I heard it. A *ping*."

"A *what*?" the provost opened his eyes wide with confusion.

"A *ping*. Like a, well, high-pitched *ping*. Like the sound that the machine that cost over a million pounds makes in the delivery room in the opening birth sequence to Monty Python's *The Meaning of Life*. You're British; you should know," he leveled at the provost. "The machine that goes *ping*!"

"Wow, all these scientist folks *are* mad," the politician's wife Tabu'ed in my ear and nose.

Dr. Inchbald continued, "This *ping* marked something that finally went off in my head, in my heart, in my hand—steadying all three by what I can only call a miracle."

Please don't clap again, I silently beseeched the politician's wife. By some other miracle, she didn't.

"Do explain!" Dr. Sterling urged.

Dr. Inchbald tried his best to comply. "I've come to the conclusion that God is sovereign, even over science, and that I cannot pretend to fully know His ways. They really are mysterious, as the saying goes. And they are not of the mind of men, no matter how hard we try to wrap our minds about these ways. I can marvel at the intricacies of the human body, which really are pretty miraculous to behold. In fact, I don't know how one can go to medical school and not be in greater awe of a Creator than ever before.

The original, in both senses of the term, *pings* into the banal; the heavenly pokes in, pokes through."

Several guests nodded, a few looked confused, one or two took a hard swig of the liquors now circulating.

"But to cut to the chase," Dr. Inchbald stated, no doubt seeing the same reactions I saw as he glanced around the table, "when I see death, I know it is *wrong*."

"Obviously." Dr. Rieland snickered.

"But *really, really wrong*. In-my-gut wrong," Dr. Inchbald almost pleaded. "It was not meant to be. It was not meant for us. We were not built for it. Everything in my body, at a cellular level, let alone a metaphysical one, twists against it. Not just *my* death, but the death of every living thing."

The politician's wife next to me sniffed. "Yes," she said. "I had a beloved shih tzu who escaped from my purse and got struck by a car. I held her broken body as she breathed her last, looking at me with bewildered adoration the entire time. I was heartbroken. When I think about it, it felt so *wrong*."

We all sat there in silence, serious or otherwise, but unified, thinking of dead pets, birds fallen from their nests, whales washed ashore. Of unborn babies, abducted children, hospices and the elderly. Of loved ones wasting away, suffering, shattering against a windshield, bleeding from a wound. Of aging. Growing weak. Losing one's mind. Of ourselves.

Buried. In the dark. Devoured by insects. Turned to dust. Burned. Cremated. Turned to ashes. Was this really all there was, forever? That we were lost to ourselves and to each other forever?

Wrong.

Wrong!

Dr. Sterling interjected into all of our ruminating thoughts.

"Yes, I would have to conclude that no matter how misleading the title of the theory of relativity, absolutes rule the physical as well as the metaphysical. For me God's love is so great that it can attract even the farthest, most lost, most seemingly random cell to Him. That we desire to respond, to have right relationship with Him, is the secret. To set it all *right*. For everything to be *all right*."

The politician's wife was dabbing her eyes with her napkin now. "Poor Fifi," she whispered.

Darkness surrounding. Light at the table.

"Which it is, which it will be, depending on how you view time." Dr. Inchbald smirked as he finished Dr. Sterling's thought.

It was only when we stood up to say the parting grace that I remembered Dr. Sterling sat confined to a wheelchair. As the rest of us filed from the platform, two waiters came to lift him off. One of the waiters broke protocol and actually spoke to a parting guest. As he set his side of the wheelchair down, I heard him ask Dr. Sterling a question.

"Sir"—the waiter knelt down beside him—"I wondered if you could tell me what you consider to be the strongest force in the universe." He rushed on, "Please forgive my intruding, but I was curious as to your opinion, your being such a great scientist and all."

Dr. Sterling put his hand on the waiter's shoulder. "Excellent question!" he marveled.

"I'm a bit of a science-fiction buff," the waiter admitted, "and I read all the science magazines. Always have. Before I had to quit school, science was my best subject," he added proudly.

Dr. Sterling nodded in praise. "Well, what a delight and an honor to meet a fellow with similar interests. Yes, I don't think I've ever been asked such an excellent question."

The waiter beamed.

"Love."

The waiter's smile froze, and then it started to melt. He gave Dr. Sterling a confused look.

"The answer to your query is *love*," Dr. Sterling repeated.

"I'm afraid I don't understand," the waiter hedged. "I mean, love is an abstract, an emotion. It's not a force or a substance or even a theory."

"Are you so sure?" Dr. Sterling's eyes danced.

We were waiting for the rest of the procession to go through the dining hall doors, so the waiter risked a few more moments of conversation. He leaned in even closer to Dr. Sterling, resting his arm intimately on his wheelchair. Dr. Rieland threw the waiter a withering look, but Dr. Sterling seemed delighted.

"Please, sir, do go on," the waiter urged, ardently, seeing only the doctor's delight, and delighted in response.

"Well, I used to have this hunch," Dr. Sterling began, "but years of experience have only confirmed it."

"What?" the waiter asked with bated breath. Now several of us were listening intently. But Dr. Sterling continued to speak only with the waiter.

"There is nothing more powerful, more radical, more transformational than love. No other source or substance or force. And do not be deceived, for it is all of these things, and then some! Often folks like to dismiss it as a mere emotion, but it is far more than that. It can't be circumscribed by our desires or dictated by the whim of our moods. Not the Great Love of the Universe, as I like to call it. Not the Love that set everything in motion, keeps it in motion, which moves through all things and yet bulldozes nothing, not even our will. Try it. Just try it and you'll see. If you love that Great Love first, because It loved you first, and then love yourself as you have been loved, and then love others from that love . . . *Wow! Bam!* Life without that kind of faith—that's death. Therein lies the great metaphor, Miss Drake." He nodded toward me. "Life without faith *is* death. For life, as it was intended to be, is love. Start loving and you'll really start living. There is no other force in the universe comparable to that."

Through the tunnel of my mind, I heard the silvered tinkling of a coin dropping.

The great doors opened off the dining area, and the line started moving from high table. In celebration of Christmastide, voices from the college choir lifted into the air "O Holy Night" as the recessional:

> Long lay the world in sin and error pining.
> Till He appeared and the soul felt its worth.
> A thrill of hope the weary world rejoices,
> For yonder breaks a new and glorious morn.

The waiter stood up, wrapped in a sort of awe. The candles flickered in the reflection of the benighted windows like tiny lanterns floating on a dark, still lake.

> Fall on your knees! Oh, hear the angel voices!
> O night divine, O night when Christ was born . . .

The waiter began pushing the wheelchair of the man at whose side he had just kneeled.

He knows our need, to our weakness is no stranger,

Another waiter came to help him ease Dr. Sterling down the final steps.

Behold your King! Before Him lowly bend!

The waiters wheeled Dr. Sterling around the corner to the old-fashioned elevator, or "lift," as the Brits call it. The kind that makes you feel as if you are being cranked up or down by a monkey working a cumbersome pulley in a metal cage, and which gives the disconcerting effect of passing through the skeleton of a building. The large formal staircase to the SCR antechamber loomed ahead of me. I found myself already missing Dr. Sterling's dear company as I dug into the first step.

Truly He taught us to love one another,
His law is love and His gospel is peace.
Chains He shall break, for the slave is our brother.
And in His name all oppression shall cease.

The music followed us through the open door:

His power and glory ever more proclaim![4]

Mounting the stairs, I looked over my shoulder as the waiters began extinguishing the candles. I felt TDH take my hand, steadying my attempt on the steps in my dress shoes. The door closed gently behind us and, like Wordsworth's traveler emerging from the valley, "the music in my heart I bore, / Long after it was heard no more."

⚜

"More Madeira, my dearah?" The provost tipped the prismatic decanter over my delicate demi-glass.

In the SCR, where faculty gather, I joined the throng in praise of Dr. Sterling's work and dazzling intellect. Like Dr. Inchbald, he handled all the fawning with disarming humility.

"It is amazing that you can be both a believer in God *and* an accomplished scientist," our perfectly coiffed senior dean said, sniggering as the result of, I suspected, holding Madeira a little too dearah. "And that you can be both given, your, well, uh, your . . ." he stammered, now caught uncomfortably in his inebriated trap, ". . . state," he finished, clumsily raising his glass.

"You mean my wheelchair?" Dr. Sterling asked.

We all shifted our weight uncomfortably in the circle.

Without a shadow in his pleasant tone, Dr. Sterling replied, "Yes, I've had this facet to keep things interesting since birth."

Then turning with a look of particular kindness toward the senior dean, Dr. Sterling smiled broadly. "Like you"—he nodded as he raised his glass back—"I am not a mistake."

CHRISTMASTIDE

TIDE OUT: HAVE A HEIMLICH/UN-HEIMLICH CHRISTMAS (HOME, BUT NOT HOME, FOR THE HOLIDAYS)

> *Some say that ever 'gainst that season comes*
> *Wherein our Saviour's birth is celebrated,*
> *The bird of dawning singeth all night long:*
> *And then, they say, no spirit dare stir abroad;*
> *The nights are wholesome; then no planets strike,*
> *No fairy takes, no witch has power to charm,*
> *So hallow'd and gracious is the time.*[1]
>
> —WILLIAM SHAKESPEARE

I was in the air. Flying from London to London. From Big Ben to my Ben. He had chosen my ring; he would be waiting for me in the airport when I arrived. My sister had told me so, furtively, on the phone last night. I was having trouble breathing, certain the air pressure in the cabin was dropping. I kept waiting for the oxygen masks to dangle, followed by an ecstasy of fumbling among my fellow passengers. But all remained quiet and still. Cocooned in white noise, we sped above the clouds toward a slash of fiery horizon and then blackest black, nothing but darkness visible beyond.

Oxford lay far behind me, as if in a dream. Unable to sleep, I closed my eyes and traced my daily wanderings throughout the town in my mind. Even Oxford's infrastructure was conducive to contemplation, revelation. Its walls seemed infused with mystery. When I walked through the stony passageways, I often *felt* voices from ages past murmuring great mysteries. It was tempting to think that resting my head against this stony chest would betray a heartbeat, or by putting my ear to this shell, I could hear the distant but undeniable advancing and then retreating of whispered wisdoms. The walls were saturated with thoughts of endless minds across hundreds of years into the present, like a fine chain linked with hopes for the betterment of humankind. "The finest City in the world," sighed John Keats. "The finest thing in England," Henry James declared. "There is *nothing* like Oxford," Francis Kilvert proclaimed. Over an expansion of years since these writers, and now high in the sky, I had to agree.

I opened my eyes and looked down at the magazine resting unopened in my lap. A gift from TDH, along with some chocolates, in a cheeky care package he gave me to enjoy as I traveled home. Its title, in bright red capital letters, seared through the silence: *TIME*. I heard the telephone troll's chuckle; he had brought his goblin friends this time, scattered along the Beethovenian evening sky like some mindscape from a Forster novel. The universe sat brooding on the wing outside my window.

"Coffee or tea?" The flight attendant's request startled me.

Panic and emptiness, lady, I thought. But recalling J. Alfred Prufrock, I said, "Coffee" as I fiddled with my spoon.

The man beside me had fallen asleep slumped against my shoulder. I felt his drool seeping through my shirt, but I did not move him. In fact, I did not move at all. *If I sit still enough, long enough*, I reasoned, *perhaps I can make time sit still too. Perhaps the plane will never land but remain suspended forever between two Londons, forever between decision and consequence, singleness and union, fear and faith.*

I shifted in my seat, coming back to the present. Under *Time* sat a Bible, also unopened. It seemed to be burning a hole in my lap. I finally purchased one at a small Christian bookstore on my way to get groceries. An impulse buy. Now, however, it was only partly an act of retaliation; the other part an act of companionship, perhaps. A copy to bring home with me, legitimately. Its spine was still stiff with newness.

Holy Bible. The words embossed in gold on the cover stared back at me whenever I lifted the magazine. How can Christians really believe these words are "alive," that they have actually been revealed to us by God? And, therefore, that they own some sort of power? Besides, anything "original" would surely be threadbare by now, tire-tracked with various mistranslations, amendments, political agendas. How can mere words have the ability to shift us from our temporal cages to eternal freedom, to purposefully move us from one point to another, let alone to restore us and everything we know?

Whoa. That seemed eight seconds too long on the bull for me.

One day at the tiny gym I visited on High Street, after a string of hits from Bon Jovi, I heard a Scottish pastor on the radio claim, like TDH, that Scripture has real, explosive power. Not the power of suggestion, reprimand, or even persuasion. Not nice pleasantries or comforting self-help tips. But the power of spiritual DYNAMITE! It blows your worldview apart, shatters your complacency, forces you to choose, to act, to love. It is radical *and* holy . . . without amendment . . . without apology.

I began to worry that perhaps I was getting in over my head here. It was occurring to me that believing in the Bible was an all-or-nothing affair. Either you believe it is the revealed Word of God, or you don't. It is like being a little bit pregnant. Impossible. Either you are in or you are out. Having eliminated *lunatic*, given the unavoidable seriousness warranted of my attention, was it now *liar* or *Lord*?

I still was not sure. Yet why did reading this text give me goose bumps—literal *goose bumps*—more consistently than anything else I had ever read? Why did my life and how it related to the lives of others hitherto now make more sense, and yet more than ever, in and of itself, not seem *enough*?

⌀

"Are you okay, miss? You look a little pale. Are you airsick?" the flight attendant asked from under her immaculate beehive. She looked as if she had weathered much altitude.

"I'm fine, thanks. More homesick than airsick, I would guess."
I smiled weakly.

"Homesickness is a blessing, you know," she said over her
shoulder as she handed out the napkins. "It means you actually
care enough about folks to ache for them, and vice versa. Not
everyone has that luxury."

Taking a deep breath, I murmured, "How do I tell a wonderful man who cares deeply for me that this love of ours is not
enough?" But the man seated next to me continued snoring, and
the attendant had moved on to the next row. Drowning in the
hum of the cabin, I was speaking to myself, or so I thought.

"Nuts?" the flight attendant half-asked as she reached back
and set a package on my tray.

TWELVE

TIDE IN: AM I MY SISTER'S KEEPER?

Defenseless under the night
Our world in a stupor lies;
Yet, dotted everywhere,
Ironic points of light
Flash out wherever the Just
Exchange their messages:
May I, composed like them
Of Eros and of dust,
Beleaguered by the same
Negation and despair,
Show an affirming flame.[1]

—W. H. AUDEN

D o you want to talk about it?" a voice gently asked.
Bummer, I thought. I hate talking to strangers on airplanes. I like to bury my nose in a book and pretend no one else is there.

I craned over the man still asleep against my shoulder and realized that it came from the woman seated by the aisle. The slumberer between us had his other arm outstretched heavily across her lap, but she had not moved it either. Slender, with skin the color of darkened cinnamon bark, she wore a red-and-gold scarf. An enormous pile of books sat on her tray. She was older than I, but I could not quite tell her age. With genuine concern on her face, she leaned in under my reading light. I now saw that she had exquisite eyes. Kaleidoscope eyes that seemed to constantly change hue. Like a cat's. Like a girl's in a Beatles' song.

"Well, sister?" she waited. I had to look away from those eyes, not accusing but seeking. Sympathizing. I then noticed that one of her books was a Bible; it was well worn, dog-eared, with all sorts of papers sticking out. I looked down at mine. It lay naked and pristine on my lap, the neon sale-price sticker still on the cover.

"I'm not a Christian, you know," I shot out, instinctively covering my Bible with my magazine. "Just some wider cultural reading."

"I see," she said and waited. She did not look away.

"I've had a lot going on in my mind . . . in my, well, soul." I felt compelled to say something. "It's hard to explain. It's not worth explaining, I guess."

She kept looking at me with those eyes, so I stammered on, "No one at home will understand, least of all my fiancé, especially when I tell him that I can't build a life with someone who isn't at least asking the same questions I am."

"What kind of questions are you asking?" she inquired simply.

"You're not quite British, are you?" I replied, curious.

"A funny question to be causing you such turmoil," she laughed.

"Sorry, I mean you sound British, but you don't . . . not quite."

"You sound American, but not quite." She smiled. "I'm South African by birth, though I've spent much of my life in India too. I've been living in London now for some time."

"Are you on pleasure or business?" I politely asked my fellow traveler.

She smiled widely. "I'm lucky enough to be traveling to Toronto to help start a series of exchange programs for girls who otherwise wouldn't be able to afford such an educational experience. I benefited greatly from such an experience. I'd like to help create the same opportunity for others. And you?"

"Going home for the holidays. I'm studying at Oxford. I hope to teach literature one day." I paused. "Most likely, however, to privileged white kids," I couldn't help adding sardonically.

"Salt and light are needed everywhere," she replied with complete earnestness.

Gee whiz, I'm sitting next to one of those feel-good, do-good Christians, I supposed. *And I'm stuck in the window seat.*

Sartre's description of hell passed before my eyes. In French. Then in English. Another Canadian habit.

She gave me an admiring look. "Ahhh, teaching literature. A noble calling! For we are all stories."

I had to admit, even when it should stoke suspicion, flattery does melt it.

"And a fellow member of the Commonwealth too?" She nodded with tongue-in-cheek delight. "Good colonial company.

Home and not at home, 'eh,' as you say?" She disarmingly chuckled at her own joke before I had the chance. "But tell me, what is
now so uncanny about home for you? What are these questions
that obviously disturb you so?"

I remained silent, uncertain.

"Try me." Again, those eyes.

"Okay," I ventured, "you know, all the biggies. About God.
About us in relation to God."

"Like what, for instance? There are a lot of biggies, and a lot
of smallies, you know," she said invitingly.

"Well"—I took a breath—"such as, why is there suffering
and evil in the world if God is good?" I took another breath
and raced on—it all started coming out like an existential ava-
lanche—compressed and then springing forth from weeks of
wrangling with TDH: "What about, ironically, 'acts of God,'
such as devastating earthquakes or floods, or a guy walking his
dog and getting killed by a falling branch? Or unintentional
accidents? What's the use of a jellyfish or a mosquito? Why
can't the lion lay down with the lamb? Why do babies die?
Why is wealth so unevenly distributed? Does God only exist if
I believe in Him? And by the way, do people really go to hell"—
suddenly my eyes began to tear up, in spite of myself—"and only
some go to heaven?"

I could have gone on and on but for that pathetic lump in my
throat. And the man seated in front of me who looked back men-
acingly. I shrank back embarrassed, but she seemed undisturbed.
Even riveted.

"All very good questions, every single one," she replied. "Let's
see. The problem of evil. Man's (and animals') position in the
order of things. Hmmmm. The existence of God. The dilemma

of hell. The promise of heaven. You *have* been busy, girl." She laughed, but in a *with* not an *at* kind of way.

I smiled in spite of myself. To my relief I felt my eyes clearing and the lump disintegrating.

"By the way, I'm Veronica." She held out a delicate hand. I took it, surprised by its firmness.

"Easy to remember," I said as I introduced myself, "because that's my aunt's name. I'm Carolyn." Her initial greeting of me as "sister" echoed in my head.

"Well, Caro, if I may," Veronica began, "personally, I guess when it comes down to it, I still don't know how to reconcile the fact that I believe in the existence of evil and the kindness of strangers." She started straightening her pile of books. "I was reading Rita Dove's poem just the other day, 'Parsley,' the one she read at the White House. Do you know it?" She jumped in, speaking the lines with tender command:

The general remembers the tiny green sprigs
men of his village wore in their capes
to honor the birth of a son. He will
order many, this time, to be killed . . .

Then she looked right at me as she finished,

. . . for a single, beautiful word.[2]

"Wow!" I exclaimed, moved. "What word?" I could not help but ask.

"*Perejil.* The Spanish word for 'parsley,'" she answered. "Something clean and green and fresh brings on the slaughter of Haitian black field-workers, because they could not roll their Rs in what the dictator considered perfect Spanish. God spoke the world into being, and it was good. Then we tried to speak over God's good because we want things in our imperfect language, and we now have the world as we willed it—lack of communion causes miscommunication . . . ." She tapered off for a moment, admitting quietly after some thought, "I don't get it all either. But I do know, in my core, it is not God-based but human-generated. I am not surprised, then, that the way in which God brought everything into being is the way in which we most warp it all in our fallen state. And then, in turn, what He made flesh to dwell among us and deliver us. Yes, words have unspeakable power."

"But isn't God's silence as good as His acquiescence?" I interjected.

"What would you like Him to say that He hasn't said already?" she asked simply.

I turned away, looking out the window.

Veronica's words cut the wake of my averted gaze: "It would seem to me that it's your turn to answer."

As I took a bite of my plain, stale bun (I gave up trying to spread the icy butter with my flimsy knife), it occurred to me: perhaps this emptiness is my doing, and not His.

Veronica warmed her butter packet between her palms. "I like to think that God has a particularly soft spot for oppressed people," she said as she buttered her bread with ease. "The Jews, the African slaves, the Irish, the poor—He brings them to Him more easily, perhaps, because of that worldly oppression, or perhaps they recognize their need for Him more because of it. I guess it's an equation where it really doesn't matter what comes first, the chicken or the egg, as long as it comes. I know it must sound like an atrocious justification in worldly terms, but if you remove the limited lens and look through an eternal one, the power of reason shifts; faith in rationales wanes."

I remained silent, swept up by the soft force of her voice. As she ate, her beautiful profile resembled a stately cameo on an ancient coin.

"Friend"—she smiled tenderly, and suddenly I felt very safe with her—"if you will allow me that, if 'sister' scares you . . ."

No cynicism lurked in her voice, no matter how hard I tried to detect it. Only kindness, only gentleness from this persistent passenger. I met her gaze.

"No matter what culture tells us, faith is not the opposite of reason." She took a book from the bottom of her stack and deftly opened it to a back page. "Since you are a fellow lover of literature, I know you will humor me." She grinned.

She had me there. I was already craning to see what page she wished to share. I'm like an addict when it comes to books. Compelled to read, understand, savor, wrangle with, be moved by, learn to live from these silent companions who speak so loudly. Surely some language must have a word for such a "book junkie"?

A Christian . . .? The term crossed my mind.

"I was just reading this earlier today on the bus to the airport," Veronica said, interrupting my thoughts. "I've been reading Flannery O'Connor's letters. I love O'Connor. I love her because she was a woman, because she was a thoughtful Catholic, because she was dying a slow and untimely death as she was writing, but she maintained her dignity and humor."

Flannery O'Connor, I thought disappointedly. I had not read her yet, but an image of a woman in thick-rimmed glasses who could not possibly have anything relevant to say to me loomed in my head.

Veronica passed me a book opened to a letter dated 1962. I took it from her, more to appease her than to closely read it. Maybe it was because I initially skimmed it, or maybe it was because I underestimated the power of alphas and omegas—for whatever reason, the first and the last sentences drew my attention:

> Dear Mr. Corn,
>
> I certainly don't think that the death required that "ye be born again," is the death of reason . . .
>
> Satisfy your demand for reason always, but remember that charity is beyond reason, and that God can be known through charity.
>
> Regards,
> Flannery[3]

The flight attendant returned with coffee and tea. Fearless, Veronica set her cup perilously on top of her stack of books. "Wasn't it Thoreau who stated that the masses of men lead lives of quiet desperation?" she asked. "I think of that one a lot." She sighed. "It's so easy to fall into the game of justification, Carolyn. C. S. Lewis put it well when he wrote about our tendency to try to justify or explain away Christianity. Believers claim, for instance, that because it has endured, it is worth something. 'See the rift?' he points out. 'Believe this, not because it is true, but for some other reason.'"

I wondered how many of my fellow passengers were despairing, caught justifying, or explaining away?

"Only you know if you are turning from one world toward another," Veronica said as she stirred her tea. "This new life doesn't seek to etherize us but to make us fully alive in that living, and even in our inevitable dying. And then, as if that were not enough, it promises us to yet live, truly, again, forever. You would be a freak if you weren't at least a little freaked-out." She smiled.

"Thank you, I think." I smiled back, then said, "But Veronica, things seem so much simpler if I just stop going down this road. I feel like one of those heroines in a choose-your-own-ending book. If I select the page where I can return home, love my family, marry a good man, then I can have everything neat and tidy. I can do as I please and not answer to anyone, let alone someone whose existence I cannot prove beyond a doubt. But if I choose the other . . ."

"Belief is really hard work." She shrugged her shoulders. "*And* it's radical work. I mean, imagine if we *really* implemented the golden rule, among individuals as well as nations. If we *really* did everything from holding doors open for each other, to helping raise each other's kids, to feeding and clothing one another. If we *really* took God at His Word, that He is *real*, and so love, and grace, and accountability are too. Like Mother Teresa telling us to love until it hurts, with a smile."

"Veronica," I said quietly, "I don't know if I can do this. I am no Mother Teresa. I am not even close. It's no use. I think I may need to leave it alone."

"You can try drinking it away, or partying it away, or simply ignoring it away. But that's actually what proves to be of no use to anyone, yourself or your neighbor. I understand; I have been there."

She took a deep breath, looking at me steadily. "Caro, friend, you are no longer the person you were when you first arrived in Oxford. Oxford has changed you. Or, rather, what God is working through you at Oxford has changed you. You have been brought across, over, beyond. You are now in a different place. Of course you will continue to love, to question, to study, to learn, to do everything as before and more, just from a different place. This change changes everything."

The man between us suddenly shifted in his sleep, knocking Veronica's tray table with his knee. I marveled at how deeply he had slept the entire time. Her tea jostled in her cup, but not a drop spilled. I discovered, however, that my cup had left a ring on my magazine, blurring the *T* and *I* so that the title now seemed to read *ME*.

Veronica lifted her cup to her lips. "It *is* a trip," she admitted, "and not for the fainthearted. For instance, instead of simply loving, you will ask yourself how best to love."

"*How best to love*? Is this sixties' jargon?" I tried scoffing. I found it was getting harder to scoff.

"The Lord is sovereign, even over the sixties." Veronica smirked, but then grew serious. "A lot happened at the time of O'Connor's letter. Martin Luther King was a man who ingeniously and genuinely modeled his politics on his Bible. He said much of great importance, obviously, but one thing really struck me. He claimed that a man who won't die for something is not fit to live. That made me wonder, what would I really die for? And then it made me wonder, what does that say of a God who would die for *us*?"

She paused, sipping her tea. I remained suspended. She left me there.

<hr />

Later the pilot's voice crackled over the intercom. The ascent of descent. My ears began popping. *Strange*, I thought, *how this proverbial stranger sitting (almost) next to me on the plane was actually proverbial.* As I watched her rise to open the overhead bin a few seats up and pack her books away, I noticed that she walked with a severe limp. It was obviously painful for her to stand, but she smiled warmly at others, just as she had at me, while making her way along the aisle.

"No one will understand," I bemoaned when she returned.

"Some will," she replied.

"No one will listen; no one will really hear," I continued.

"Some will, eventually, or perhaps." She shrugged. "Beyond speaking the truth in love, that's not your territory anyway."

"I will no longer belong," I said sadly.

"To whom?" Her beautiful eyes danced.

I fastened my seat belt and braced for a different kind of impact.

THIRTEEN

TIDE OUT: FORSAKING ALL OTHERS
(INCLUDING THE SELF)

I was much too far out all my life
And not waving but drowning.[1]

—STEVIE SMITH

I saw him before he saw me. I recognized the familiar stance before I could even make out his face. Leaning, legs crossed, against a column by the baggage claim. Impeccably dressed, my farmer-philosopher. No longer mine.

He gave a huge grin when he saw me. We kissed. Something pressed between us: a small, velvet box.

"Don't," I said, pulling away.

His eyes shone with hurt.

We did not speak much on the drive. I never saw the ring.

At home we searched for something to eat. He stood with his back to me at the kitchen counter; I could see his shoulders shaking. Suddenly he turned with an accusing look: three years' worth of love and laughter turned in an instant to pain and confusion.

I looked away.

"Is there someone else?" he managed to ask.

I did not answer.

"Tell me. Do you have another lover?" He was fighting to remain calm.

Perhaps, I thought. "No," I said.

"Let's go away this weekend." He pulled himself together, a statement rather than an invitation. "Just us."

I stood outside of my body; I saw two people close together in a small kitchen, yet miles apart. I heard myself agreeing. I reached for him, but then let my hand fall.

I didn't feel hungry. I didn't feel anything.

Late Christmas Eve a sea of red felt stretched across the width of our entire living room floor. We did not have a fireplace, so we hung it from our only formal chair: a larger-than-life Christmas stocking designed to decorate a house or garage. In a fit of giggles, my sister and I began madly stuffing treats into it, thinking ourselves quite clever.

"Mom will pee her pants when she comes down in the morning." Kelly laughed at one of her trademark eloquent phrases.

After my brother, Matt, left home, my mom, sister, and I agreed to keep gifts to stocking contents only. This year, however,

Kelly and I decided to outsmart the small-stocking limitation by not technically breaking the rule. Anticipating seeing Mom so happy, in spite of her scolding, was motivation enough.

I had to agree with Kelly, as I continued to fill the supersized stocking with things we knew Mom needed or might enjoy, but she would never buy herself. Then I turned to the immaculately wrapped pièce de résistance. We both went silent as I poised it carefully at the top of the stocking. Inside was a simple but poignant figurine of a woman from bygone days, seated on a bench and holding a rose in her hand. The entire piece was white except for the red rose. Its inscription on the bottom read "My Love."

Mom had admired the figurine in the collectors' shop, though way beyond our means, or so she thought. Mom had not considered all that two determined sisters can do. *Means* is not limited to "money."

"Oh, it's lovely." Kel sighed. "Mom hasn't had anything lovely in so very long."

I nodded, suddenly unable to speak. I admired how Mom, as always, had so masterfully made a home. The furniture dated from her wedding more than twenty-five years ago. Even the curtains had been hemmed and let out repeatedly to fit the varying windows of countless moves.

Things had been touched up here and there with polish, with paint, with a new patch of fabric. To outside eyes these items must have looked worn, even outdated. To me, however, especially with different eyes now, they seemed all the more precious for their fixed brokenness.

My love, I thought. *How does love turn out for any of us?*

But I still hoped my mom would cherish the gift.

"I think it's cool you're thinking about Jesus. Hmmm, I've never really given Him any serious thought," Kel said as she ate the popcorn we were supposed to be stringing. She had a slight buzz from drinking something electric blue; I wasn't sure what it was, but she loved neon-colored drinks. "Oh maaaan," she whined distractedly, "I just sewed my popcorn tinsel to my shirt."

Simply put, my sister is one of my favorite people on the planet; I could never have enough time with her. Thank God (even as an agnostic, I have always felt that way) she was born. I would have been a far-too-serious preschooler had she not come along. I poked at dead things; she cried over them. I hoarded my Halloween candy all year until it ended up too stale to eat; she immediately shared hers and then devoured her portion with glee. She was beautiful, bright, loyal, and matter-of-fact. When everyone else was congratulating me on winning the scholarship to Oxford, she did, too, without an ounce of jealousy or surprise. But then she reminded me that, because the MPhil academic gown did not have sleeves, I had better have toned arms in time for my graduation picture. And use self-tanner.

Of everyone with whom I first shared my consideration of faith upon returning home, Kelly was the only one who did not, well, pooh-pooh me at first. She did not agree with me, but she did not disagree either. Maybe a lifetime of giggling together earned me the privilege of being taken seriously.

Sitting there together amid the preparations for Christmas morning, I suddenly blurted out, "Kel, I've come to wonder if the greatest gift parents can give their children is joy irrelevant of each other?"

"What do you mean?" she mumbled, picking at the thread in her shirt.

"I mean owning joy that is not dependent on another person. A gift from some other first true love."

She gave me a searching look, so I poured out in greater detail my struggle with God from my first term at Oxford, fleshing out previous short notes and phone conversations. A working student with an adoring boyfriend, Kelly had been just as busy with her life as I had been with mine.

"Carolyn, I can respect your search, and I can respect your answers. And I will always love you, no matter what you do, decide, or practice," Kel replied after listening carefully. "But I need to pursue my own path." She took my hand. "As your little sister, I often feel as if I've been in your shadow. I can't stay in your shadow, especially for something like this."

I nodded that I understood.

"I'll try not to pester you too much about it." I smiled softly instead. "But I'll keep you posted, okay?"

"Perfect." She smiled back. I leaned in to help her carefully pull the threaded popcorn out of the Polo shirt she had saved up so diligently to buy.

⌐━⪻⪼━⌐

All around us the cornfields stretched out, barren and buried in snow—a wasteland with sharp, dry stalks sticking up randomly in broken rows. The sun was setting, so Ben had to cock the visor over his left shoulder. We spoke of trivial things. His studies. My studies. Updates on our friends postgraduation. I fiddled with the radio, keeping the background noise constant as the various stations went in and out of static every few miles.

By the time we reached his parents' summer home on the lake, the fog had rolled in so thick that our headlights were bouncing back, blinding us. Ben had to inch up to the house, pulling cautiously up the driveway so as not to skid into the ravine.

Ten-second intervals, I noticed. The foghorn went off at ten-second intervals. I waited and counted as Ben fumbled with the keys in the dark.

Somewhere out on the water, the foghorn echoed its lone lament. Warning us of rocks. Danger ahead.

Inside, the uninsulated Craftsman felt freezing cold. His parents' retirement project, it was a beautiful shell of a house caught in the ambitious transition from blueprint to home. Tarp covered gaping holes in the frame, flapping frighteningly in the dark like some great, caged bird.

Ben built a roaring fire in the master bedroom, the only room in the house that was finished and that could be closed off from the rest of the cavernous chill. It also held the only furniture: a chair and small desk, a mattress (no box spring or frame), and a bookshelf hosting a few scattered philosophy volumes. The fireplace came in handy; there was a small space heater, but it had to be run in intervals or else it shorted out the fuse. Only a few rooms had electricity, so we carried a flashlight with us. One toilet functioned, thank goodness, but there was no hot water. Since nothing worked in the kitchen yet, Ben had packed a simple meal: bread, cheese, wine.

I sat motionless on the mattress in front of the fire, uncertain what to do. Ben poured the wine and passed me a glass. "Cheers"—he grinned awkwardly—"as you must say now."

I took the glass and rolled the wine on my tongue. I held it up to the fire, looking through the garnet liquid into the flames, mesmerized by the shifting hues of both.

"Why?" I heard Ben say.

I looked at him, startled.

"*Why*?" he repeated.

I tried to look confused, to dodge the responsibility, the discomfort of any real answer, but I knew what he meant. I shrugged.

"I'm not sure exactly, Ben." I began wading through all the letters and phone calls between us.

"All I do know"—I spoke to the flames—"is that this won't work if we are on such different spiritual pages. This faith, and its subsequent way of being, is starting to become a real consideration for me . . . You have made it clear that it is of no interest, or even relevance, to you."

Ben nodded, swallowing his wine.

"I can respect that," I said sincerely, looking at him hard now. "But I need you to respect my position too. It'd be hard enough to be in a marriage where we differed so significantly, but to start out that way . . . well, it seems to me a recipe for disaster, don't you think?"

"I'm not so sure, Carolyn," Ben reasoned. "I mean, can't you do your thing, and I can do mine? My parents do it all the time, and they've been together forever."

"I don't want to live in a separate part of the house from you, Ben, let alone in a separate part of my soul from you . . ." I struggled to explain, but I didn't have the vocabulary yet.

"I've tried to believe, Carolyn, honest I have. Especially when I thought that not doing so meant losing you." Ben spoke so ardently that I ached. For him. For us.

I moved in closer to him, wrapping my quilt around him too.

"But I just *can't*," he whispered.

I took his hand and looked at his face, part shadow, part flame.

"Come with me," I pleaded.

He looked at me, and then he looked away into the flames.

I held my breath and waited.

"No." He shook his head, still avoiding my gaze. "No."

I exhaled.

It was over.

I appreciated his honesty, but I also knew, on some level, though there would be holidays yet to celebrate, family dinners, obligations, farewells, letters . . . it was over.

"I love you, Ben. You know I do."

He nodded again, finishing his wine.

"And you know that part of me always will." I thought of this dear man beside me with his impish grin and bright mind. Kind. Restless. Certain, so certain of everything, except me.

"So what *are* you saying, Carolyn? What do you mean?" Ben winced, then reached out to touch my cheek. I fought the impulse to feel guilty.

How best to love him?

I took a deep breath.

Honesty, I thought. *True engagement.*

"I don't want to end up somewhere you're not, Ben," I said, "and I don't want to be alone on the journey—not for the rest of my life. I mean, you are so *sure*, and I'm *not*. I'm just beginning something here, very important, I think, and I don't know where I'll end up. But if you are closed, and I'm still open, we just can't travel together." I took his hand. "Ben, the only thing I am sure of at this point is that I can't marry a man who won't even consider kneeling."

Ben gave an almost imperceptible nod with an air of defeat.

We sat in the quiet, my words frozen above us. The fire waned, but neither of us moved to stoke it. Wrapping ourselves in more quilts, we ate peacefully together until the room grew completely dark.

Ben got up, stretched, and went over to the mattress. He held out his hand. It was too cold to undress.

The foghorn called again, beckoning sailors to the safety of the harbor.

He wrapped his arms around me.

We slept.

Home from Oxford, I found that Christmas this year was no different, at first.

My father showed up in a rage, pounding on the door late Christmas Eve. As always, I let him in.

"You think you've done pretty well for yourselves here, don't you?" he stormed. "You think you don't need me? You sit around here enjoying all these beautiful things"— he gestured about the room, at the wedding ghost furniture—"celebrating Christmas together, eating, being merry, laughing, enjoying yourselves without me, without any thought of me." He began wailing. "No, no one invites *me*. No one has any concern about where *I* might be, what *I* might be doing, where *I* am living. Well, I'll tell you, I live with nothing! I have nothing! I am all alone." He sat down, intent on staying.

"Dad, you've created that for yourself." I could not help myself. I felt my usual need to argue rising up in my throat like bile. I took the bait no matter what.

Yet this Christmas Eve, as soon as I said it, I became aware of it, for the very first time. But my awareness came too late. Dad went crazy. He stood up with that empty look his eyes had begun to take on more and more lately. He started yelling obscenities. Then he began telling me what an ungrateful, difficult daughter I was. How cruel we all were to him.

"Your old man is pretty smart, you know. Yes, I'm pretty smart. Why don't you ask me how things are going?"

I tried to get him to sit back down. When his moods escalated like this, I grew afraid, and survival trumped pride.

"How are things going, Dad?" I asked him quietly.

"Are you mocking me?" he yelled. "How can you ask that when you know perfectly well it's been hell for me?"

"What are you up to, then, Dad?" I tried another angle, fighting to stay calm. He was a very large man. His eyes were fixed on me, then beyond me.

"I'm worth a lot of money, you know." He suddenly lowered his voice as though conveying a secret. "Don't let anyone fool you about your father. I could've easily made a million this past year."

"Really?" I feigned interest. I knew all about my dad's *business ventures*.

He leaned in. Somehow he still smelled of that beautiful pipe smoke and the ocean. I fought the tired longing to close my eyes and breathe it in.

"But I can't tell anyone. It's complicated, honey." His voice grew gentler. The storm had, for the moment, passed. He sat back down. "Get me something to eat," he ordered.

"Would you like a sandwich?" I asked, still quietly. Quiet begets quiet—usually.

"Sure. And some milk. Thanks, honey." He smiled. "Now, what was I saying? I wish you would stop interrupting me." He grew irritated again.

"That you might have made a million this past year," I prompted him, steadying the mast.

"Yes. Are you mocking me?" He peered at me from under heavy brows.

"No, Dad. Talk to me," I said as I went to make his sandwich, my movements methodical, controlled.

"Well, never you mind how I made it. Your father has his ways, you know. Too complicated to explain to a girl like you. Just trust me. Maybe when you're older and out from under your mother's influence, I can teach you; you'll understand. I can't let her know I have a dime . . . Where's my sandwich? What's taking you so long?"

I blindly slapped together a few things on some bread.

"Here you go," I tried to say lightly.

"My milk?" He snapped his fingers.

If it weren't Christmas, I thought angrily . . . but then I forced myself into survival mode.

My father stopped all conversation and very daintily ate his sandwich and drank his milk.

I thought about how, entirely by self-motivation, he earned an electrician's license, a real estate license, a mortgage broker's license. An accomplished artist, he had also taught himself to sail, to install telephone wires, and to golf semiprofessionally. His mother, an orphan and then a teenage immigrant bride, herself abandoned and then divorced, worked twenty-hour days to achieve a successful business; my father continued this legacy of self-made financial accomplishment. This man who used to pull quarters from my ears and feed me shrimp on his lap. The owner of hearty laughter once filling the house.

"This next project, it'll be big," he said strangely, suddenly standing up. "You'll see."

"Dad . . ." I started.

"I need to go. I am so busy. Way too busy to be wasting time here talking with you," he half-joked.

"When will we see you again, Dad?" I asked. "I have a Christmas gift for you. Just a little something from England I thought you'd like."

"You know how Christmas depresses me," he answered flatly.

I remembered back through a childhood of Christmas Eves. Kelly and I decorating, Mom doing the best she could with meals and gifts, Matt staying up late to put together the dollhouse, excitement falling through the air like snow, blanketing everything in expectation. All a-tingle I was tucked in bed with my sister, watching the warm glow of the candle against the frosted panes of glass. Eyelids growing heavy . . .

My father moaning with self-pity. Or gone. Claiming it was too painful to stay. Barely acknowledging presents. "Christmas depresses me." An explanation he deemed sufficient for bewildered children.

But I persisted in giving him gifts anyway. That's what good daughters do.

I was tired. It was late. I was relieved when he stood up.

"Yep, I'm too busy," he said as he stretched dramatically. "I will call you."

Yes, I thought sadly. *You will call me all night, again.*

"Tell me you love me," he stated blankly at the door.

"Dad, don't . . ." I replied.

"Tell me you love me. Go on." He grabbed my arm.

"Of course we love you, Dad," I replied, the old fear and disgust rising in my throat.

"Tell me you love me! You. Not we. *You."*

"I love you, Dad," I said emptily. I just wanted him out. Out of my house. Out of my life.

I did. And I didn't. So messy!

And then, without warning, that warm feeling came up in me, in spite of myself.

Man, I thought. *It just made things hurt more. Or did it? Would I hurt more without it?*

I thought of his own fatherless Christmas Eves. Of Veronica quoting a saint, to love until it hurts. Of the Gospels I was now reading. Father, Father, "why have you forsaken me?" (Matt. 27:46).

"Don't you ever forget I'm your father," my dad grumbled, somewhat appeased but still menacing. An injured lion caught in a trap. The limb was not quite gnawed off yet, but it was bleeding all over now.

How could I? I could not help but think bittersweetly.

"You're pretty hard to forget, Dad." I shrugged and smiled.

"You're my special girl, named for me, remember. You're mine. Always remember that." He began to cry. "It's so hard, Carolyn. It's so hard."

"I know, Dad, I know." I tried hugging him, but it came out an awkward dance of bodies not in step, arms missing each other, cheeks crashing.

"Merry Christmas, Dad," I said as I watched him walk out

into the snow in his mismatched boots. He got into one of his mysteriously rotating old cars. I recognized tonight's as the one with the missing door handles in the backseat. The car sputtered into the night. I remained shivering in the doorway. My sister came upstairs and put her arm around my waist.

"You don't mind that I stayed downstairs?" she asked.

I shook my head, relieved that Mom remained heavily asleep as usual after her evening drinks.

"I can handle it," I said as I shut the door.

By morning the fog was gone. So was Ben. He had taken his parents' old truck back home. He left me his car keys on the pillow, along with an envelope. Inside was a sonnet by Pablo Neruda, in typeface:

I don't love you as if you were the salt-rose, topaz
or arrow of carnations that propagate fire:
I love you as certain dark things are loved,
secretly, between the shadow and the soul.

I love you as the plant that doesn't bloom and carries
hidden within itself the light of those flowers,
and thanks to your love, darkly in my body
lives the dense fragrance that rises from the earth.

I love you without knowing how, or when, or
        from where,
I love you simply, without problems or pride:

I love you in this way because I don't know any other
   way of loving

but this, in which there is no I or you,
so intimate that your hand upon my chest is my hand,
so intimate that when I fall asleep it is your eyes
   that close.[2]

Underneath, in his own hand, Ben had written, "Good-bye, my love. I hope you find your God. I hope He is worthy of your love."

With the gentlest and most deliberate of movements, I folded the letter. Then I opened my discounted Bible until its spine cracked, slipping inside the small, perfect square.

FOURTEEN

TIDE IN: MORE THAN A NEW YEAR

Each home has its unbelievers and its believers; and
thereby a good war is sent to break a bad peace.

—St. Jerome

W hat's going on with you and Ben?" Mom asked as she sat at the kitchen table in her pink kimono housecoat, doing the crossword in the newspaper. It was the day after New Year's. Our stripped Christmas tree watched us from the corner, forlorn.

"We're not getting married, Mom," I replied simply.

She kept working on her crossword. I wound red and green tinsel around my fingers, making neat little nests in which to rest the ornaments we were preparing to pack away. I could hear the frenzied scribble of Mom's pen.

Suddenly the penny dropped for Mom. Then her pen.

"What do you mean you're not getting married?" she said,

looking up at me over her reading glasses. "You are perfect for each other!"

"No, actually, we're not," I said, tucking a delicate glass-spun ornament into one of the nests. "Not in one very fundamental, important way. Not yet anyway."

"What on earth do you mean? What about all your plans?" Mom sounded desperate. "You were going to come back and finish your studies here, then work here, then take over the house."

I was? It all seemed so long ago now.

"Other things have, well, come up." I shrugged.

"Is he cheating on you?" Mom gasped. "Remember, it don't mean a thing if you ain't got that ring!"

From the kitchen her favorite radio station blared golden-oldie tunes in the background as on any other morning. I wanted to scream over the sound of the Four Aces about the hands dealt us in life: "Mom, you got that ring and it still didn't mean a thing!" Instead I simply shook my head.

"Well then, sweetheart, what's the problem?" Suddenly she grew very serious. She came and put her arm around me. "If there's something you need to tell me . . . if you're . . . well . . . we can work it out . . . I'm always here for you. Like Gram used to say, you can always make things stretch to feed one more mouth at the table."

"No, Mom, it's not that." My irritation melted into an immense flood of love for her. Love for her unconditional love of us. I stood up and hugged her, feeling her familiar frame separated from mine by folds of silk. Slight but strong. Such delicate shoulders to carry such great weight. This beloved body from which I came.

I sat back down with her at the table. "Mom, I have something to share with you," I started uneasily.

"Yes, of course. What is it?" She patted my hand.

"Well, I don't know how to put this exactly, but . . ." The music from the radio rushed into the void between us.

> Three coins in the fountain
> Through the ripples how they shine.
> Just one wish will be granted
> One heart will wear a valentine.

I coughed, clearing my throat. "I'm thinking of becoming a Christian."

"What?" she replied, not with judgment or antagonism, but with a neutral little intake of breath.

> Make it mine!
> Make it mine!

"A Christian," I repeated. "I've been doing a lot of thinking at Oxford and . . ."

> Make it mine![1]

"Well, isn't that nice, honey." She smiled kindly. "I hoped you would be doing a lot of thinking at Oxford! My goodness, you had me worried there for a minute. A Christian! But what do you mean 'become'? Why, you've always been a Christian."

I could not stifle my laugh: Mom wore a clear look of relief. She was probably ecstatic to know that I was not doing drugs or sleeping with my married thesis supervisor.

"Mom," I explained, "I haven't been a Christian. I mean *really* a Christian."

"Oh, nonsense," Mom continued cheerily, returning to her crossword puzzle. "Most decent people are Christians. And you are more than decent." She smiled. "You are, well, *perfect*."

"Thanks, O unbiased one!" I laughed again. "But really, Mom, I'm discovering that being good or moral or anything else, for that matter, doesn't automatically make you a Christian."

"You certainly can't tell me that people who go around lying and murdering are getting into heaven, can you?" she asked in her most Libran fashion. "Your grandfather was an altar boy, remember? Actually, come to think of it, he did have a crisis of faith as the result of the Catholic church . . . couldn't bring himself to agree with the pope. But yes, we are good, Christian people. Ethical. Moral. Kind."

"Mom, listen," I tried to say gently. "It's not about character, or acts, or genes, or even tradition."

"Then what is it about?" She peered at me from under her reading glasses. I could not tell if she was in earnest or just tolerating my views. Often Mom's slide into bitterness is hard to detect at first through the rhetorical question or humor. But then it walloped you. Much like a Philip Larkin poem.

"It's about faith," I stated.

"Faith in what?" came the same hard-to-read tone from Mom.

I breathed in. "Faith in Jesus Christ." I breathed out.

Dead silence.

For some reason, *Lord, have mercy* popped into my head.

Empty phrase or ardent prayer? I had not tried actual prayer yet. I mean, formally speaking. Prayer, I reckoned, was a tricky matter and not for novices, let alone common flounderers such as I.

Mom got up and fiddled with the radio, moving the dial two decades to a sixties station. She returned, looking somewhere between uncomfortable and bewildered, so I tried to say something, anything.

"Mom, I feel as if something is missing in my life—something more profound than I can give words to; something more than just yearning for a dependable dad, or financial security, or a nice home."

Mom looked pained. Her face seemed to say, "Haven't I given you enough? Aren't we enough?" but she remained quiet.

"Mom, you've given me all you could." I tried to speak to the look. "But I am starting to suspect that when it comes down to it, only faith gives joy, suffering, life, death—well, pretty much everything—true meaning in the end. I'm beginning to wonder: if I take Jesus at His word, will I grow closer to knowing God and closer to what is truly God's best for me?"

"It's a pipe dream, a cloud of smoke." Mom looked at me with wistful eyes, her mouth turned down a little. "You'll feel differently when you're older, sweetheart."

"I have to say, Mom," I concluded, "this new good—or should I say, this good news—seems *better*."

"Better than what, dear?" she asked tightly.

I hesitated. Just that alone touched a nerve. Mom began to close down. I could see it.

Wait. Don't go, Mom. Don't check out, I urged in my head. *Man,* I thought, *why is it so hard to talk about this with the people you love the most?*

I scrambled, trying to reach out truthfully but afraid of coming up trite. *Oh, wait. Wait! Quick! How best to love?* I grasped at any straw, praying (yikes—again?) that it could be spun into gold.

Suddenly Mom launched into her usual argument, the one I had heard for ages. But now I heard it differently. "How can I be expected to believe in a God who would sacrifice His only Son?" she shot out severely. There it was: Mom's mighty maternal Achilles' heel.

"Mom, how can we believe in a God who wouldn't?" I leveled at her.

Mom gasped in shock. I half-expected her to respond in a whirlwind of Hungarian, as she usually does when extremely moved. That unique language had the power to comfort as well as strike complete terror in us as kids. I'm surprised God did not write the Ten Commandments on the tablets in Hungarian.

But Mom remained silent. For a moment I did too. I had to admit I was a bit stunned myself. I sat back, recalling many talks late into the night with TDH. With him I was defensive, on edge. But with Mom, I just wanted her to be happy. Desperately. As I began feeling out this possible faith with her, I found myself wanting her to believe it too. Why? For *her* good? Or for *mine*? Or for some truth here at stake—that perhaps this "good" was indeed . . . *good*? So good, in fact, that the need for it ultimately outweighed the need to have all the answers?

"Mom, I know you would give your life for me in an instant," I said, this time more gently.

"Of course. You bet I would! For any of my babies. Like *that*!" She snapped her fingers.

"Well then, how much more must God feel about each of us as *His* children?" I trusted this computed in mom-mathematics.

"I have heard you say that the worst fate that can befall someone is to lose a child."

"Oh, my goodness, yes. Children should never die, let alone before their parents," Mom agreed passionately. Mom's affectionate heart really is something to behold. Better get out of the way!

"What if God wants to be with each of His children?" I rolled with such heart. "By sacrificing His only Son, as I see it," I began, feeling my own way, "I think God sacrificed Himself, but *even more*."

Mom listened, intrigued, forgoing for the moment even her crossword addiction. So I continued, "Mom, I've been reading the Bible for myself, and people who think He is a passive God, an uninvolved God, a God who is distant or who doesn't care . . . to be frank, it looks like they're wrong."

"Is the Bible required reading at Oxford?" she finally asked politely.

"Yes . . . no . . . well, not exactly." I could not help smiling. "You say that you can't believe in a God who would sacrifice His only perfect Child for all of His imperfect ones. I used to think the same thing. But reading the Bible has required me to consider how, in extending us grace, God not only sacrificed Himself, but something even dearer than Himself. He went the whole nine yards and then some. Not a precise and petty measure, Mom, but an overflow, an outpouring of abundance, as I've seen you do for us."

Mom looked uneasy. "My, you have done a lot of thinking at Oxford," she finally said, in English, and in a tone that, again, I couldn't quite decipher. A mix, perhaps, of admiration and annoyance. Mom loved and excelled at a good debate, but now she hung up her gloves and retreated into her crossword.

"Your grandfather used to argue with your grandmother about how we originated from the apes." Mom started into one of her stories as she turned off the radio. Soon it would be time for her to leave for work. Mom never complained about the long hours she worked, but I knew this was the secretaries' most efficient season, before the rush of term descended with all the demands of faculty and students. "My poor mother would beg him not to tell anyone or else he'd be considered a communist. But Grandpa persisted, saying how much we resembled apes, and how Jesus was, in fact, the first communist. Living on nothing but the generosity of others. Preaching that everyone should give everything away. Having such a soft spot for the poor and such. Then he brought home a monkey, just to prove his point, not Jesus but Grandpa, and poor Gram had to keep it in the garage. A constant thorn in her side until she announced, 'Daddy, either the monkey goes or I do.'"

"I'm assuming Grandpa kept Grandma," I said wryly.

"Yes, the monkey went, but not without a good fight." Mom nodded with satisfaction, adding quietly, "Gee, I adored my dad."

I knew my mom had loved her father deeply. *She shouldn't have any trouble with fathers*, I thought. Shouldn't she have a particularly soft spot for Jesus, then, and what He claims? Or perhaps she is afraid that no other father can hold a candle to hers? Or that by becoming a true Christian, might she somehow betray the memory of this father with all his own pushes and pulls with faith? I wondered if all fathers had died along with hers that cruel and snowy April. But certainly paradise for Mom would be reuniting with both fathers, earthly and eternal?

I know when separated from Mom I could only be comforted by the promise of seeing her again. But Mom maintains that we dissipate into nothingness upon death. I had to admit that this increasing point of disagreement now worried me greatly.

"If man is ape or angel, Mom"—I laughed in all seriousness—"I'd like to think I'm on the side of the angels." I could not help myself. I had some of Grandpa in me too.

"Well, I'm sure this is just one of those little miscommunications. Don't be rash. Give it some time." Mom began clearing the table.

I looked at her quizzically. "What are you talking about?"

"I'm talking about Ben, of course." Mom had changed topics quickly. "It's good to have you home, Caro." She kissed the top of my head. "We missed you dearly. I missed *my* girl. I just want you to be happy. I love you so. One day, when you are a mom, you'll understand. You'll want something that keeps your baby safe and happy too."

Yes, I thought of the so-called restored world that the Bible promised. When I thought of trying to live as a thoughtful believer in the current world, however, I almost choked on my coffee.

But I swallowed hard and kissed her back.

Another tidal wave of love swept over me for her as I trailed after my mom as she got dressed. Of course, I have always loved my mother. But this wave felt slightly *different* somehow. It was a love—how to put it?—very *conscious of loving*, without fear or judgment or reservation (or even concern at the paradox), a love that encompassed her brokenness and her beauty. A love that lived and died and rose and then, somehow loved even harder, even better.

Anew.

Had this love first been given to me in spite of, or because of, my own brokenness and beauty?

Yes, it seemed, as I watched Mom drive off, following the usual numerous tries for the ignition to catch. For as long as I could remember, I had felt cherished by my mother. She often referred to her children as her "baby chicks." Now Jesus' description of God's own love for His children through the same metaphor came to my mind; "O Jerusalem, Jerusalem, you who kill the prophets and stone those sent to you, how often I have longed to gather your children together, as a hen gathers her chicks under her wings, but you were not willing" (Matt. 23:37). The mother hen has been known to collect her chicks under her wing even in the threat of encroaching flames. Sacrificing herself so that they may live.

Life is messy. Life is beautiful and terrible and messy. So why would we expect a faith in this life that is easy to understand? Why expect a gift wrapped up neatly within the tissues of our brains and tied with a nice bow of material clarity? I thought of TDH's image of things coming full circle in grace. Funny, again, how nothing is wasted. If my long days in retail taught me anything, it was that a round gift is the most difficult to wrap.

Matt drove me to the airport. I hugged my brother hard as my luggage was loaded. He looked so proud, so happy for me, returning to Oxford to pursue my dream. His eyes were misty as he hugged me back.

After all the usual good-byes, he leaned in for one more hug. "Hey, Mouse"—he used his pet name for me—"so you still thinking of becoming a Christian?"

"Yeah, I've been rolling it around. A lot has been happening to me away from home, Mattie . . ." I looked at him earnestly. That dear, dear face. My big "brudder," with whom I had always felt cherished and safe.

I held his hand, feeling him rock back and forth, heel to toe, heel to toe, with his usual energy—the manic energy of comedians who care too much not to laugh.

"Well, let's make sure you're not bald and barefoot, handing out flowers at the airport when I pick you up next," he interrupted me, partly joking but partly serious.

Flowers in an airport?

I felt the sting. Then the indignant defense rushed in. Then the anger. Then the sadness. And, then, without warning, the Love. Within an instant. That tsunami Love, which threatened to flood out everything.

So messy!

And then washed clear.

Brother. Matthew. Gift of God. The tax collector who became an apostle. The unloved who became beloved.

Flowers in an airport.

First the thorns, I thought. *Then the rose.*

HILARY TERM

FIFTEEN

BOOK ENDS

Back in our silences and sullen looks,
for all the Scotch we drink, what's still between's
not the thirty or so years, but books, books, books.[1]

—TONY HARRISON

"Caro, welcome back! We missed you! So good to see you! How was your trip? How is everyone at home?" And, inevitably, "Are you still getting married?" The questions came fast and furious on the heels of warm greetings and hugs from inside the Boars Head, a cozy pub tucked around the corner from Oriel College. A collection of ties hung on the wall over the fireplace, the sign of a distinct tradition. Newcomers who did not know the rule and inadvertently entered wearing a tie had it snipped off and tacked to the wall. No ties allowed. In fellowship you can be yourself: no formal airs, the cutting of "conventional" ties a prerequisite for such fellowship. It made me think of the description of family according to Jesus, defined not by genes, accomplishments, accoutrements, or attire but, radically, by faith.

Sitting down I looked at them all, so very different and yet so very authentic in their friendship. Isn't life funny, that it can bring such an eclectic group so joyfully to one table?

"Well, tell us"—Hannah, of course, rushed in loudest and first—"how did things go with Ben? Are you two still getting married?" Then she paused and leaned in, sotto voce, "Does he think you're going completely nutters? And does your family think you're going nutters, too, for considering becoming a *Christian*?" She practically mouthed the last word, suddenly protective of my privacy in the crowded pub. But it was too late; several pub goers held their drinks suspended in midair, waiting to hear about my love life. Of both kinds. *Great*.

"We're not getting married," I stated matter-of-factly. Then I looked at all the other faces staring at me and repeated it for them too: "We're not getting married," I said again. "Okay?"

"Well done, lass," someone behind us slurred back.

"Marriage is a trap anyway," a woman chimed in from the next table, her friend adding, "Hang in there, luv. There's plenty more fish in the sea."

Another stranger asked, "Can I buy you a drink?" When I looked over, I saw an elderly man who gave me a wink. I laughed.

"Okay, everyone," I addressed the listening crowd. There is about as much privacy in a British pub as there is in the MCR phone booth. "It was hard, but I'm back, and I'm still standing. Gossip session is over now." I pulled up a chair, sneaking in as close as possible between Linnea and Hannah. "Thanks a lot," I muttered at them.

My friends huddled around me protectively as I filled them in on my visit back home.

"I'm really sorry that your loved ones weren't happier about your search, Caro," Mark offered up. "It's strange but it's often hardest sharing the most important thing with those who are closest."

"Sometimes I think the good news is almost easier to share with strangers," Rachel observed, "maybe because so much isn't on the line, relatively speaking (if you pardon the pun)."

"It's the most important thing to share," Mark insisted. "Of anyone we should be sharing it with—"

"But therein lies the rub," Dorian interjected. "No wonder Eve's temptation was intellectual—not sexual, or sensual, or physical, or even, ironically, spiritual, but highly intelligent—a rationalization of her desire, her hubris. Our heads can deceive us just as much as our hearts, if not more so. But then Satan brought Eve and Adam both down because of their intimate relationship. Anything of real value lies in relationship, and yet relationships are where we find ourselves the most vulnerable."

At the mention of Eve and intimate relationship, Edward perked up. "Didn't you two at least sleep together one last time?" He smirked at me. "You know, for poetry's sake?"

Hannah rolled her eyes.

Earlier that day, rays of sunshine poured through the stained-glass windows of the Duke Humfrey's Reading Room, dappling my otherwise dim working space with primary colors. The wintry light gave a false impression of warmth. Wrapped in an old scarf and moth-holed sweater (an old cardigan of my father's), I felt like Scrooge's assistant, Bob Cratchit, as I rubbed my hands together, trying to uncramp my fingers after a morning of gripping a pencil in the chilly air.

Being allowed to read in this section, which was situated at the very top of the Bodleian Library, was a specialized privilege. The dark-wood paneled rooms with doors like huge chocolate bars held some of the world's rarest books, priceless manuscripts, and historical documents. Many books were still chained to their original shelves from centuries ago, reminiscent of the immense wealth books represented in the past. Before our culture of mass production, a handful of books marked a small fortune, a roomful of books easily worth an entire farm.

Somehow the old, enclosed reading room managed to smell like lilacs. I breathed in deeply. Despite the beetle infestation. (Yes, sad to say, it had been discovered that beetles were ingesting some of our civilization's wisdom. Occasionally one gorged itself too much and fell with a gluttonous plunk onto your desk from the rafters.) I breathed over the problem with looking for God at Oxford, or with God looking for me at Oxford. As a result I found myself now at odds with both things I previously held most dear: my family and my studies.

Neither did it help that my social circle had widened so dramatically compared to back home. Hitherto I had grown up inconspicuously mediocre, literally: midsize town, midsize schools, midsize cars. Even my struggles were, relatively, midsize. But now I dined regularly with people of position, influence, and fame. I studied with their children and helped guard their anonymity. An old high school friend half-joked that she was surprised I still spoke with her, a college dropout. But homesickness prevents the intoxication of being impressed. How many times I enjoyed a lively conversation with someone famous over an extravagant meal, and yet I would have exchanged everything for a simple cup of tea with my sister!

As I sat there irreverently doodling in the Duke Humfrey's Reading Room instead of taking notes, something else lurked beneath my hesitation about presuming greatness, in others as well as in myself. Noteworthiness according to worldly standards suddenly seemed relative. Fame is fleeting, fickle, relative to others' interests and tastes. Self-worth that is subject to others' judgments remains alive only as long as the delay of condemnations.

By contrast, greatness, when you have God, it would seem is absolute.

Perhaps righteousness was not boring at all. (I could not help but think of TDH's hometown of Boring, Oregon, and smile.) Perhaps righteousness commanded respect and my full attention. And, perhaps, in trying to know God better, becoming righteous made you known to God—the only fame that matters. Perhaps the magi were so wise because of the true star they followed.

I looked around Duke Humfrey's. *Books, books, books between us*, I thought. *Between all the people I love most and me. Actually one great Book stands between us*, dropped like a beetle burrowing into our false senses of permanence, disturbing our slumber like a cock crowing at the dawn of thought.

Of course folks from home were proud of me, and I'm sure a bit put off by me and this new God—this God of the elitist educational experience, this God of what could seem the studying of no real consequence.

After lunch with my friends, I tried to assert my scholarly significance by working away in the bracing, more "modern" building of the English Faculty Library for the rest of the afternoon. Having lost track of the time, I impatiently checked out my books and raced down the block to make the connecting bus. I did not want to be late to the much publicized evening lecture. In my haste I ran smack into a tall figure also carrying a stack of books. Dead authors flew irreverently everywhere. "I'm so sorry," I gasped, bending over to save Milton's beautiful blank verse from being trod on by a preoccupied tourist.

"No harm done," I heard a familiar voice say. I looked up, way up, for he was indeed very tall, especially against the demure dignity of the little, ninth-century St. Cross Church. We stood surrounded by the picturesque Holywell cemetery, if you can call a cemetery that. With the late afternoon sunlight settling around his head, TDH resembled some sort of mythological god.

Ooh, that was rather pagan of me, I inwardly mocked. *Well, why stop there?* So I continued to think, which is not always a good thing.

"How *are* you?" he exclaimed in his warm, larger-than-life TDH way, practically sweeping me off my feet with his hug and then picking up all the books in one fell swoop. "Let me carry your books for you?" He grinned, with his usual cheeky gusto. I had to admit, it surprised me how much I had missed him.

"Just this once," I said, suddenly growing irritated. Why *did* he irritate me so?

I had not seen TDH since leaving for Christmas holidays. By the end of last term, after countless evenings patterned on me pummeling him relentlessly with questions about his faith, and his answering things as thoroughly and thoughtfully as possible, I began to feel I was way out of my league . . . on so many levels . . . although I would die before letting on. But, thankfully, Christmas vacation intervened, and I was able to swim back to shore. Barely.

Do I refuse to consider this faith so seriously because the messenger is attractive and thoughtful and intelligent and a gentleman? I thought of Kelly's hesitation to consider the faith because she wanted her independence from me, from someone who loved her more than could possibly be expressed. Are things of the utmost importance sidelined because those who convey them are too good, or in TDH's case, if I were to be honest, too good to be believed? Should these not, in fact, be valid sources we trust the most?

Obviously the plank in my eye is bigger than my sister's. Watching the traffic skid along the dirty slush, I felt far less pious than when I had been at home for the holidays amid all that freshly fallen snow.

Squinting at TDH aglow in the sunset, I decided that for now it was far easier to remain irritated at him. He was just a man, and like all other men he would mess up, eventually. All I had to do was be patient.

TDH balanced our books on one arm and hooked his free arm through mine rather jovially. I felt exposed without my books in their usual hold against my chest. He took my left hand.

"No ring I see," he said gravely. "Are you okay?"

Tears started welling up in my eyes. I was glad we were walking side by side so he could not see my face. I nodded and broke free. "I'm late. I really need to dash—" I managed to say as I pulled my collar up around my chin against the bitter chill. TDH passed my books to me with a puzzled look on his face. I bolted and just made the bus, plopping down in the back, out of breath. The frozen Botanic Garden rushed by. My family surely thought I was crazy. Most of my oldest friends thought I was crazy. Even some of my professors, former and current, thought I was crazy. And I had just broken up with a good man who loved me like crazy.

Maybe I *was* going crazy . . .

Sitting alone on that bus, I felt, well, very alone. "Where *are* You?" I said, partly to me, partly to God.

My eye caught a Calvin Klein ad of a perfectly chiseled man wearing only a fig leaf. *Did Adam look like that?* I found myself wondering. Biblical questions kept incessantly popping up now in all shapes and sizes.

"Just left Logic Lane!" cried the bus driver.

Only in Oxford, I thought.

"Next stop, Angel Meadows!" he sang out.

Okay, very funny, I almost said aloud. *Almost.*

I wasn't crazy.

Not yet.

SIXTEEN

WHAT IF JESUS
HAD BEEN A WOMAN?

Life on the planet is born of woman.

—ADRIENNE RICH

The stage production of Shakespeare's famous love story *Romeo and Juliet* proved painful.

To my right, Rachel worked furiously on her to-do list in the little journal she always carried with her. To my left Linnea and Dorian huddled together, intensely discussing something I could not make out. I looked down the row. Hannah left ages ago, complaining she had old laundry to get to that stunk less than the play. Edward, looking like a sexily stubbled lion lazing in the sun, had stretched his legs out in Hannah's vacated space. Hands folded on his chest, he seemed to be enjoying the stilted performance with a wry grin. Later, when I asked him how he tolerated it to the end, he assured me, "Cheese is the genre in which I feel most at home."

We were on the sixteenth minute of Juliet's dying (for the second time) when I felt a tap on my shoulder.

"Do you want to blow this Popsicle stand?" a strong Yankee voice attempted to whisper from behind. I was surprised that a few audience members cared enough to shush us.

"Would I!" I smiled back and took TDH's hand as he pulled me off the bench to my feet. Sweeping me both on and off my feet was becoming a habit of his.

"Hey, Romeo," Edward hissed jokingly down the aisle, "take it easy with the girl. She belongs to us." He narrowed his eyes and added, "To the dark side." Edward enjoyed ribbing his Christian friends almost as much as he enjoyed self-deprecation.

❧

Edward and I once sat in his room late into the night, talking about whether or not men and women can just be *friends*—a loaded topic for discussion in a dark room, at a lonely hour, with an attractive member of the opposite sex.

"I don't think it's possible," he argued. "The sexual attraction and the possibility of accident will always underlie things, like the signal of a submerged submarine scanning the horizon of hope."

"So men and women are doomed forever, by biology, to be separated? To not even own true friendship?" I asked while snacking on his store of pretzels.

"That's what marriage is for." Edward surprised me, suddenly growing serious. "I think marriage is the only place—maybe because the sexual tension gets settled, or maybe because they decide to stick together through so much, or perhaps both—where a man and woman can be true friends."

"Interesting. Continue . . ." I replied, intrigued.

"The problem is, I can't." He shrugged.

"You can't marry, or you can't continue?" I asked, drawing circles in the salt at the bottom of the bowl.

"Both I guess. I mean, I wonder if there really is any such thing as a *real* marriage, as a relationship of perfect submission to one another, of a love greater than you or I could ever imagine." Edward furrowed his brow.

Wow, I thought. *Does someone like Edward have these thoughts too?* His demeanor seemed far too serious for this to be a pickup line.

Tasting the salt on my tongue, I decided to answer him at face value: "I am beginning to think there may be, although I won't make any promises, not yet anyway."

"Caro," Edward groaned as he leaned back, "why is it that just when I go to focus on what seems to really matter, it grows fuzzy in my vision? For instance, I begin to suspect that marriage may reflect something deeper—okay, don't laugh—a more *divine* relationship, for lack of a better phrase."

"I'm not laughing," I assured him. "Quite the opposite. Go ahead."

Edward studied me hard and then decided it was safe. "And yet, just when I veer toward this great thing that feels right and good, I lose sight of it. I lose *traction*."

"What do you mean?" I topped his wineglass.

"I become distracted," he said with a heavy sigh, as though giving up on something.

"Oh."

"I don't know. Things happen, I guess," he tried to explain. "My mind wanders. Someone interrupts me, like Coleridge's stranger from Purlock knocking at the door, like a great grim reaper, interrupting his poetic process, cutting down his muse. The candle flickers and then goes out. And I can't get it back, or not quite. There is this momentary ache. And then I'm not sure if I *want* it back."

"Why would you not want it back?" I asked, playing with the candle wax.

"Because then it would take me under; it would undo everything I have done, everything I have created for myself." Edward leaned in and blew out the candle.

I sat with him in the darkened silence.

After some time Edward admitted drily, "It's far easier to just leave after sharing the cigarette."

I arched my brows at him. "Climbing out the window before dawn, are we?"

As I excused my way past spectators with TDH, my attention returned to the stage. An ungainly, leotarded Romeo was crawling clumsily out of a makeshift prop balcony complete with real roses and thorny stems. As he got stuck in a straddle over the ledge, even as a woman I grimaced on his behalf. I looked back down the aisle at Edward. He was grimacing too. I thought of the portrait of his mother, done by a famous artist, that Edward kept by his desk in his room. Beautiful. Fragile. I wondered what it must have been like for him to find her hanging in the closet. He was so little he had to have strained to touch her feet. But he did touch them. They were ice-cold, he said.

"Farewell. Farewell. One kiss and I'll descend."[1]

Before us sat tiers and tiers of beautiful pastries and delicate sandwiches, piled high with strawberries, an array of preserves, and heavy cream on the side. I sipped my Earl Grey tea, curling the bergamot and orange blossom around on my tongue—a perfect blend of the masculine and feminine steaming from my cup. High tea at the Randolph Hotel was TDH's idea. His treat. There is nothing like it. It even outdoes breakfast at Tiffany's.

"What's the occasion?" I leaned over the table to ask him, always suspicious.

"Just wanted to enjoy your company and surprise you with something thoughtful, as I know you've had a lot on your heart and mind lately." TDH smiled.

"I'm fine."

"Well, it didn't seem like *Romeo and Juliet* was helping much. From a distance you looked miserable to me, lost in your thoughts." TDH frowned.

"What are you, some kind of Shakespearean stalker?" I said, trying to joke things off.

"Caro, I care about you."

"You are a Christian, and I'm not. We can't date by some secret law of the universe. So why do you care?" I thought sardonically of Edward's belief that men and women cannot be friends.

"I know I've made that clear," TDH replied, "and I trust one day you'll understand completely, without feeling so judged."

"Or excluded, or not good enough, or wrong," I seared.

TDH silently sipped his tea.

"A simple thank-you would have been lovely," he said as he set his cup down.

I squirmed, feeling a bit sheepish. I shook it off. "Thanks for the gesture." I swallowed hard as I tried to digest the authenticity of his actions. "Thanks for thinking of me." I managed a weak smile.

"Now there, was that so bad?" He smiled back broadly and refilled my gold-rimmed china teacup. "So tell me how you are doing, and be honest."

Why not? I thought, as I took the most delicious-looking pastry from the top tier. I was on a man diet, not a food one, as Hannah would say.

Countless devoured pastries later, we slumped back, satisfied and on a sugar high. I was touched that TDH insisted on picking up the bill. I was also touched by how much he clearly enjoyed the tea. He was probably the only person alive who could have devoured more scones smothered in preserves and crème fraîche than I. And I marveled at how TDH spoke so easily of his poverty. I didn't speak of mine at all.

Like Forster's poignant hero Leonard Bast, I was more likely to shift distractedly in my seat, unable to fully enjoy the production for want of my missing umbrella, accidentally taken home by the person next to me. But TDH seemed to enjoy wholeheartedly the productions of life in spite of his missing umbrella. Or more precisely, maybe it was because he trusted that someone else had the joy of its use.

TDH guided me through the revolving door into the brisk evening air. He then swung me around with the grace of a dancer, so that he stood between the street and me. A gentlemanly reflex on his behalf, it was partly to lend his help in navigating us through the jostling crowd, and partly to come between the oncoming traffic and me.

I walked back around him to my original spot.

He swung me back around again, gently but firmly.

I returned to my spot.

We must have looked like two crazy partners caught in an awkward dance where both parties insisted on taking the lead.

"What are you doing?" I finally shot at him, irritated beyond belief.

"I'm walking between you and the traffic," he replied, unperturbed.

"I don't need your help," I stated as a matter of fact.

"No, you don't," he agreed, it seemed in earnest.

I hated that, when he responded respectfully. It knocked me off balance. But I was onto his ploy.

"I am entirely capable of walking on the sidewalk alongside traffic," I insisted.

"Of course you are," he said in the same kind tone . . . again. I listened for the condescension . . . craned for it. But it was not there. I had to think quickly. This was slippery, new territory.

"So what's your problem, then? Why do you keep insisting on putting me on your inside arm?" I huffed.

TDH stopped walking. "Because it's the right thing for me to do," he said, looking straight at me.

"The right thing for you to do! Says who? Stalin?" I stopped, too, and shook his arm off me like a plague. He stepped back. *See, he'll back down*, I thought.

So I went on both walking and talking, fortified. "What a

patriarchal act of subordinating assumption," I grumbled. He stood there, watching me storm off.

"I don't need your help," I repeated. "I don't need any man's help." My voice began rising above the bus exhausts and blaring horns of the intersection.

"No. No. *No*. Thank you very much!" I shouted at him over my shoulder. I barely glimpsed his face, but in it I thought I saw that same messy look . . . that look of, well, compassion? Even when someone is ticking you off. I almost wanted to turn around, to turn back and rest in that look. Almost.

No. No. No! I reminded myself, dashing ahead of him to cross the intersection before the light changed.

⌘

"For women, Christianity is irrelevant and derogatory," Dr. Lynbury stated authoritatively. We were seated six at a table in celebration of the annual meeting of the Association of Feminists in Academia. I didn't bother asking her if she had ever read the Bible, I mean actually read it. Even I had given up asking that one some time ago, especially among academics.

"What does Jesus know about being a woman anyway? If He really wanted to come as a servant, He should have come as a woman," Dr. Rajan said with a laugh. "On the very bottom rung of life. A woman with children. No, make it a divorced woman with children. Lots of them. With no child support, and no education, and no opportunities."

Listening, I nodded, putting my head down as I sipped my tea. I had thought all these things, too, for quite some time. But more recently some new things reared their heads as well.

First, there was that handy intersection of place and time where Jesus inserted Himself into history. I kept wondering why He didn't come now, in my age, in my lifetime. Like the *petit prince* in my own little desert. But as I read the Bible more and more, I realized just how radical and, well, *timely* His timing was. That aside, however, if He had come as a woman, it didn't seem that *she* would have been listened to anytime in world history thus far.

Then there was the consideration that a "historical Jesus" must remain within the limitations of human notions of time that do not allow for simultaneous tenses of being. If homesickness had taught me anything, it was how funky the nature of time must be. At any moment in my day, I can stop and imagine my sister's daily living, or a friend's, in a parallel universe to mine, so to speak. I can see in my mind's eye what they might be doing at the same time that I'm doing something in a different time zone miles away. But does that nullify their existence, their goings-on, or mine? Does it change my ability to imagine them, or be buoyed by them, or be saddened at not being with them? Not at all. Homesickness only makes the afflicted more in tune with how absolutely plausible a concept like the Trinity really is.

Being a woman did not exclude me from this phenomenon. Maybe it even highlighted it? *Wait. I'm a feminist, so how can I be having these thoughts?* I chastised myself. *I am a liberated woman.*

What does that mean, really, a "liberated woman"—for *anyone* to be liberated? Free from what, exactly?

Sure, there were obvious sound causes, including equalities any idiot could grasp, such as equal pay for equal work. Human rights, not gendered ones. But in this world, one thing would just eclipse the next. There was always going to be something unjust, something askew, even in a sophisticated system . . . even as a result of such a sophisticated system.

The power of women to choose, yet silencing those who can't choose; the right of a woman to pursue the same education, salary, life options as a man, but denying many of the very things that grew from such opportunities, if they did not measure up to a man's way of being—sometimes I got all of it, and sometimes I got none of it. It seemed I had all of the privilege but none of the certainty, all of the provision but none of the contentment. What was worse, I was beginning to sense holes in this logic, but I did not want to nest in them. I still wanted desperately to belong—belong to those who themselves wanted to belong. It is all driven by such want. In this case, what *do* women *want?*

The speaker cried, "To take back their power! To reappropriate their appropriated language!"

I thought, *Isn't this the same as desiring to have one's value reinstated within a cultural exchange? To be justified? Is it possible it's all the same—just different lingo?*

How was Jesus as *He* relevant to me as *she?* I squirmed in my seat. I could not deny the fissures I was feeling. *Just stop it,* I told myself. *You are becoming the enemy. Traitor!* I smiled it all down as I continued listening to the banter at my table. Besides, being a feminist and a Christian seemed a no-win scenario. If Jesus had been a woman, feminists would have seen her as just another woman in subordination to a man. Even worse, to *the Man.*

All of this seemed the worst kind of paradox: a feminist Christian, or a Christian feminist. It's an implosion of such difficult terms. Again, so messy!

So, in the wake of discussion following the speaker, I remained silent. Simon and Garfunkel silence.

"There are a lot of amazing stories about very intelligent, memorable, even powerful women in the Bible," I finally ventured feebly.

"Sure, prostitutes, handmaids, multiple wives . . . sounds very powerful to me," the woman on my other side scoffed.

Countless women in both Bible testaments are shown in favorable lights, but especially in the New Testament, I now know, I thought but did not say. *Many demonstrate incredible discernment and are entrusted with wonderful information, not by men but by God.*

"Then there's the problem of a male God altogether," another guest piped into my thoughts.

Oh man, here we really go now, I inwardly groaned. *How can these women so steeped in Mary Wollstonecraft and the original concerns of "feminism" even go down the road of gender in heaven? Besides, Lord knows, the world needed more of fathers, not mothers.*

It was time to wheel out the cake. There were *ooohs* and *ahhhs*. The candles on the cake represented the number of years women had been allowed to participate in the Oxford Union. I strained to make out the inscription. Virginia Woolf's words appeared in pink icing script: "To raise bare walls out of bare earth was the utmost they could do."

"Now it looks like the modern woman can have her cake and eat it too." The speaker raised her glass triumphantly.

I downed my champagne and accepted unabashedly a corner piece decorated with two huge pink flowers.

"Can I stay with you?" Daphne, my dear friend from undergraduate days, pleaded. She waited all afternoon in the porter's lodge to catch me. I literally jumped with joy at seeing her.

"Of course you can stay with me; stay as long as you like," I told her over tea once we were up in my room.

"You may not be so sure once you hear why I'm here." She began crying. After a brief fling with a pub owner, Daphne found out she was pregnant. The abortion had used up most of her paltry savings, and she was trying desperately to collect herself, emotionally as well as financially, before heading back home.

"I'm here for you." I hugged her. I could feel her down-to-the-bones sadness.

"You mean, you'll still talk to me?" she croaked.

"Of course I'll still talk to you. What on earth do you mean?" I looked at her carefully. It was not like Daphne to play coy; it also was not like her to appear so broken. I ached for her, my former study-and-giggle buddy.

"Well, it's been going through the grapevine back home . . ." She hesitated, peering at me through tears.

"Yes? What?" I froze.

"Well, it's been circulating that you're thinking of becoming a Christian. Or perhaps you already are. You always were the most symbolic of all of us, the most proper too." Daphne smiled shyly.

"Great," I grunted. "There's something to be remembered for."

She managed a laugh. "You know what I mean. You're so *endearing*, Caro. I could see *you* becoming a Christian. But *me*?"

"What on earth is that supposed to mean?"

"Nothing." Daphne avoided my eyes. "Just know I'm grateful that you'll have me. I was worried for a minute that . . ." Her words tapered off.

"That I would turn you away and throw a Bible after you on the way out the door?" I finished.

"Precisely," Daphne replied, looking back at me.

"Come on, sister." I put my arm around her exhausted shoulders and led her to my bed. She protested, but I told her I would be out late, so I would sleep on the cushions on the floor when I got back. Until then she was to make herself at home.

After getting Daphne settled in, I went to meet Rachel down at St. Ebbe's Church. She had invited me to visit the women's weekly Bible study with her. As a general rule I was hesitant of Bible studies, but curiosity got the best of me. Plus I liked Rachel a lot, and I had decided to make a conscious effort now to give reliable, likable sources a chance.

Around a welcoming fire I met a beautiful tapestry of women from many different walks of life. Most were believers, though there were a few searching ones like me. After introductions I told them about Daphne, referring to her only as my 'friend,' of course.

"Why didn't you bring her?" Sylvia immediately asked. Earlier Sylvia had shared how she became a Christian after having a baby as a teenager. Her parents kicked her out, but one of her teachers, who happened to be a Christian, took her in. Over the years Sylvia got married and had three other daughters while managing a prominent political career. As she said, "All of them, strong and beautiful and wise. The delight of my heart." Her eldest would be getting married this summer, with her half sisters as bridesmaids. "My rose pillars," Sylvia called them. "Each one."

"Oh, she wouldn't have come," I answered quickly in regard to Daphne, sure of myself.

"You don't know if you don't ask," Sylvia replied.

"Yes," another woman piped up sincerely. "We would have welcomed her."

Sylvia added, "We could have given your friend some community and support. Maybe next time. For now we'd love to pray for her."

"Pray for her? Doesn't that sound condescending?" I cringed.

"Condescension is your genre," Sylvia replied as she passed the snack plate. "Incarnation is His."

⁂

At the intersection I felt him take my other arm as I turned away. Again, gently but firmly. "Caro," he said. *Dear one*, I thought I heard him add.

I swung around, facing him, so angry I could spit. Who did he think he was? Didn't he realize that not only did I not need a man to protect me from any danger, but I did not need a man, *period*.

I pulled away as he let go of my arm. *Jerk*, I thought. *Here it comes. Some sniveling excuse for trying to be a man, some lie about trying to help me, when in fact it's all about power, control, getting into my pants.*

"Whoa, take it easy, I'm just practicing being a gentleman," TDH said, taken aback. Then he paused and added, "You honor me when you allow me to serve you."

"What?" I shook my head to clear my ears.

Unnerved, I stammered, "I don't need to be served." Just what was he up to? I recovered my footing and shot back, "I don't need anything, let alone your machismo and hollow offers of help."

For a moment he looked wounded. *Aha!* I thought. So I added, "Besides, there isn't really any danger present anyway. What are you? Some kind of crazed knight? It's just an ordinary street. It's everyday traffic, for crying out loud."

"'Ordinary' can change in a heartbeat. And if it does, when it does, I would take the blow. But more important than that is that you can rest in the fact that I want to take the blow," he explained.

"Geesh, it's not as if we're married." I rolled my eyes.

"No, we're not, but that's totally irrelevant. I'd be offering the same gesture to my mother or any other woman on the planet." He shrugged. "But!"—he raised his finger in serious good humor—"if I were your husband, I would be absolutely desperate to serve you in this and a thousand other ways."

What to say to that?

I had to admit it didn't seem all that Neanderthal to me. In fact it seemed rather a want-win situation with a big win for Team Woman.

Suddenly, like *The Grinch Who Stole Christmas*, I began to feel my heart grow three times its size. But unlike the Grinch, I did not scoop up Suzy Who or relieve my mutt of its heavy antlers just yet. Rather I threaded my arm through TDH's and allowed him to walk between the symbolic traffic of life and me.

He smiled at me, pulling me closer with friendly firmness, shielding me from the freezing wind as well. He wore an old, woolen army coat that smelled somehow of home—the lake after a summer storm; fields of chamomile and buttercups, dive-bombed by larks; autumn leaves with a trace of musty pine from a fire on a cold winter's night. A coat for all seasons it was.

"Don't push it," I muttered, growing uncomfortable at how comfortably I rested in the crook of his elbow.

SEVENTEEN

SEHNSUCHT

In Xanadu did Kubla Khan
A stately pleasure-dome decree:
Where Alph, the sacred river, ran
Through caverns measureless to man
Down to a sunless sea.[1]

—SAMUEL TAYLOR COLERIDGE

A week of heavy rains ensued after Daphne left. One particularly dreary afternoon, while studying in the Radcliffe Camera, I came across a cartoonlike illustration by the Romantic poet and artist William Blake. A man held a ladder up to the moon, with the caption underneath reading, "I want, I want." One of Blake's talents lay in his ability to appeal through the childish to actually very adult themes. He wrote reams of children's poetry, very much aware of who does the actual reading in the nursery.

I got up and wandered over to the reference section. Flipping through the worn, tissue-paper pages of *The Oxford English Dictionary*, I stopped at the entry for *want*. It reads: "To desire and need. To be desired or deemed necessary. To crave, and to lack." *How can it be all these things at once?*

Then it occurred to me that perhaps another synonym for *want* is *human*. Poverty is a form of want, occurring when your means do not meet your needs. I had grown up with poverty simply being in relation to one's financial status. But now I was beginning to see that there are all types of poverty, most having nothing to do with money.

To be pursued, desired?—when you are the one also pursuing, desiring?

For the writers I was studying, I recalled that another common name for a mole was a "want." This term could also apply to someone who was blind, either by defect or deficiency. Burrowing into our want. Not being able to see the whole for our holes.

I closed the dictionary and, in a digressive mood, wandered again to the collection of Bibles. I opened one to the story of Jacob's ladder in Genesis.

Before leaving for Oxford University last summer, I remembered how I stood at our back screen door, yearning but unable to put the desire into words. I pressed my hands against the mesh until tiny fine crosses stung into my palms. *Sehnsucht.* The German word for "longing," which C. S. Lewis identifies as the inconsolable crux of the human condition; an ache that reminds us of that eternal joy and beauty for which we were made.

What? What is there? Only the hush rising up from the

evening haze settling on the unlistening grass. No crickets. No birdsong. The smell of a storm. In the distance thunder was tearing through still sky like the opening of an envelope.

⌐⌐⌐⌐⌐

The rain continued pounding into the night. He stopped by to borrow some printing paper. "I saw your light on, so I hope you don't mind."

"Here." I passed him the white pages. He turned to go.

I took a breath. "Wait . . ." I stammered, "I owe you an apology. The other day at high tea, when you offered to walk between the traffic and me, you were just trying to help. I shouldn't have made such a fuss. I'm sorry."

"Thanks, and you're welcome. I didn't realize the sidewalk could be such a minefield." He smiled.

"It's just that, well . . ." I struggled to put it all into words, "I'm not used to trusting men . . . I mean, my brother is terrific, of course, and Ben was gentle and sweet, but as a general rule . . ."

"Tell me."

I hesitated.

TDH respected my hesitation. "How can I help?" he asked gently. I shrugged.

"Well, you have certainly been sampling many different areas of the faith. Have you tried praying about what concerns you?" he suggested. I shot him a wary look.

Prayer is weird. There's no way around it. The concept of it seemed bizarre. Talking, possibly out loud, to Someone unseen who might or might not be listening? *Weeeird.*

I did not understand how it worked. I mean, if God knew

everything about us, including what we needed, why bother asking Him for anything?

It also weirded me out when Christians offered to pray for me. Pray for me, as if they knew something I didn't. As if they (unwittingly or not) acknowledged, by their very request, my want. Anyway, I did not want anyone to know my want. If they knew my *want*, they might not want to know *me*. Hey, if I fully acknowledged my want, *I* would not even want to know me.

"I'm never good enough." I inhaled. "I'm never enough!" It bellowed out from me, without warning. "I can't fix it all! And I won't be forced to do it alone. To have some man leave me to deal with it all."

"Whoa, whoa, whoa! What does all this have to do with walking between you and the traffic?" TDH looked bewildered.

"Everything, don't you see?" I tried to keep from yelling, aglow with indignation and anger. "Of course you don't see, because you're such a . . . a *man*. How can you ever see how condescending men are to women? How horribly they treat us? How they use us and then discard us, get us to love them, and then pull the rug out from under us? Denying us promotions, child support, the dignity of their devotion. Wives, daughters, girlfriends . . . it doesn't matter. It's all the same, a power trip for them. For *you*."

I began to pound against his chest. This had never happened with Ben. With him things remained quiet, easygoing. He did not seem to rattle my armor, so everything stayed neatly in check.

"Yes, get a woman to really trust you, and just when she reaches for the hand holding her soul, you do the old switcheroo and open it to reveal an empty palm. You love us and leave us. You love us and leave us with children. You crush us with your expectations of our bodies, of our abilities. You take advantage of our desire to be loved or at least affirmed by you. You have us sit on your laps, stroke our hair, only to leave us when we need you most." I sobbed, "You leave us tired. Oh, so tired. And alone . . ."

TDH stood there, motionless, which only infuriated me further.

"And you want me to believe in this God of yours? This *male* God? This *man* Jesus? This unknowable, invisible, indefinable"— I spat out the last word—"*Father*?"

TDH said nothing as my hands continued to flail.

"You delight in confusing us, in misleading us. And then you get angry when we don't play the game anymore, when we choose independence instead. Or escape. Or denial . . ." I trailed off.

I thought of . . . Daphne, abandoned, legs spread-eagle as the life was literally sucked out of her; my mother, desperate in her steaming bath, razor suspended above her wrists at the sound of my sister's infant cry; the fear my paternal grandmother must have felt, pregnant and penniless, trying to dodge the blows of an angry drunk; all those generations of women, burdened and denied. Even rock wears down under years of relentless water.

"And it all starts with promises only to be broken, impossible demands, and no, absence does not make the heart grow fonder . . ." I was whispering now. TDH caught my hands and held them tight. I started to resist, but he stood firm. I bowed my head. "Do you know that Ben is already sleeping with someone?" I moaned. "Only weeks after declaring undying love for me? I let him go, but still . . ." I fought the urge to rest against TDH.

"Caro, Caro, you are upset," he said without a shred of the condescension I was straining to hear and, in turn, accuse him. "And in many ways, rightfully so," he relented warmly.

He waited until my breath regulated a little; then he squeezed my hands tighter.

"But I won't let you take it out on me." His voice rose up steady and genuine in a way I could not put my finger on but which struck at the core of my being.

I tried freeing my hands, to recoil from the unexpected challenge, but he continued to hold them firmly.

He looked right into my eyes, his own eyes alight with kindness but with a flint of something set. "I can see that going home at Christmas was hard; something in you seems especially conflicted since then."

I looked away.

He continued, "But Caro, you can't just carve up all men based only on what you've witnessed. Not all men are like the ones you describe. Unfortunately, many are. But many are not."

A statue of two figures clasping hands—wrestling or in prayer?

I noticed that although his face had grown very gentle, his jaws were tight. "Caro, with all due respect, surely you don't believe all that?" he half-stated, half-asked.

I said nothing.

So TDH kept going, "That is not my father. Or my grandfather. Or my brothers. Or any of the men I respect and know as close friends. That's not me either. Nobody is perfect, but I know lots of men who strive very hard to be the real thing, who know God intimately and answer to something far greater than themselves. They are men who are humble, who respect women, who devote themselves in marriages and families. They are men whose genuine, disciplined lives model God's goodness in a myriad of ways. These men, they exist. Trust me—I know that is a particularly difficult premise for you—but please, trust me," he pleaded.

Reeling inside, outside I stood perfectly still.

"As Christ showed us, one righteous man has the power to change the world," TDH spoke into my stillness. "He did. Forever. For men, and for women. For all of us. Not only to be our food and our drink, but also our rest." He stopped and gave me such a deep look of compassion that for a moment I thought my heart would break from its beauty.

He squeezed my hands now passionately, holding them up to his heart. I closed my eyes and tried to envision such rest. I tried even harder to imagine what it would be like to have *the rest*.

"Remember the film *Rocky*?" he suddenly asked.

What on earth . . . ? I thought. My eyes shot open.

"The one about the lovable but at first lowlife boxer who gets a shot at the world heavyweight title?"

"Yes, yes, of course I know *Rocky*." I cut him off, impatient that he could insert pop culture at a moment like this. Then again, he was American.

"Do you remember the scene between him and Mickey, his manager? When Mickey asked him, 'You wanna know?' and Rocky replied, 'I wanna know!'"

"Know what?" I said with some disbelief at where this could possibly be going.

Unfazed, TDH went on, "And Mickey said, 'Because you had the talent to become a good fighter, and instead of that you became a leg breaker for some cheap, second-rate loan shark.' And Rocky replied, 'It's a living.' But Mickey said, 'It's a waste of life!'"

He continued to hold my hands firmly in his. "Christian

214 SURPRISED BY OXFORD

men—real, thoughtful, active Christian men—fight for something larger than ourselves, Caro. We fight for real life, the life God calls us to."

I looked at him, eyes wide, then narrowing.

"We are not perfect. God only knows how imperfect we are," he rushed on before I could fury in. "But we try. God also knows how hard we try. In good faith we try, and so, by grace go we. Anyone will tell you that trying to wear a halo too tightly will give you a headache."

I nodded only too strongly in agreement. TDH surveyed the response as ground safe enough to continue.

"Caro, as your heart heals and you learn to fully lean into the reality that God cherishes you, I think you will see that other men who have a personal relationship with God are capable of cherishing you too. And then you'll enjoy mutual cherishment with God, and perhaps someday, with one very special man."

He let my hands go. I felt all the air go out of my body as I lowered them.

Now it was my turn to just stand there, blasted and bewildered.

This anger is tiring, I thought. All I wanted to do was crawl into bed and sleep for years.

"Look, I care about you, Caro," TDH addressed me calmly, "but I won't be your whipping post for men gone wrong. You are understandably angry, and my heart goes out to you, but your view of men, or at the very least, committed Christian men, is horribly skewed. You will rob yourself of great joy and rest if you persist with the current version. Bless you, but you have some work to do with God on this one."

"Good night," I said starkly. He would never understand.

TDH stood there, palms up and open.

"Leave," I managed to get out. "I want you to leave."

He walked past my desk and opened my Bible to somewhere; I didn't care. He placed my empty teacup on the page to weigh it open. Then he was gone. The door clicked softly behind him.

Silence.

Just my rage and I. Rather, now just the weight of all that rage, the weariness of all that distrust, the indignity of all that injustice, the haplessness of all that waste, and I remained. Immense sadness swept over me and carried me onto my bed. Spent, I curled up and wept.

***

I had a dream, which was not at all a dream.

He walked back through the door.

"In the cross, there is integrity," he said, looking right at me.

I went to the Bible open on my desk, careful to remove the teacup without disturbing the page. But the cup had left a wet ring around a passage, I noticed, from Ephesians:

Stand firm then, with the belt of truth buckled around your waist, with the breastplate of righteousness in place, and with your feet fitted with the readiness that comes from the gospel of peace. In addition to all this, take up the shield of faith, with which you can extinguish all the flaming arrows of the evil one. Take the helmet of salvation and the sword of the Spirit, which is the word of God. And pray in the Spirit on all occasions with all kinds of prayers and requests. (6:14–18)

I traced the ring with my finger, circling the words over and over. Then I turned back to my bed, climbing under the white down comforter my mom had sent me—another luxurious gift at her sacrifice, another extension of her care. Even across an ocean I could feel wrapped in her presence. The parallelisms of time and compassion bridged the rift between us.

Drifting . . . "He will cover you with his feathers, and under his wings you will find refuge; his faithfulness will be your shield and rampart" (Ps. 91:4).

Drifting . . . *Is it possible the best armor is both gentle and firm?*

Drifting . . . and then I slept.

Eighteen

Butterflies in the Bookcase

I looked to heaven, and tried to pray;
But or ever a prayer had gusht,
A wicked whisper came, and made
My heart as dry as dust.[1]

—Samuel Taylor Coleridge

I slept for what felt like a blink of the eye, but the numbers coming into focus on my alarm clock informed me it was late the following morning. Panicked at first, I then vaguely recalled that it should be Sunday. Vacant, I got up and automatically went to my bookshelf, pulling books out as old friends, trying to find the right one to fill me.

I passed over the Bible.

Then I saw it. Or I should say *them*. Three small butterflies

217

rested at the back of my bookshelf, hidden behind my *Webster's New World Dictionary*. Their wings spread out like fragile Oriental fans. Painted eyes looked back at me, unblinking.

Startled at my discovery, I removed the books around them carefully so I could get a better look. They seemed far too weak to put up a fight. God knows how long they had been trapped in that bookshelf. Gently I tried coaxing one onto my finger. It climbed on feebly, opening and closing its tissue-paper wings ever so slowly in effortful greeting. Starved and parched, its body an imperceptible weight on my finger, but still breathtakingly beautiful near death. Perhaps even more so.

It seemed to me that not every answer can be found in a book. Not even in the Bible. What to do when words themselves seem hollow? When Scripture seems irrelevant? When prayer seems irreverent? When I feel . . . nothing?

Maybe because I felt nothing, I eventually opened my Bible to the story of Lazarus in the Gospel of John. Lazarus, a dear friend of Jesus, fell gravely ill. His sisters sent word to Jesus; as a result, Jesus traveled to Bethany, back to the same region where the Jews had tried to stone Him only a short while before. Upon His arrival Jesus found that Lazarus had already been dead in the tomb for four days. Martha rushed to meet Him, telling Jesus that her brother would not have died if Jesus had been there in time.

Jesus replied, "I am the resurrection and the life. He who believes in me will live, even though he dies; and whoever lives and believes in me will never die. Do you believe this?" (11:25–26).

Martha answered yes. Then Mary came out of the house and fell at His feet, weeping. Jesus asked to see the tomb and wept, too, joining in their suffering. Then Jesus did something miraculous, not for Himself, but for the benefit of others so that they might believe in God. He raised a man from the dead. Lazarus emerged from the tomb, still wrapped with strips of linen. Jesus then turned to the surrounding gawkers (which surely we all are), saying, "Take off the grave clothes and let him go" (v. 44). I imagine the onlookers agape at *agape*.

When I first read it, I found myself reasoning that Lazarus was not really dead. There must have been some sleight of hand involved there in terms of medical logistics or bodily misunderstanding, like a potion mishap straight out of *Romeo and Juliet* or a rerun of *Gilligan's Island*. But four days is a long time, even for someone initially mistaken for dead but who is alive, to be shut up in an airless tomb. Even the Bible tells us that Lazarus had started to stink. Then I jumped in with the skeptics and asked why Jesus did not prevent the death in the first place. But then I saw that even Jesus pointed out how that would nullify any humanly graspable illustration of the purpose of the story, like blaming a book for having a plot, or shouting at the heroine in a horror movie not to open that door. Like any of us staving off the inevitability of death, I continued to rationally explain away the story from every possible angle, and yet . . .

And *yet* . . . something kept fluttering beneath its surface, anchored by the undeniable authority of the final line: "Take off the grave clothes and let him go." There was no other way to put it than to say that I detected something bigger happening here: A love that turns back to a place of danger to retrieve its beloved. A love that illustrates itself in acts and words and trust. A love at work in the seen and the unseen. A love that weeps over us, releases us, raises us, removes our grave clothes, and tells us we are free to go.

Do you believe this?

An upstart love. A radical love. An uncontainable, indefinable, incomprehensible love. A love that invites and defies and eternally transforms.

For the ancient Greeks, the same word *psyche* stood for both "soul" and "butterfly."

Dare I believe this?

The question hangs in the air like the scent of myrrh in a tomb.

In the opening and closing of butterfly wings, I heard a still small voice: *"What is your Jacob's ladder?"* I thought of Sylvia's words: *Not you, condescending*, but angels, ascending and descending.

To acknowledge that this very ordinary place at this very ordinary moment is holy? That it is holy because God is there, even if you did not know it at first? At the rock by your feet; at the top of the steps? Perhaps such knowledge has to be dreamed to be believed. Or as U2 later sings, "believed to be seen."

Where does your want lead you?

Maybe when it came to prayer, there wasn't some minimum or quota; some right or wrong way; some preferred pose, volume, tone, words, opportune moment, or ideal setting. Maybe I did not even have to say anything profound. Maybe I did not even have to say anything at all. And neither did God. You cannot have intimacy without relationship, it occurred to me, or without shared silence.

Maybe there *was* something to this prayer thing. Articulating my needs whenever I needed to (and especially whenever I did not think I needed to)? Burrowing into my want and coming through it transformed? After all, rather than doing something

for God, maybe prayer did that something for *me*, and by extension for all of us, lifting me out of my need as I entered the
compassion of lifting others. A ladder extended from, extended
to, our want of Him.

"Butterflies are like prayers, child," she said. "Just let what is caught
go." My grandmother and I loved watching butterflies together,
walking amid clouds of them in the summer, trying to get them
to land on our fingers. Such vibrant, winged friends of my childhood—so unlike the weary ones among these books. "Prayers
offered in the state of dryness are those which please Him best,"
wrote C. S. Lewis.[2]

With great care I took each butterfly from the bookcase and
let it go out the back staircase casement, blowing it gently from
my finger over the unbloomed gardens below. With wings unused
to freedom, I feared they would fall. But then, shaking the dust
of the books from the dust of their wings, they began to flutter,
suddenly alive with motion. Lifted and lowered on the breeze.

Significant specks rose from near death to heaven and then
well beyond my sight.

NINETEEN

PROFESSOR VON X

Take away paradox from the thinker and you have a professor.

—Søren Kierkegaard

A rustling, coughing crowd of students filled the lecture theater in the St. Cross Building to capacity. You could cut the atmosphere of anticipation with a knife. A bright beam of light shone on the podium only, leaving the rest of the room in darkness and heightening the effect of a theatrical production. One of the greatest postmodernist critics of our time would be appearing shortly. He owned controversial status in relation to two of his main areas of interest: the relativity of truth, and women.

I did not see how he was that different from most men.

When he did finally appear, I felt as if I were a spectator at the equivalent of an academic Super Bowl. The crowd went wild;

it took Dr. Condorston several bows and nods of the head before it was quiet enough for him to begin. I half expected him to tap his conductor's wand on the podium, lift his hands, and begin Beethoven's Fifth. But he didn't; in fact, far from it.

"Today I wish to address the nature of truth. Or rather," he clarified after a dramatic pause, which caused the undergraduate girls seated at the front to swoon, "the *lack* of a nature to truth." After sipping his water he leaned heavily against the podium as though burdened by the weight of needing to enlighten the masses. "Truth," he explained, "as anyone must come to believe in present times, can only be relative in nature. And relative implies, then, no nature at all. If truth exists in meaning, and meaning is a system of constant deferral, as I have clearly established in my extensive publications, then we, as human beings, exist in a constant state of deferral, unable to attain true meaning."

Several students seated ahead of me leaned in, pencils scribbling furiously.

On my way to the lecture, I practiced reciting from Milton's *Paradise Lost* as I strode Longwall Street (British pragmatism embedded even in their infrastructure, given that the old road literally ran the length of a long wall). For our assignment next week, among other expectations, Dr. Nuttham required that we memorize several lines from the epic poem.

"What?" we all gasped in unison.

"Consider how easy you have it," he replied. "Many of the Romantics knew much of Milton by heart—how can you study these writers if you do not know what was in their hearts as they themselves wrote?" Then he added, thoughtfully, "While you are at it, I also suggest that you memorize the first few chapters of Genesis. So you know what was in Milton's heart too."

"Why memorize it? Why not just read it carefully?" argued Susan, our Yale graduate.

"Because what you memorize by heart, you take to heart," replied Dr. Nuttham simply. "It shouldn't be called by 'rote' but by 'root,' for you get at the source of the text, its foundation. Once you really absorb the words, the words become your own. Then, and only then, can you mull them over on your tongue, appreciating them as you would good wine, enjoying them as the company of a good friend. Besides," he added, "we always value something for which we've had to labor."

"Postmodernism posits that meaning can never be deciphered, in and of itself," the honorable speaker launched in. "Rather, meaning exists in a system of signs—signs that constantly signify other signs, but which are incapable of taking us to the source of the sign itself."

Isn't this just Platonic theory revisited? I thought, looking around at the figures about me, obscured in the dim lecture theatre. *Or wait, maybe even older. Perhaps I'd call it Revelation*, I mused. *Or "seeing through a glass darkly"*?

Dr. Condorston grew more excited. "And the self-consciousness of this! What a modern phenomenon!"

Man, I thought, *if the ancients realized there lay nothing new under the sun, where does that leave us?*

"Such an assessment of truth owns serious repercussions for the church," Dr. Condorston now himself pontificated, "for where does this put something like the Bible? A text that asserts itself to be truth, to be the 'revealed' Word of God." He pulled himself up further, "To even, dare I say, call itself 'holy'?" Dr. Condorston could barely disguise his disdain.

Shrugging, he allowed himself to wallow in it, at least a little. "Bertrand Russell claimed, 'So far as I can remember, there is not one word in the Gospels in praise of intelligence.'"

The Gospels don't spell out everything, I counterargued in my head. *Rather, they are enacted in deeds, principles, or parables. In symbols or syllogisms. Any student of literature knows that metaphor is far more precise than the literal, although there were plenty of both in Scripture. Surely a literary theorist could see it much more clearly than the rest of us.*

For example I thought of how objectively intelligent, even shrewd, Jesus' responses were when He was put on the spot. I know I could never think like that—how many could? Especially in the worst viva voce (or Oxford oral examination) imaginable? As when the Sadducees questioned Him about marriage and tried to trick Him by asking Him which husband the wife with seven husbands will have in heaven. Jesus beat them at their own game, trapped them in their own net, by answering, "You are in error because you do not know the Scriptures or the power of God" (Matt. 22:29).

That seemed pretty smart to me.

Maybe Russell got caught in the eternal deferral of meaning?

"What is truth?" Pilate asked Jesus before accepting his condemnation from a timeless crowd. It occurred to me that Pilate, too, deferred the answer.

Now I really needed to turn off the internal chatter, I scolded myself. The scary thing, however, was my temptation to volley back from the Christian side of the net. Why was that happening? Was I not still wavering? Nestled in the luxury of noncommittal plush?

I decided to take a breath and force myself to focus on something more superficial. This will cause a break in my uncontrollable impulse to see things through that annoyingly persistent Christ lens. Opening my notebook, I began drawing a caricature of Dr. Condorston. I etched out a stick figure, and then studied my model to see how best to clothe him. He appeared gentlefolkly disheveled, as most academics do. Or I should say, as most male academics do. I have never been certain if this was a carefully cultivated guise or not: the tweed jacket with the patched elbows, button-down shirt, corduroy pants, loafers, weathered leather satchel—everything tasteful, in hues of brown and grey. Appropriately worn, even a little threadbare, they are a sign to the world that academics, no matter how notable the discovery or the contribution, does not pay, will never pay, as athletics does. It is as if somehow dousing intellectual pursuits in beige renders them dignifiedly approachable.

So I colored in his clothing I thought very appropriately with my pencil. Then I gave him a dollop of Heathcliffean hair.

Thinking of Virginia Woolf seated in the British Library among the absence of women, present and historically, I looked down with some admiration at my version of her little Professor Von X likeness as Dr. Condorston gusted on. I added a stroke here, a detail there.

"So words as we use them can never convey the idea itself. We are doomed to miscommunication, caught forever in a vortex of inaccessible meaning receding forever from our grasp."

I thought of the Jewish term for God: *Yahweh*. The name so holy that it was a blasphemy to even speak it, so meaningful it could not be expressed in words. Milton identifies the main reason angels have wings as not so much because of their intermediary status between earth and air, or brute and divine, or even their ability to fly, but to shield their eyes from the glory of God, for its brightness is blinding. As God tells Moses, it is death to look on His face. I had an orthodox Jewish friend who typed her word for God as a blank in her papers. I thought that fascinating and very unhypocritical of her.

"While this plurality lends us multiple truths, in and of themselves important and worthy . . ." Dr. Condorston's voice echoed throughout the amphitheatre.

Isn't that just Aristotle now? Okay—I mentally slapped myself—*You've got to stop it. Just stop it and pay attention. This is one of our culture's leading critics, so he must be good.*

"We are limited by our own self-referentiality." Dr. Condorston set down his water glass with his last word. Both struck the attentive atmosphere like an anvil.

"Duh," I said . . . out loud. Louder than I anticipated. The word hung suspended, palpable, like words always do when spoken into an unexpected silence. But I couldn't help it. We agreed there.

Dr. Condorston stopped his lecture. He stepped out from behind the podium, peering into the darkness.

"Who said that?" he asked, to my mortification. I felt myself sinking down in my seat.

"Who said that?" he repeated, growing more irritated. In spite of my fear and horror, however, I tried desperately to keep from sniggering, which is a bad habitual response of mine to grotesque moments, or moments which combined the incongruent experience, the bizarre. It was not uncommon, for instance, for me to get a fit of the giggles during a moment of silence. Entirely inappropriate, I know, but often that just made me want to laugh harder. And then if I threw a glance at my sister into the mix, it was game over.

But I had to admit the thought of an otherwise self-possessed specialist in discernment (isn't that another name for a theorist?) squinting angrily over his glasses into a sea of darkened faces in a moment of silence while he tried to make out the source of some great "duh" did strike me as a little funny.

A few ingratiating undergraduates, starstruck by our speaker, looked toward me, betraying my hiding spot in the crowd. Why isn't there a good fire drill when you need one? Sure, the alarm always goes off just as you have emerged naked from the typhoon-shower in your college room, but what about when you are far more metaphorically naked and in need?

Dr. Condorston stepped to the edge of the stage, leaning over almost to the point I thought he would topple right off. But he hung there, like a raptor on a treetop, and slid his glasses down his nose. Giving me a look that could wither Eden, he pointed at me with a cue card and said sternly, "You, in the red cardigan . . ." I tried slumping lower in the chair, regretting my bright choice of wardrobe color immensely. "Yes, you." His voice stuck me in place.

I smiled weakly. "Yes?" I managed to squeak.

"Ah, that eccentric creature, a girl student. Stand up and introduce yourself." He raised his voice at the sound of my lowered one. *Vampire*, I thought as I gave my name.

"Miss Drake. Hmmmm. Aren't you one of Dr. Nuttham's protégés?" He seemed to be flipping through a Rolodex in his head.

I nodded. Oxford could be a small world; this had its good and its bad tendencies.

"I should have known," he sniffed. Somehow I couldn't imagine a Miltonist and a postmodernist having tea together. Maybe some pints, however, but only if they got very, very drunk.

"Producing a thesis on the influence of the metaphysical poets on the Romantics, aren't you?" he continued.

I nodded again.

"I should have known that too," he said drily, evoking a few chuckles from the audience.

I started to defend myself, but my voice evaded me. Instead, I stood there, as crimson as my Topshop cardigan. Linnea reached over and touched my leg in moral support. When I glanced at her, she looked terrified.

"Miss Drake"—I had never realized just how spondaic my maiden name sounded before—"have you ever heard of the Moro reflex?" Dr. Condorston asked, looking smugly out over the crowd in a play of stump-the-student (as students, we used to play it in reverse whenever we had a substitute teacher).

Yes, in fact, I had. We learned about it in high school biology. Moreover about the Moro, I nannied often for extra pocket money, and I loved children, so I was aware of the reflex that caused babies to arch back and flail their arms in preparation of impact, if they fear they are going to fall.

"No," I managed to croak, however. I thought it best to play dumb. Sometimes this is the safest vantage point according to Wendy, my incredibly beautiful, blonde, *and* smart sister-in-law.

"No, Dr. Condorston, I don't," I said with increasing volume (thinking, too, of Wendy's other adage, "Never let your roots show," pertinent in its, again, precise metaphorical wisdom). I took a breath. "I would be delighted to know the connection to your lecture."

Taken aback, Dr. Condorston leaned back. Then he leaned forward again as when people are tempted to shout at the blind; it seemed as though by lunging at me, even from a distance, he could make his words more imposing.

He began to give a minilecture on the Moro reflex. Often, I wonder if "lecture" is the professor's verbal genre in real life as well as the classroom. "The Moro reflex, named for its discoverer, the Austrian pediatrician Ernst Moro, is also known as the startle reflex. The most obvious of infantile reflexes, it normally remains present until approximately half a year in age. The absence of this reflex indicates a profound disorder of the motor system. Persistence of this response, however, is noted only in infants with severe neurological defects."

I cocked my head and widened my eyes, as Wendy had shown me. I decided not to push it and twirl a highlighted strand. Somehow I suspected the professor to be the Lolita type, but I was too old for such games. The cock-and-widen maneuver alone, however, must have worked, because Dr. Condorston appeared flattered by the attention. Somewhat disarmed but with even greater command of the stage, he continued, "This reflex is a response to an unexpected loud noise or when the infant feels as if it is falling."

Again, more frenzied scribbling from the students in front of me.

I cocked my head to the other side. *Gee, this is hard work*, I thought. *My eyes can't get any wider.* I felt like the tortured character from *A Clockwork Orange*.

"The response is concise and predictable. In reaction to this imposed 'falling,' the infant spreads out his arms, then closes them, and then begins crying." Dr. Condorston paused, and then added thoughtfully, "It is believed to be the only unlearned fear in human newborns."

That gave me pause too. The fear of falling is our most primal reaction? The startle at being fallen? So fresh from birth, so innate in our physical being, that the lack of this impulse implies some sort of structural deficiency? And yet, how we become accustomed to this fallenness after being steeped in the world even for a short while. How this newborn startle reflex recedes as it gets replaced with postlapsarian developmental "normalcy."

Dr. Condorston bore a hole through me with his eyes. I managed to flutter back my dry ones.

"Clearly," Dr. Condorston stammered, and then regained his arrogant composure, "clearly this indicates humanity's Darwinian roots in the need to cling to something tangible, like a branch or its mother, in order for a baby to survive."

Or the truth? I thought. *As humans, don't we need to cling to the truth as we would to a parent or to a tree? To keep from falling? Or because we are fallen?*

"All of this points to how relative truth is . . . the baby is wired to respond to a perceived threat, not even always a real one. At the biological level of our very being, we cannot perceive what is true, we can never reach for some perfect truth, and so we are at the mercy of a combination of instincts, drives, emotions, reflexes . . . a flailing infant in the deterministic and yet deferred universe of life!" Swept up by his ingenious example, Dr. Condorston ranted like an overdramatic Shakespearean actor now, quite literally with his perfect Queen's English accent.

Suddenly Dr. Inchbald's conviction from Christmas high table rang—could it be—*true*? Fatally deterministic, yes, if life centered only on you.

Dr. Condorston did not seem interested in hearing a response from me, so I did not offer one. "Let's take another example from the 'scientific' world, shall we, Miss Drake? After all, we are not limited to the discourse of humanities," he stated authoritatively.

Is there any other discourse ultimately? I inwardly arched my brows, thinking again of Philip Sidney.

Dr. Condorston paced to and fro on the stage like a caged sphinx, rubbing his chin while collecting his thoughts. I took this as a cue to sit down, but he reprimanded me, commanding that I remain standing. All I required was a dunce's cap. I felt like a destitute schoolboy, palms outstretched and waiting to be whacked by the teacher's ruler in a Dickens novel.

"You look like you have something to say." Dr. Condorston studied me carefully.

Everything!

Suddenly Dr. Sterling's face, awash in Christmas candlelight, came into view. Followed by Dr. Inchbald's, then Dr. Deveaux's, then Milton's (imagined), then countless other faces, then countless other things . . . all I had read and studied and observed and queried . . . it all came rolling together in one big cosmic ball. One that seemed far too big to volley back to Dr. Condorston. Too hard to put in words! Argh! The deferment . . .

No, I corrected myself. *Inexpressibility differs from deferment.*

I thought of a quotation I saw on TDH's desk once amid the scatterings of his pages on the church fathers. It was from John of Damascus: "God is infinite and incomprehensible, and all that is comprehensible about Him is His infinity and incomprehensibility."

Now my eyes grew wider of their own accord.

"So, Miss Drake." Dr. Condorston turned his full attention back on me and asked outright, "What say you besides 'duh'?"

This is not a good time to giggle, I reminded myself. Dr. Condorston may be on my examination board for my Romantics' antecedents and influences topic papers. *Hmmmm.*

"What say I to what, exactly?" I asked politely, partly to buy time, partly because I really did not know what he was getting at.

The entire row of undergraduates between us crouched down as though caught in a firing range.

"What say you to the nature of truth?" he clarified impatiently.

We stood there looking at each other, a podium with the Oxford crest between us.

"Let me put it another way, Miss Drake," he said, with the air of a weary mother frustrated with her child. He paused, searching for words like bullets to load a gun. "Do you believe in absolute truth?" he finally leveled at me.

Yeats's lines flashed before my eyes: "And what rough beast, its hour come round at last, / Slouches towards Bethlehem to be born?" Dr. Nuttham was right; poetry does befriend you if you take it to heart.

Dr. Condorston coughed. "Miss Drake?" he prompted.

The room was so still you really could have heard a pin drop, as the saying goes. Instead, I heard the snap of the point breaking off a nearby student's pencil.

I took a deep breath. "Absolutely!" I exclaimed, my voice, yet again, resounding louder than anticipated in the well of silence.

For a moment Dr. Condorston looked startled. So startled he teetered on the brink of his perch. I half-expected him to flail his arms and cry out. Instead he retreated back to center stage. I could not tell if it had been the volume or word or the (unexpected) enthusiasm with which it was spoken. Sometimes tone speaks more than the word itself, I have found. Then I wondered, *What do theorists have to say about deferred tone?*

"Miss Drake," he finally said, "surely you must realize how— to put it colloquially, or at the very least, politely—"

I waited, partly inflated by my own arrogant academic adrenaline of the internal battle, partly intrigued by something else stirring within me.

"Just how crazy such a position is?" He emphasized his words mercilessly. A few sniggers rose from the audience.

Condemned so publicly, I shuffled a bit uncomfortably. Sure, some of it had been love of a good jousting, even if unspoken on my end. I had to admit that the academic pride part of me stung. But I was surprised to find that the rest of me did not hurt at all; in fact, quite the opposite. And then—unexpectedly, too— that strange but increasingly familiar feeling swept up, in spite of the anger, embarrassment, dissatisfaction. Insisting its presence among them. Poking its head through the muddied frost like a persistently purple spring flower.

I suddenly felt moved by a wave of compassion for the man who seemed so small, having stepped away from the massive teak podium. With my cheeks burning, I was so set to despise him.

Oh, dear, how messy!

"I am giving you a rare opportunity, Miss Drake," Dr.

Condorston spoke, sweeping his hand as though to underscore his act of conversational generosity. "I am giving you the chance to rethink your answer."

I paused. It felt good to unwiden my eyes. I simply looked at him. *Is this my Moro reflex?* I asked myself. *Am I arguing against him because that's my knee-jerk response with condescending men? Am I arguing against him for the thrill of the game? Or is my fear at falling due to something akin to, and yet far more than, a survival instinct?*

I cleared my throat. "I don't want to be confined or defined by your ambiguities," I said loud enough to be heard but quiet enough to show I was at my most serious. Like my mother. I took a deep breath. "Absolute truth remains my final answer."

Resembling a game show host at the end of some amusement that actually seemed to cost him dearly, Dr. Condorston waved me off with a fistful of his cue cards. He motioned for me to sit; then he took up his glass and chugged down the remainder of his water before retreating to finish his lecture from the authority of his podium.

I drew the empty glass in his hand into my picture, but I did not enjoy it as much as I expected to.

TWENTY

THROWING THE BABY OUT
WITH THE BAPTISM WATER

A rush of tourists, clucking contentedly,
fluttered after him as he scattered
the grain of the Word. It was they who had passed
the ruined temple outside, whose eyes
wept pus, whose back was higher
than his head, whose lopsided mouth
said Grazie in a voice as sweet
as a child's when she speaks to her mother
or a bird's when it spoke
to St Francis.[1]

—Norman McCaig

"You owe him an apology," Hannah announced in her distinct unapologetic way. We were standing in the porter's lodge. I went to check my pigeonhole, certain of finding something there from TDH. We left each other friendly notes on a regular basis. I riffled through my mail, trying to seem nonchalant but deeply disappointed at the absence of his familiar handwriting.

"Yeah, whatever." I brushed Hannah off. "He can come to me. I'm not catering to him. I didn't say anything that he didn't need to hear."

Hannah held her eyes on me. I ignored her loud stare and changed the subject.

"What makes you so eager to attend a C. S. Lewis Society meeting?" I smirked. "I thought you weren't into old white guys, or *dead* white guys, for that matter."

"I don't know," Hannah said shyly. "I suppose I really enjoyed his books as a child, and I'm intrigued at what else he had to say. I didn't realize what breadth he covered as an author."

"He's pretty outdated, isn't he?" I quipped, thinking of Dr. Lynbury's *humph* when I mentioned that I was planning on referring to Lewis's *The Four Loves* in my essay on Shelley.

Hannah shrugged, reciting in response, aptly, Lewis's friend J. R. R. Tolkien: "The old that is strong does not wither, / Deep roots are not reached by the frost."[2]

"Touché," I conceded. Conversations with any student of Dr. Nuttham's were becoming increasingly plagiarized.

"Didn't you enjoy Sheldon Vanauken's book, *A Severe Mercy*?" Hannah asked.

I nodded. TDH had given his copy to me, and then I had passed it on to Hannah. A favorite former teacher of mine claimed that books become alive not only when read, but when shared. Indeed Vanauken's was a book to be shared.

"It is a powerful book," I remarked. The moving story of a couple studying at Oxford with the likes of the Inklings, a famous literary group in Oxford in the 1930s and '40s, including Lewis and Tolkien, it tells a true story of love, loss, and faith.

"It is a *beautiful* book," Hannah corrected me. "Well, the speaker tonight hails from the book's inner circle. I think it will be a fascinating talk. The primary text for consideration is *The Screwtape Letters*. I loved those!"

"You would." I smirked again. Lewis wrote *The Screwtape Letters* as a parody of devils trying to thwart God's good will. It is a clever little collection in the epistolary style, written in the tradition of something like Jonathan Swift's "A Modest Proposal." In Swift's essay a "sophisticated" speaker argues for an absolutely ridiculous cause: the devouring of Irish children in order to manage the "surplus" population. In Lewis's case a senior demon named Screwtape craftily advises his nephew, a young demon named Wormwood, on how to turn his "Patient," an ordinary man living in wartime England, toward "Our Father Below" (or the devil) and away from "the Enemy" (or the Christian God). Wildly witty and yet also a serious depiction of our flawed humanity so in need of God's grace, it paints a poignant picture of spiritual warfare. It is the kind of book that should have a mirror on the cover.

"I was surprised at how funny the work was," I admitted. "I expected Lewis to be all gravitas and no giggling."

"He *is* surprisingly funny," I heard a voice say behind me, "and self-deprecating, and amusing, and shrewd," the voice continued to say, adding, "for a dead white guy."

I turned around to see the provost of the college, Dr. Nicholby, standing behind me. I turned red. It was obvious he had overheard our conversation. And, as luck would have it, he was an elderly white male.

Dr. Nicholby grinned at my color change. "Have a good

time tonight, girls," he added, chuckling his way out of the lodge.

I stood there, mortified.

"Pick you up here?" Hannah called out along with her trade-mark belly laugh as she left for her tutorial.

The college bell clanged seven, marking the second seating for dinner in the hall. The first seating happened an hour earlier, a casual affair suitable for starving undergraduates who were much more likely to want to run in, eat, and run out to the pub. The second seating attracted more graduate students. Dining by candlelight while wearing your academic dress, the formal second meal produced a relaxed atmosphere more conducive to good conversation. A student Bible clerk always opened the meal with grace, and then the provost would recite a short Latin prayer after the meal. I was sorry to miss college dinner but excited to participate in a little bit of Oxford history: whether I was a Christian or not, whether I was a lover of old, dead, white guys or not, it seemed a shame to visit Oxford and never once attend a C. S. Lewis Society meeting, followed by a pint at the famous Eagle and Child (otherwise known among locals as the Bird and Babe), the pub frequented by Lewis and his circle.

I poked my head in the lodge, but Hannah was not there yet, so I wandered over and checked my pigeonhole. It was about the seventeenth time I had checked it today. Still nothing from TDH. No olive branch of a note, no peace offering of a loaned book, not even an invitation to a talk or a pub gathering. Miffed, I almost overlooked the simple white envelope with the college crest in the top left corner, addressed in elegant handwriting to "Miss Drake."

Curious, I tore it open in haste. A clipping slipped out, which appeared to be a photocopy from a book. Immediately I recognized the excerpt from Lewis's introduction to *The Screwtape Letters*:

> I like bats much better than bureaucrats. I live in the Managerial Age, in a world of "Admin." The greatest evil is not now done in those sordid "dens of crime" that Dickens loved to paint. It is not done even in concentration camps and labour camps. In those we see its final result. But it is conceived and ordered (moved, seconded, carried, and minuted) in clean, carpeted, warmed, and well-lighted offices, by quiet men with white collars and cut fingernails and smooth-shaven cheeks who do not need to raise their voices. Hence, naturally enough, my symbol for hell is something like the bureaucracy of a police state or the offices of a thoroughly nasty business concern.[3]

A small, separate piece of paper that had been tucked behind the larger page fluttered to the ground. I picked it up and saw that it was written in the same elegant hand as the formal address of my name on the envelope. It read,

> Not bad insight for a dead white guy, wouldn't you say? Remember these words when you are tenured one day.
>
> The older I get and the more world-weary I become, the more pained, frustrated, and saddened I grow at people insisting on throwing the baby out with the bath water. Without fail, it seems due to their own self-importance, or their own addiction to prejudice, or their own perfectly reasonable,

self-validated "reasons." Over many, many years, I have yet to witness any other explanation.

Lewis rightfully argues that it is the "ruthless, sleepless, unsmiling concentration upon self which is the mark of hell . . . For humour involves a sense of proportion and a power of seeing yourself from the outside." Chesterton, another dead white guy and friend of Lewis' (of course, aren't they all brothers?), reminded us that Satan fell through force of gravity.

Miss Drake, you can become part of the world's bureaucracy, and seek all the hollow rewards that it so proudly promises but never quite delivers . . . or you can base your identity, your worth, and your self-esteem in what the world understands not, let alone promotes, validates, or remunerates. Such a reference point, when seen with eternal eyes, offers abundant recompense beyond all human understanding. And then, strangely, somehow, all else falls into place.

The baby is yours to throw away, to drown, or to love and nurture. Even an old, tired, almost-dead white guy is shown mercy in the manger. Rethink "in spite." For I know that this same mercy extends to you too.[4]

There was no signature. I examined each page, looking for any sign of the sender's identity. Nothing. Then I remembered the envelope. Quickly I turned it over. Luckily, I had torn the letter open across the top of the envelope. Still intact, a discreet but commanding wax seal read, "The Office of the Provost."

I looked up to see Hannah leaning in the doorway. "You look pale enough to have seen a ghost!" she exclaimed. "Don't just stand there or we'll be late! Are you ready to descend into the pit of dead white male authors, O ye of much prejudice and little apology?"

I rolled my eyes at her and tucked the note into my jeans pocket. *How one missive changes everything*, I marveled, as we locked arms and giggled into the night.

"Where are you off to?" the senior dean inquired politely. We were passing him in the bustle of Carfax, where he was trying to flag a taxi. Silver-haired and always impeccably dressed, he carved an imposing figure. I introduced him to Hannah and told him we were off to a C. S. Lewis Society meeting.

"Oh," he sniffed.

"Would you like to join us?" Hannah offered brightly. I can't always tell when she is being polite or facetious. It is a terrific talent of hers I envy.

"Thank you, but no thank you. Lewis is not really my cup of tea," he replied aloofly.

"Why not?" I asked, eyes wide, trying my hand at Hannah's (and Wendy's) game.

"All that hibberty gibberish about Christianity is, well, irritating," he replied, raising his hand again, but the taxi, already full, had the nerve to bypass the senior dean unceremoniously.

"Fair enough." I shrugged. But Hannah pressed on, which surprised me. I can never quite tell for which team she is playing, but then again, I should talk.

"Why is it irritating?" she asked, looking up at him earnestly.

"Try getting baptized against your will, and you'll see," he replied tersely.

"What?" Hannah and I cried in unison.

"You heard me. I was baptized against my will," he repeated.

When we stood there, aghast, he continued, "When I was a child, our church rector forced me to get baptized, at my parents' overt and not-so-overt influence."

"How can someone be forced into baptism?" I asked.

"I was five years old. Five years old, for goodness' sake. I trusted the rector. I was terrified. He held my head under the water." A dark cloud passed over his face as he added, almost inaudibly, "And that's not all he did."

"I'm so sorry," Hannah offered. I was speechless.

"Yes, well, thank you, but I do not need your sympathy." The senior dean straightened his demeanor along with his tie. "Baptism means nothing. I'm sure countless people do it every day without a second thought. At least I fared better than my brother—me, no real long-term complications. But he ended up having a real religious conversion as a teenager at some bizarre summer camp or other. At least it was short-lived. He later came to his senses and got *deconverted*."

"Deconverted?" I asked, making sure I'd heard things correctly.

"Yes, that's right, *de*converted," he pronounced. "That's when you decide to consciously undo the damage that organized religion has done to your mind and your dignity. You turn away from God; you reject all this Christ nonsense. It's really the only reasonable solution if you've been silly enough to become converted in the first place. *L'amour de Dieu est folie*—'the love of God is folly.' Indeed." He fastened his top button against the cold. "So French!" he added with a mutter.

A taxi pulled to the curb. The senior dean opened the door; the cab yawned empty. "Finally!" he exclaimed. "I prefer to ride alone." He started giving the driver instructions as Hannah stepped forward to close the door after him, but he stuck his hand out to stop it.

"Wait!" he cried, his face suddenly red. Very red against his silver hair.

"I don't believe I have my wallet." He fumbled through his coat jacket. Then he arched in the seat to check his pants, too, growing more visibly distressed with every outturned pocket.

"Sure, mate, I've heard that one before," the driver brogued lackadaisically as he started waving the senior dean out of his cab like a bad odor.

"Wait, wait. I'm late . . . I'm late for a very important date," he pined, harried. I forced down a smile at the image of our senior dean as the white rabbit from *Alice in Wonderland.*

Hannah and I looked at each other and then opened our wallets. "How much does he need?" Hannah asked the driver.

"About ten quid, gorgeous. Unless you want to get in with him," the driver winked, "and then it's free."

Hannah rolled her eyes. We quickly muddled together a couple of crumpled five-pound notes. I added a few pound coins for a tip and good measure. Hannah passed the collection to the driver.

"Oh, no, no. This is awkward," the senior dean stammered.

"No worries." Hannah shrugged.

"Enjoy the ride," I followed, sincerely, as I shut the door on his protests and thumped on the cab to go. I stepped aside, but an incessant drumming sound caught my attention. I looked back at the cab.

A gloved finger tapped madly on the glass. The driver finally got the message and let the window down a crack, revealing the senior dean waving wildly without his usual composure.

"Thank you!" the dean called out. He seemed genuinely touched.

"You're welcome!" We waved back.

"*De rien*," I echoed, in French.

<hr />

When we arrived at the Pusey House at St. Cross College, I braced myself for a sea of chin-wagging men, as the Brits like to call self-absorbed, pretentious conversationalists who tend to thrust out their chins and wag them. *Here we go*, I thought at the debonair gentleman who warmly welcomed us at the door. From his patched elbows and crest-dotted tie, I knew in a moment he shopped at Academics-R-Us.

I could not have been more surprised, however, once I passed through the door into the unassuming lecture room, lined with simple chairs and a single stool at the front, no podium. A wave of color washed over me, from saris to skin tones. All sorts of people from all walks of life crowded the room, including visiting scholars from as far away as Japan, missionaries from Africa to Iceland, a group of girls from a school established for the poor in Haiti, a conference of pastors from Australia, two very prominent U.S. politicians, the usual Lewis pilgrims (largely Americans), and then, finally, handfuls of students as curious as I. We all joined the "regulars," who lived and worked in the district, academic or not; as a student at Oxford, one tends to forget its town-and-gown constitution.

I scanned the room, hoping to spot TDH but didn't. Hannah waved at Andy and Evelyn, a committed Christian couple engaged to be married that summer. They motioned for us to sit with them, just as we had when Bishop Tutu came to speak so powerfully about God's love as an active, radical force at work in our lives today. The love that he said is so relevant and real, capable of clothing and feeding the poor, healing the sick, driving out demons in all senses of the term. That healing could really happen, if we were willing. If we, ourselves, had faith. After he left the pulpit at St. Mary's, walking humbly amid a buzz of photographers and journalists, I stayed in the ensuing emptiness—the space that somehow feels quieter, emptier, after the dispelling of a crowd—and read a borrowed Bible long into the night.

"Dorothy Sayers wrote, 'The greatest sin of the Christian is to be joyless,'" the speaker began. "As reflective and active Christians, one of our most important duties is to be joyful. This may sound like an oxymoron"—he chuckled—"but it's a good reminder that 'all joy reminds,' and that, as recipients of grace, we have much to be joyful about."

Dare I believe in the joy?

"We tend to think of Christians as dour-faced, poor, pious beings who must slug out life in the dim hope of a better one. Words like *duty, chastity, repentance, sin* and the like, though necessary and with their place, often get undue emphasis and certainly don't help matters," he confessed.

That's the understatement of the millennium, I thought, pursing my lips. By now, however, I had learned to keep "duh" to myself.

"The poet T. S. Eliot calls the greatest sin 'to do the right thing for the wrong reason,'" the speaker continued. "At what point do we become legalists in our faith? When are we going through the *motions* without *emotions*, or worse, going through the motions because they have taken the place of faith? In this state we are no better than the Pharisees whom Jesus set on their heads or bobbing dolls on a dashboard, with glazed, empty smiles. Ultimately self-deception is the great absurdity. As Brennan Manning wrote, 'In philosophy, the opposite of truth is error; in Scripture, the opposite of truth is a lie . . . the really real is God.'"

The really real is God. I had to admit that struck me.

"*Even better than the real thing,*" U2's song played in my head.

"'A great number of people leave off praying at the very moment when their devotion is beginning to be real,'" the speaker went on, inserting St. Teresa of Avila into my thoughts. Nietzsche's famous line loomed up on my end: "When you look long into an abyss, the abyss also looks into you." But it is the dare that scares, as I also thought of Emily Dickinson, a woman who certainly would have admired my persistent lugging of all those soles upon my arrival: "Is Bliss then, such Abyss, / I must not put my foot amiss / For fear I spoil my shoe?"

My mind flashed to my mom's favorite passage from the Bible, John 14:1–4.

> Do not let your hearts be troubled. Trust in God; trust also
> in me. In my Father's house are many rooms; if it were not so,
> I would have told you. I am going there to prepare a place for
> you. And if I go and prepare a place for you, I will come back
> and take you to be with me that you also may be where I am.

It's a strange choice for someone who so adamantly discounts life after death, and yet the joy Mom derives from reading this passage seems real. As Tolkien puts it,

> From the ashes a fire shall be woken,
> A light from the shadows shall spring;

Renewed shall be blade that was broken,
The crownless again shall be king.[5]

"Laughter is eternal if joy is real," U2 would later sing.

Is it a cop-out to want this? After all, did I love this passage from John because my mom loves it, or because it is beautiful, or because it is true? Are these necessarily exclusive? Is it not okay to love something all the more because someone I love, loves it? And that someone also loves me? And ultimately, does any of this make it any less true? I was not so sure anymore. The push and pull in my heart certainly kept me on my toes.

The speaker began wrapping up his talk: "As Gandhi famously said, 'I like your Christ. I do not like your Christians. Your Christians are so unlike your Christ.' Who can blame him? I know I have often thought the same thing, and I'm sure most, if not all, of you have too." The speaker looked at us meaningfully.

Gandhi and my brother should have a drink together, I thought.

"The gravity of being a Christian must be matched, if not outweighed, by the levity of being one. You cannot truly live the gospel and be a serious hypocrite." The speaker smiled and then thanked us.

When I'd first arrived I had felt like Eeyore in a roomful of Tiggers. No one seemed to notice the dark cloud of judgment raining over my head, or if they did, they did not give it any notice or gravity. Slowly it dissipated and lifted. To my surprise the ambience among such soulful conversation felt, well, *merry*. People embraced each other warmly and welcomed any hesitant newcomers into their circles with a hand on an arm, or with a strategic cup of tea or glass of sherry. In addition to lecture format, discussion was encouraged in small groups. Eventually, in spite of my prejudices against (believe it or not) white men and those whom I believed must be naive social recluses, I was enjoying myself, stimulated intellectually and spiritually, and, most of all, in community.

Rethink "in spite."

The crumpled letter from the provost in my back pocket poked me as I sat through the extensive Q and A session. I imagined the crossed *t* of "spite" as the culprit, prompting me to consider how insightful and deliberately active my Christian friends were proving. It was easy to skim the surface and yet dive deeply at a moment's notice with them. While studying I discovered reams of thoughtful writers, loving activists, people who were careful about what they believed and how they acted for social good from those beliefs. Contrary to media snippets from American television in the MCR, the Christians I was getting to know were far from gay-bashers or unabombers. Rather, they stood boldly for cultural catchphrases that others seemed to merely hide behind, such as *race, gender, class, poverty,* and *social justice.*

Yes, that's it. These Christian people were *deliberate*. They were pursuing despite being persecuted. They were deliberate in discerning and knowing their own hearts, confessing their own faults, desiring forgiveness, and being grateful for grace. They were then deliberate in exercising the same forgiveness that had been granted to them, deliberate in at least genuinely trying to sidestep the continuous trap of self-reference and judgment. Most of us would balk at being called "evil." But it takes a lot of courage to be self-evaluative before other-judgmental, to be conscious rather than oblivious, to be actively loving rather than apathetic.

"Lord, have mercy," the group closed in prayer.

I did not eat or drink anything at the following social. Somehow I already felt full.

With the crowd dwindling Evelyn came over and hooked her arm through mine. "I saw a lot going on in that head of yours during the talk." She smiled warmly. "Spill?"

If Evelyn were a goddess of Homer's, her epithet would be easy-to-be-with Evelyn. A highly intelligent Stanford University graduate with a quick smile, she did not own a thread of pretension. Evelyn relished working with children. She left family, friends, and funds to relocate to Oxford with her fiancé while he studied theology and literature. *Now, that takes a sense of humor*, I reckoned. Together we took long walks in the Magdalen College gardens among the deer. She was the one who had pointed out Lewis's former college office to me. She listened to all of my thoughts, my background, my various shames and shams, without judgment. One afternoon I poured out some of my darkest secrets to her. Evelyn was the one who told me that Christ washed us clean, that our histories did not matter, that the only stories that did matter were the ones written in His blood after we accepted His grace. For once, I saw past my usual gothic response to such idiom, *feeling* instead of *blocking* the meaning. And in the way she took my hand, I believed her.

"Oh, Evelyn, so much pushing and pulling," I almost cried out to her after the talk. "One minute I think I will give my life over to Christ, and the next I chastise myself for being so crazy, gullible, naive."

"Which state is more naive, Carolyn?" Evelyn looked right at me. "Denial or acknowledgment? Unquestioning unbelief or questioning belief?"

Darn Stanford and all its intellectual training.

"I'm tired, Evelyn. It's been a hard week." I began packing my bag to go. "Can you let Hannah know I'm going to pass on the drink at the Bird and Babe and take off?"

"Are you sure you want to go?" she asked, helping collect my things.

"I have a headache," I lied.

"Good excuse to avoid your Lover." She winked as she tossed over my gloves.

TWENTY-ONE

PSYCHOMACHIA

The mind is its own place, and can make
A heav'n of hell, a hell of heav'n.[1]

—JOHN MILTON

O vernight, spring startled into being. Unfolding before me was the perfect morning to go for a run. Hearty daffodils danced as far as the eye could see with a yellowness that dazzled the eyes. Swallows dipped in and out of the pussy willows. The cows lowed behind the fence to my right, nuzzling the first generation of wobbly calves. With oars moving in hypnotic synchronicity, rowing crews skimmed the river Isis, which wove like a grey ribbon unfurled through the still-groggy fields. A few tagalong clouds emphasized the blueness of clear sky.

Christ Church loomed behind me, its stone-walled majesty

253

wearing a cloak of greenery. I now understood the origins of "ivory towers" and "ivy league": postcard-perfect, a centuries-old castle of learning nestled amid a countryside that made the rest of the world envy such a small island.

After stretching at the gate, I started a slow trot along the path. My footfalls softly crackled along the pale gravel, pounded into a firm, packed dust from years of use. I picked up my pace and found my meditative speed. Soon my steps were falling into the rhythm of all the life pulsing around me. The brilliant sunshine tricked me into thinking it was warmer than it was; cold air burned my lungs as I started to breathe harder. The effect became exhilarating, however, and I was off at a clip.

I looked around at the spotted calves, the freckled fish in the inlets as I coursed by, the speckled bird singing in the tree, the sun like bright paint spattered through burgeoning foliage onto verdant forest ground. I could not help but chant Gerard Manley Hopkins's poem as I ran:

> Glory be to God for dappled things—
> For skies of couple-colour as a brinded cow;
> For rose-moles all in stipple upon trout that swim;
> Fresh-firecoal chestnut-falls; finches' wings;
> Landscape plotted and pieced—fold, fallow,
> and plough;
> And all trades, their gear and tackle and trim.
> All things counter, original, spare, strange;
> Whatever is fickle, freckled (who knows how?)
> With swift, slow; sweet, sour; adazzle, dim;
> He fathers-forth whose beauty is past change:
> Praise him.[2]

Glory be to Dr. Nuttham's regular memorization requirements, I thought with a chuckle. As I rolled Hopkins's words around on my tongue (no easy task), it occurred to me how dappled I am. How dappled life is. Gifts and talents are easily virtues or vices. Doubt is not at odds with faith; irony or cruelty does not cancel out beauty or truth. God knows all of me, including the darkest parts. Sometimes I can even see heaven easier for the clouds than for the perfect blue. And He loves me still?

I rounded the first corner along the water and prepared to sprint along the riverfront, mentally challenging the rowers to a race. My reflection in the water became my doppelgänger urging me along. Self-derision, along with a good music track, was one of my best workout tools. Running along the bank, reflected in the water, I could keep myself in the corner of my own eye. And, like any girl, I could measure how big my rear end had grown eating all those bangers and mash (yummy sausages smothered in creamy mashed potatoes) followed by what the Brits call pudding, which usually and happily entails a decadent dessert drowned in custard.

But today somehow the competitive-reflection experience felt different. It felt, well, *reflective*. Instead of pulling a Narcissus as I panted at my image along the water, I thought about how easy it was to create parallel lives for oneself. Becoming a Christian would be no safeguard against this temptation to alienate myself from even myself.

You owe him an apology. Hannah's words rang in my head. Pride is a cheap shot in the arm. It keeps you from recognizing just how annoying and shortsighted and judgmental you are; it keeps you from the prickle of your own flaws. Once its numbing effect wears off, however, you feel even worse. You feel stupid . . . and, well, very, very *wrong*.

But forgiveness is too risky—asking for it and giving it. I do not want to forget all the injustices, and I do not want to grovel for mercy at another's whim. I did not ask TDH to be such a good man, to be a foil to the usual self-absorption I saw at work more often than not in men. My pace quickened now; wonder at the scene around me melted into the old anger, and I used that to fuel my legs. I ignored the familiar ache starting to act up in my left knee. I certainly did not need anyone's help, or anyone's forgiveness, or any more guilt.

The problem, for me, at least, was not so much that I did not ask to be born. I don't mind having been born. I was actually pretty glad to be here. It was that I did not ask God to die for me.

The kiss of life in the first garden. The kiss of betrayal in the second garden. The kiss of grace, of forgiveness, of restoration at last. The kiss returned in appreciation. Is this the difference between Eden and heaven?

Maybe, like life, the gift is so profound, such a surprise, precisely *because* I did not ask.

Run, keep running, I told myself.

My body leaned into a hypnotic rhythm, part of the effect of runner's high. My mind moved easily now with my feet, with my breath. It would be relatively easy to die for someone, especially a loved one. I looked over at the rowers. If one of those blokes fell out of the boat, and for some strange reason could not swim, and no one else could help, would I dive in? Of course, I would like to think. Even more so I would give my life in instantaneous ransom for any of my family. It is far more difficult to let that loved one go. *Especially*, I thought, *your child*. And yet our Father did both for us simultaneously. He conquered death so that we may live with Him eternally as we were made to do.

"Of course," I heard my mom's sweet refrain in my head, "you are my child."

Spring attested to this, rebirth overwhelming me, growing and greening and singing all around me. My reflection in the water glimmered and shook. I stumbled and decided it best to look ahead.

Turning the far end of the loop, I started heading back toward Christ Church. The path now wound through a dark section of forest thick with shade. My steps fell heavier on the sodden path. Curves come quickly, so you cannot see very far ahead. Anytime I jogged this part alone, I felt nervous. A woman does not have the luxury of obliviousness in a parking lot late at night; a similar threat blemishes an otherwise carefree jog along a secluded path. *Fear is at the core of what it means to be woman*, I thought with a twinge of that familiar anger. It is far more empowering to be angry than sad.

Lions and tigers and bears, oh my . . . *Lions and tigers and bears, oh my* . . . My feet struck out the rhythm in a pathetic attempt at a panicked inside joke.

I picked up my pace yet again, motivated by my uneasiness. *Were those footsteps behind me?*

> *Like one, that on a lonesome road*
> *Doth walk in fear and dread,*

> *And having once turned round walks on,*
> *And turns no more his head;*
> *Because he knows, a frightful fiend*
> *Doth close behind him tread.*[3]

I cursed last week's Coleridge memorization assignment. Moving my hand to my pocket, I wove my keys through my fingers, just in case.

Running completely on adrenaline now, I heard breathing that was not my own coming up behind me. Heavy breathing. I ran clenched, every nerve and every tissue tight.

I stopped breathing. The other breathing was *rightthere*.

Suddenly it passed me. A fellow runner, focused, steady, gave me a nod over his shoulder as he flew by. I felt his wind on my face like a spirit from the woods. My fear imploded against it. The shards then dissipated in the wake of comprehending the bold black words on the back of his plain white shirt: GOT GOD?

My knees almost collapsed with relief.

———

Lewis called it the Law of Undulation. St. Ignatius of Loyola identified it as the process of consolation and desolation, leading the Jesuits to explore it in the Spiritual Exercises. Like Coleridge's eponymous Ancient Mariner, we go up and down at sea. No wonder Jesus challenged His disciples to walk on water with Him. On stormy water. On *waves*.

We believe one minute and *waver* the next. As Screwtape tells his diabolical apprentice about mankind, it is during the lows rather than the highs that a person of faith grows closer to God.

"Lewis was actually pretty savvy for an old white guy," I admitted after the meeting.

"Praise indeed from Caesar!" Hannah joked.

I thought about Lewis's life. An esteemed professor at Oxford and Cambridge, he became a Christian later in life and married a divorced Jewish convert to Christianity, even though she was dying from cancer. An author of children's books and a classical scholar. A writer of science fiction and of critical essays. And as the author of something like *The Screwtape Letters*, a Christian able to wittily and credibly turn the devil out on his rear, while calling Christians out on their own silly games. Articulate, discerning, an outspoken Christian. Surely the latter was no easy task for an academic, let alone a British one, though when I tell Hannah these thoughts, she reminds me that Lewis was Irish by birth.

Just then I broke around the corner and was almost blinded by a final field ablaze in frost-defying flowers of every color. Phoenixlike, Christ Church rose up from the floral flames, and behind her lay the gate.

The last stretch.

It was then that I began to breathe more deeply.

To breathe Him in, and to breathe me out.

And then, I began, ever so slowly, to transform.

I did not have to carry everything on my shoulders. I did not have to be everything to everyone. I did not have to know all the answers. Could it be that sometimes glorifying God involves negatives?

My legs ached now, carrying me almost on autopilot to the

end of the path. Ahead a flock of small birds pecked among the gravel. They flew up as handfuls of confetti as I ran along, settling back to their meal after I passed. *Everything scatters from us but will come back*, I thought. *We are connected to everything, so the Fall affected everything. In a restored and truly brave new world, at the wiping away of tears and the removal of fear, the thaw will not trick, the birds will not flee, I will not run. I get it. I get it. I get all the old clichés. The lion will lie down with the lamb.*

I raised my hand to knock.

Wait, am I crazy? I thought.

Quick, knock before you lose your nerve.

A feeble tap at first.

No answer.

I turned to go.

No.

I turned around.

Yes.

A proper knock. A good knock.

The sound echoed brazenly through the stairwell.

It was early yet. Gavin, one of TDH's neighbors, had to edge past me to reach his room. He emerged from the dorm shower wearing only a towel with the cartoon character of the Tasmanian Devil strategically positioned. I tried to act nonchalant, but he caught my gaze.

Seeing me standing there at TDH's door all sweaty and out of breath, Gavin raised his eyebrows. I looked down at his

Tasmanian Devil and raised my eyebrows back. He chose not to say anything, instead nodding his greeting like a polite cowboy as he slipped by.

Maybe he's not in? I thought, feeling more dismay than I anticipated. *Has he already left for the day? Or maybe he didn't spend the night here . . .* I began to roll all sorts of ideas through my head.

Well, that's unfair, I caught myself thinking for once.

Suddenly the door swung open. TDH appeared hunched over in the arched doorway, as he had to in all the medieval doorways around here because of his twentieth-century well-nourished American stature.

I realized I was not just sweating from the run. Even my palms were clammy. I felt chilled to the bone.

"I'm sorry," I croaked. Nothing else would come. My eyes burned as I waited for my much-deserved punishment. I stood there, shivering, expecting his resentment to pour out on me, a slew of scorn, or a speech of judgment. He had every right, I knew. I had misjudged him and mistreated him. A horrible thing to do to anyone, but especially to someone I had to admit I respected greatly.

I looked down at my hands, and then folded them awkwardly against my chest, not knowing what else to do with them. Habitually protecting myself with a little bodily armor.

"Thanks," he said genuinely. "Of course I forgive you. Nice to see you!"

I waited. I waited for him to mock me. He didn't. I waited for him to belittle the argument, my feelings, my point of view. He didn't. I waited for him to dredge up the past. He didn't. I started to get nervous. Surely he would at least comment on how bad

262 SURPRISED BY OXFORD

I smelled? Even I could smell myself in the intimate space now between us. And it wasn't pretty. He didn't.

I expected him to then slam the door in my face, but he didn't do that either.

Instead, TDH moved over and held the door open wider, gesturing for me to come inside.

I could not believe it. When I finally had the courage to raise my eyes to his face, I saw he was beaming.

"May I hold the door for you?" He winked.

Speechless for once, I passed under the arch into the beloved room. Sunlight streamed through the oriel window, flooding the two chairs positioned side by side like good friends. TDH beckoned me to sit as he poured me a steaming cup of strong, delicious-smelling coffee. He offered me the sugar bowl and set a spoon in my cup.

Then, reminding me of Dr. Deveaux but with far less professorial profanity, he leaned in, saying softly, "Caro, a happy ending makes up for a lot."

This is what grace must feel like, I thought, warming myself in the sun as I rested in the chair.

TWENTY-TWO

THE ULTIMATE VALENTINE

Raise me a dais of silk and down;
Hang it with vair and purple dyes;
Carve it in doves and pomegranates,
And peacocks with a hundred eyes;
Work it in gold and silver grapes,
In leaves and silver fleurs-de-lys;
Because the birthday of my life
Is come, my love is come to me.[1]
—CHRISTINA ROSSETTI

Linnea stood next to me at the bar, drop-dead gorgeous in a flattering crimson number. Tall cool woman in a red dress. Ablaze on the bottom with a shock of black and wildly curly hair on top. "She reminds me of Medusa," Hannah whispered loudly in my ear over the pounding music, "turning all those men to stone with her gaze."

I smiled. Going out, especially somewhere on the town with Linnea, was always an adventure in male attraction and disintegration. They came like moths to her flame, and then she shot them down with only her eyes. A marvel to behold, truly impressive. She did not need words as the rest of the female race did.

It was the annual Valentine's Day bash at St. Catherine's College, the college with the most "modern" feel architecturally, the outdoor entertainment areas leading into glass-blocked partitions. This allowed you to watch all the drunk people from inside as well as outside, resulting in a sort of bizarre Alice-in-Wonderland-through-the-"drinking"-glass effect. In the midst of this modernist manifesto, I sat swinging my legs on a beam-me-up-Scotty-type stool, feeling very school-marmish in my red cardigan from Topshop.

I surveyed all the drunk blokes eyeing Linnea up and down, unwittingly planning their own demise, and took a sip of my fluorescent pink cosmo.

Just then a couple of Adonis-like men started crossing the room toward us. They each wore a rugby jersey from Cambridge. A sort of thrill rose up at the thought of dancing with a partner from "the other place," as longtime rivals Oxford and Cambridge refer to one another. Moreover, I was shocked that two such handsome blokes could appear at once, so perfectly in unison. It seemed to me that should break some sort of cardinal rule on girls' night out. Hannah was the first to notice that they were, in fact, twins; apt, since she trusted wholeheartedly in the abundant universe theory. She tossed her gorgeous hair in perfect timing to the gods' arrival at our barstools.

"Care to dance?" they each asked us, and we paired off separately. I could tell that my Greek statue was more than a bit tipsy, and I wondered to myself just how much alcohol was actually required to get such a large man-creature to just shy of weeble-wobble status. Even so, he managed to dance without embarrassing me, unlike Hannah's partner, though she did not seem to mind too much. Her Adonis was even more beautiful than mine (they were fraternal twins), so she tolerated his 1970s sprinkler and shopping cart dance moves with mouth appreciatively aghast. Perhaps I should have been grateful, but I began to tire of it all.

For a couple of songs' worth, Hannah and I managed to roll our eyes at each other a time or two without getting caught by our new hosts. Then thankfully our luck changed just as they were starting to get a little too touchy-feely. The pulsating dance music switched to something slow, allowing us to shimmy them to the edge of the dance floor without much protest. Politely refusing their offer for more drinks, I drew on every girl's favorite escape clause. "I have to use the ladies' room," I mouthed slowly, to make sure they could understand. Hannah just waved with her "Me too" eyes, as we disappeared behind the magic exit. *What a waste!* I mused, as I backhanded the stall door.

Without any real reason, I half expected the ladies' room to provide at least a temporary contrast to the scene from which I had just extracted myself. It did not. Two girls at the mirror were chatting crazily over the physical encounters that were no doubt on the immediate horizon for one or both of them. Thankfully (or not) the details were partially drowned out by the girl throwing up her fluorescent pink drinks in the stall next to me.

We exited the restroom, scanning to make sure the rugby

lads were otherwise engaged, hoping for just one safe corner to converse in, only to see more strangers groping each other in the back.

"I'm done, Hannah. I'm done with all of this." I waved my hand, sweeping it across the whole scene. "I'm going home."

"My, my, aren't you holier-than-thou?" a girl in bright tangerine-colored tights next to me cracked. I did not realize how loudly I had been shouting.

"Orangier than thou?" I yelled back at her, feigning being unable to hear over the music.

Hannah gave me a pained look. I shrugged a silent apology and turned to go, being sure to step carefully.

Am I just a prude? I thought as I snaked through the gyrating couples, sweating bodies, and glazed eyes. Why isn't this enough for me? Why can't it be enough for me? Things would be so much easier if it could be enough for me. And yet something holier than any of this sounded pretty good to me right now, I had to admit.

At the door, I saw Linnea's unmistakable silhouette aflame, dangerously close to a man with whom she was actually sharing a drink and laughing, instead of incinerating. He looked familiar. I squinted my eyes in the dark. His left hand encircled her hip with the ease of ownership. Startled, I did a double take. This time his head turned toward me just as the disco ball illuminated his face, alternating silver and pink. The identification was unmistakable.

It was Dr. Condorston from the lecture-theatre moment of (relative) truth.

Absolutely.

His wedding ring glittered me into remembrance. I heard he had a third wife now and two small children.

He looked right at me, the dappled pink light giving his face a shamed quality.

I looked away quickly and pushed through the high-tech prismatic revolving door, praying the whole time that I did not get stuck as I usually did in this stupid thing. In an act of mechanical grace, the door spat me out into the crisp night air of the quad, a welcome reprieve from the heated bar.

I counted the streetlamps on the way home to keep from thinking of other things.

Back in my room, I sat cross-legged in the dark against my bed, mesmerized by the flickering of the single candle lit on my mantel. I watched it turning blue, turning red, turning orange, and even a thread of green. But no pink, to my relief.

I opened my Bible to the beginning of the Gospel of John. I did not feel much like reading the Bible, but *if I'm going to be accused of being holier-than-thou, I might as well make the most of it*, I thought cynically.

I began reading, and the more I read, the more I wanted to read. Once the Bible gets under your skin, in its powerfully charismatic way, if you pardon the pun, then we all have favorite passages, or perhaps a certain specific passage that particularly spoke to us at a significant moment. For me, as a lover of literature, and that particular night, it was the opening chapter of John.

As I sat there in my tiny room with the slanted floor, the words started blurring on the page. Before I knew it, tears escaped my eyes. I tried blinking them away, but they kept coming.

I blinked again. Hard. The words on the page came into sharp focus. Then everything all of a sudden became very, very clear.

I knew that Jesus was who He said He was. Plain and simple and true and everlasting.

I knew that I wanted to know Him. To know Him first, and then to know Him better.

I knew that I had been an idiot, proud and imperfect, despite all my best efforts. I had been hard on myself and hard on others. Who would have guessed that when you really look at it, perfectionism (like anything else) can be a sin?

Everywhere I turned in the labyrinth, I was met by an impenetrable wall. The only way out was to be lifted up, or a ladder out of my want. There existed no act, no achievement, nothing I could *do*. The only freedom was in faith. And then I knew what I did *not* want. I did not want to return home, wherever that may be, again and again in my life, to no one, and finally, to nothing of any importance. I did not want my life to be empty, a regurgitation of excess, no matter how fluorescent, or a desperate existentialist filling of a bucket with a hole in the bottom. I did not want to live according to the meaningless exchange of bodily fluids, sweating among strangers, maneuvering amid pseudointimate relationships.

Christ offered a bridge over the gap I felt, sitting there on the floor, between my self and my own soul. Between my God and me. I wanted to know God and to be known by Him—a relationship so intimate that there was no space between Him and my soul.

But it was not as if I could shut my eyes tight, concentrate, and just make it happen as I had done with virtually everything else in my life, from the positives, like getting good grades, to the negatives, like denial. The leap seemed so impossible, so hard, too far.

Then a story from the Gospel of Mark jumped into my head. Scripture has a way of working like that. Be forewarned.

It was a man moved to faith by his love for his child. He brought his son, who had been tortured and then rendered senseless by a demon, to Jesus to be healed after His disciples could not do so.

The father asked Jesus, "If you can do anything, take pity on us and help us."

Jesus should have been insulted, "'*If* you can'?" he repeats. But instead of walking away, he continued, "Everything is possible for him who believes."

Immediately the boy's father exclaimed, "I do believe; help me overcome my unbelief!" After Jesus healed the boy, His disciples asked Him privately why they had failed.

Jesus replied, "This kind can come out only by prayer."

That man's desperate plea for the overcoming of his unbelief echoed deep within me, leaving nowhere to hide. God had called out even this very last façade, this trump card of an excuse, this very final resting place of despair. And it appeared that for us particularly hard nuts to crack, the only answer is prayer.

I wanted the real thing. The Real Thing.

"Lord, help me overcome my unbelief."

A simple prayer.

So brazen after the complete disregard for the presence and power of the Almighty in life and in death. Not even a prayer from belief, but a prayer to overcome disbelief. The lowliest of requests.

But at least, from me, the real thing.

And then, just like that, I was on the other side—the other end of the chasm. Through me, over me, beyond me. Safe. Saved.

On that Eve of St. Valentine's Day, I stepped out onto the sea and walked. I did not go under. Strangely, instead, even in my disbelief, through my ardent desire to believe, I was lifted up. The grace of it all poured out, like expensive perfume on weary feet, like soothing oil on a heavy head.

I am sorry, God. I am sorry for all the ways I fall short, for all the ways I prefer myself to You. I am sorry that I have refused Your gift of freedom from the trappings of myself. Thank You for Your offer of real life through Christ. Please fill my hunger, please quench my thirst, please give me rest as I know only You can do. Please take me and leave only You. I am Yours.

St. Mary's chimed midnight. The end of one day and the start of another. I stayed up all night in prayer, in awe, and in reverence. Everything felt new and familiar all at once. I turned back to the very beginning of the Bible. As always, and now especially, a very good place to start. It, too, felt new and familiar all at once.

> In the beginning God created the heavens and the earth. Now the earth was formless and empty, darkness was over the surface of the deep, and the Spirit of God was hovering over the waters. And God said, "Let there be light," and there was light. God saw that the light was good, and he separated the light from the darkness. God called the light "day," and the darkness he called "night." And there was evening, and there was morning—the first day. (Gen. 1:1–5)

To be one person one moment: *lost*. Then to be another person the next moment: *found*. It is the difference, as the saying really does go, between night and day. Outwardly I seemed the same, but inwardly everything had changed. I went to the window and watched the birth of the dawn. Everything, *every* thing appeared in this better light, this brighter light. The ordinary revealed its extraordinariness, like a lover stripped of mundane garments, suddenly naked and beautiful and true.

> Come away, my lover,
> And be like a gazelle
> Or like a young stag
> On the spice-laden mountains.
>
> (SONG OF SONGS 8:14)

This is the ultimate Valentine.
Dominus Illuminatio Mea. "The Lord is my Light."
Surprised by Oxford, the birthday of my life came.
Yes, my Love came to me.

EASTERTIDE

TWENTY-THREE

TIDE OUT: GOOD FRIDAY,
RIDING WESTWARD

I turn my back to Thee but to receive
Corrections till Thy mercies bid Thee leave.
O think me worth Thine anger, punish me,
Burn off my rust, and my deformity;
Restore Thine image, so much, by Thy grace,
That Thou mayst know me, and I'll turn my face.[1]

—JOHN DONNE

I could not afford to go home for Easter break. Sometimes being poor comes with a few convenient perks. While sad at having to miss out on seeing family, I had to admit I was somewhat relieved. I could hear my mom's polite refrain that faith was a private affair; that one should be "quiet" in her religion. I was not sure how those closest to me but far from faith would respond to any announcement or articulation of my "leap."

TDH was the very first person I told of my conversion. I saw him that morning on which I felt more alive than ever before. I think I startled him in the porter's lodge, almost knocking him over as I rushed at him, talking all at once. He laughed and hugged me, then later brought me roses. "For your wedding." He smiled widely. "For your *real* wedding."

Dorian and Rachel took me out to dinner. As a general rule, Hannah considered conversions strange but assured me I had not lost my noodle if I just did not go too public about it. Linnea thought it was intriguing and began asking me endless questions. My supervisor tried to convince me it was a passing phase. The provost invited me to High Table.

Now, as a Christian academic, I knew I would stand condemned by many intellectual circles for doing something as irrational as believing. Oh well. There was never fully pleasing academics anyway.

But the threat of rejection from those who were dear to me hurt far more. In particular, e-mail and phone calls are so unforgiving! They are like trying to squeeze a pound cake into an envelope so you can save on the postage. Everything falls apart, and all you are left with are crumbs. These could never satisfy, even if you tried gathering them. They could never convey the original promise and glory of the whole dessert.

I sensed how those back home could not see the cake through the crumbs. Who could blame them? It is so strange— the effect of a conversion among company. As I gradually shared the news with family and friends over e-mail and phone conversations, I began to see just how divisive this line in the sand could be. For instance, of three friends I cherished most dearly back home, I grew closer to two (immediately with one, much later with another) and lost the third completely. Some expressed reservation, others confusion; a few even admitted they thought I became a Christian out of an elite educational experience, having had too much time on my hands, or a liberal rebellion.

I began to sense, too, that coming to know God might be perceived as the result of my "going away to school," not unlike gaining the "freshman fifteen" pounds, or finding companionship in a sorority, or writing lots of sophisticated but, to many, pragmatically irrelevant papers. This God of mine to those a world away must have seemed all the more alien, all the more separated from their reality. Thus, as I was growing closer to God, it seemed I was growing farther from them. This seemed so unfair! And very lonely. "For, though I knew His love Who followèd, / Yet was I sore adread/ Lest, having Him, I must have naught beside,"[2] as Francis Thompson laments.

My sister congratulated me and then dropped the subject. Touchingly, her boyfriend, Jason, wrote me a letter full of all the usual Jason-like questions and yet also, sweetly, asking for advice on how best to love my sister. My mom thought it was very nice. I did not tell my brother or my dad right away; I could not bring myself to over the phone.

That next weekend I called Ben and heard the hesitancy in his mother's voice when she said he was not home. I asked how he was doing, how they were all doing.

"Fine," she said simply.

When I asked when he would be home, she hesitated again. "I don't expect him home until late, if at all. He's out with his new girlfriend, Carolyn."

I took a breath and asked if she could pass on a message to him for me. "You can tell him that I found what I was looking for," I said gently.

Despite the pain and discomfort of many reactions from those closest to me, I felt a deep happiness, serene and electric all at once. Later some of my believing friends would refer to this initial season in my walk with God as the "conversion high." I was no different. I felt, well, just really *good*. The world took on a surreal hue. I wondered why God's glory was not obvious to everyone. I began to swagger. I remained infatuated with my Lover. I wanted to know everything about Him. I started to go to church with vigor; I attended more and more talks, lectures, Bible studies, prayer groups. I saturated myself in Scripture, unable to get enough. I buried myself hungrily in theological commentaries, conversion narratives, and religious works.

It is a delicious and dangerous time, this honeymoon of the soul. All sweetness and light.

It literally took a reenactment of the crucifixion in a blown-up cathedral to shatter my already creeping complacency at the cost of being saved.

The ruined shell of St. Michael's Cathedral is all that remains of the fourteenth-century Gothic church in Coventry. Bombed during the Second World War, only the altar endured in one piece. These remnants would serve as the setting for the city's annual passion play.

Sylvia from my weekly Bible study generously bought tickets for those of us students exhausted from the end of term. She called it her "resurrection and restoration" gift. It would be my very first passion play. I was intrigued, not knowing what to expect at an outdoor modern production; but I was not sold on the likelihood of standing in the rain for two hours. In the end, however, I accepted, primarily since I did not want to hurt Sylvia's feelings. Although a new Christian, I had not learned fully yet the art of accepting gifts, especially from particularly gifted sources.

The entire production takes place embraced by the skeleton of the cathedral and its courtyard. The audience does not sit, but migrates with the actors, following each step in the betrayal and crucifixion of Christ. The actors are so close you can touch them, and they move in and out of the crowd. Although the production is relatively simple—there is no set except the blasted cathedral, there are minimal costumes and props, and dialogue is limited to strategic quotations from Scripture to convey the story—the effect is extremely complex. Ever so slowly I found myself becoming part of the story—being moved physically and emotionally by the play's dynamic production, and thus being drawn into imagining myself present at the most moving crux of history itself.

The actors who hurled insults at Jesus jostled the crowd in their rage and mockery. Two crosses book-ended where the third would sit. Two criminals, also crucified, flanked the actor playing Christ. One would deny Him; one would beg His remembrance. The choice on the lone hill stood starkly clear.

Firsthand I saw Him wear the crown of thorns, blood pouring down His face. Firsthand I saw His hands and feet nailed to the cross. Firsthand I saw Him bear the cross as He was whipped, stoned, spat on.

I heard the cracking of the wood under His very human weight as slaves grunted to raise the cross in the air. I heard the sneering bystanders offer Him, thirsty and dying, the cruel trick of bitter wine to drink, an ironic communion. I heard Him cry out in a loud voice, "*Eloi, Eloi, lama sabachthani?*" "My God, my God, why have you forsaken me?" (Matt. 27:46). Not just "Father," but "God." The one closest goes the farthest distance. The unwilling bent entirely to the will of God—to the very letter—of promise, and law, and love. Dying to despair, dying for us in spite of despair, so that despair may die. I thought of how Brennan Manning imagined the Lord's voice: "Have you forgotten that on Good Friday no angel intervened? That sacrifice was carried out, and it was My heart that was broken."[3]

Suffering. Emotion. Love. Devotion. That *passion* could hold all these meanings in the confines of one word. And God would take my passions and use them as a means to fill me with His true passion. As He can and will do for all of us, if we allow Him.

I stood there, tears streaming down my face. Wordless.

The star. The cross. The wise know what they signify. And oh, my star-crossed Lover, who loves me madly, truly, deeply . . . passionately—so much so that the recompense for preferring ourselves above all else, even God, is the *pietà*. There is no other passage.

Mom won't like it, I thought through my tears, *though surely she'll recognize it, too, beyond words.* That all is in measure. First act, prophecy. Second act, grace. Third act, revelation. Then came the rending of the curtain between these earthly acts. In the intermission rocks split, the earth quaked, the dead appeared, witnesses trembled and cried out: "Surely he was the Son of God!" (Matt. 27:54).

"It is finished" (John 19:30). Yet it is far from finished for us—this death, only the beginning.

But for now, the play was over. We all stood there, witnesses to our silence. Then someone in the audience started singing "Amazing Grace." It started low, but soon it grew, and the words swept over me as it started to gently rain. I smiled softly. My mom, with her own dappled push and pull with Jesus, would always say it rains at some point on Good Friday. It always seemed to. God's weeping for His only begotten Son, now swaddled in death clothes and laid in a tomb, embalmed in the myrrh gifted at his birth.

I turned back and looked at the set of this passion one more time, burning it into my brain. Into my heart. Where passion belongs. This broken Man set so symbolically against this broken cathedral: the ultimate sacrifice upon the insistent altar.

In quiet solidarity the crowd dispersed, various pilgrims trickling back into various cars. Once in our rattling Rover, we drove home in silence, each of us lost in our own thoughts.

I felt the cross behind me as we rode into the night.

TWENTY-FOUR

TIDE IN: CONFESSIONS OF
AN INTROVERTED CONVERT

*You are so young, so before all beginning, and I want
to beg you, as much as I can, to be patient toward all
that is unsolved in your heart and to try to love the
questions themselves—like locked rooms and like books
that are written in a very foreign tongue. Do not now
seek the answers, which cannot be given you because
you would not be able to live them. The point is, to live
everything. Live the questions now. Perhaps you will
then gradually, without noticing it, live along some
distant day into the answer.*[1]

—RAINER MARIA RILKE, *Letters to a Young Poet*

R egina took me in for Easter weekend. She owned a unique
ability to provide people with just what they needed. In

academia, Regina herself was a rare specimen. A respected female fellow of the college, she was an esteemed historian, a successful mother, and had been a loving wife. She stayed at home raising her four children, writing and teaching part-time, until her husband, a famous historian at Oxford, suffered a massive heart attack and died. Regina stepped into his place, finishing his lectures and submitting his grading, at first to help the students who had been initially left in the lurch, and eventually, talented and beloved, she assumed the position entirely.

Now, with her children grown and on to their own adventures in various parts of the globe, she was a vibrant grandmother dedicated especially to women's issues and supporting diversity in Oxford colleges. A long line of admiring students constantly vied for any crumb of her attention outside her office door. A mentor figure, she was a clever, funny, sophisticated, hip wisp of a woman, who somehow managed to be down-to-earth. And oh, did I mention? She was also a committed Christian.

I remember the very first lunch I had with her. She treated me to soup and salad at the Museum of Modern Art, around the corner from St. Ebbe's Church. I knew her casually, but I did not know yet that she was a believer. I was a brand-new convert and spouted out my conversion before the soup arrived. She laughed at my joy. "Thanks be to God!" she cried, giving me a huge hug. "Let's eat, and then let's go to Evensong and celebrate together!"

I had never thought of going to church as a form of celebration before. So celebrate we did. After chapel, back in her office, she poured me a whiskey. "À votre santé!" She clinked my glass. "For now you know true health."

I looked at my whiskey tentatively. I had never celebrated

with anything like it before either. This dainty lady across from me, however, downed hers easily.

"Drink up!" She smiled warmly. "You're going to need all the fire you can get if you're going to be a woman *and* a believer in academia." Then, turning her glass in her hand, she added, "If you're going to be a committed Christian in our world at all."

I swallowed the golden liquid down with a shudder and then settled back, feeling the warm afterglow. "Regina," I began, "how did you do it? I mean, *why* did you do it—forfeit a promising career when you married, stay at home, and then work now so tirelessly to help the underprivileged study and thrive here? Especially in the face of all these, well, *men*."

Regina sat quietly for a few moments, looking pensive. Then she stood up, sweeping her arm across her office. She began banging on things, smacking her printer, knocking on her computer monitor. She thumped on her stack of ungraded papers and roughly pushed aside the committee work to be reviewed and signed on her desk.

Maybe she can't hold her whiskey after all, I thought.

But when she turned to face me, I could see without doubt that she was completely clearheaded.

"Carolyn," she began earnestly, "all of these 'things' mean nothing in and of themselves. They are just objects, just means to an end. What does it matter what committee you serve on? What promotion you get? That book you labor to write and push to publish, someone will end up resting a coffee cup on, without any care as to your sacrifice. Your children are only young once. Your marriage provides you a chance to put someone else first daily. Such things refine your soul." A fond, faraway look passed over her eyes, and I caught myself remembering that she was a widow.

"Jesus wanted freedom for women too," Regina continued, "but His notion of liberation is very different from our limited one. His teachings are for the most part genderless; they apply to everyone. What is important is that my identity doesn't lie primarily in being a professor, or being a wife, or even in being a mother. Those things will always fall short. Entire careers get swept away at a moment's notice at the presentation of a pink slip, a vote of the elders, an accusation of a student, a cut in the budget. Marriages face infidelities, for instance, and end up like car wrecks from which people can recover but are never again the same. Children grow up and move far away and forget to write or call—as they should." She smiled wistfully. "The point is, if you have your identity in any of these things, it's surefire disappointment. Anything man-made—or woman-made, for that matter—will and does fail you. Having my identity in Christ first and foremost gives me the courage—yes, the *courage*—to live my life boldly, purposefully, in everything I do, no matter what that is."

I studied this woman in front of me, small as a wren but majestic as an eagle.

"Living your faith is risky, but it's worth it." Regina swooped down beside me. "So you'd better rest up, and drink up." She winked.

When I really thought about what Easter meant, the reality of the cross unnerved me. "I'd rather stay in the manger," I told Rachel the morning after the Passion Play while sitting by a cozy fire at a teahouse around the corner from Christ Church. We had planned to walk the meadows before catching my train to Regina's, but the weather turned. We looked over the wall at the daffodils and crocuses, somewhat blighted by frost and now bent under the heavy rain, but persistently poking their vibrancy into the gray of the day.

"Sure," said Rachel. "Who wouldn't want Christmas every day? The ultimate Neverland. I get you. A newborn baby. Sweet-smelling hay. Gentle animals and great kings adoring. Sure beats the stench of blood, the hurling of insults, the wretch of tasting vinegared wine."

I nodded, though I felt annoyed, betrayed. Peace and joy and comfort and love and all that stuff—these were some of my favorite things. I wanted to wrap myself up in them, nice and cozy, as a new believer. Spring should promise these, but Good Friday did not allow for that too comfortably.

"Rachel," I ventured, "sometimes I'm afraid . . ."

"What do you mean?" she asked.

"Well . . ." I stammered.

They called our number for our order. Rachel returned with a tray laden with goodies, a big pot of tea, and two dainty teacups. My mom was an excellent cook; even one of her reheated dinners late at night far surpassed any expensive restaurant food. But still, I had never eaten so consistently well, let alone "out" so often, before my scholarship money, I thought with gratitude. The still-warm scones tasted all the better against the sound of rain outside.

Avoiding her eyes as I ate, I thought of something TDH told me his father once said: "Sometimes the loftiness of one's gifts outweighs or exceeds the depth of his character." Maybe my so-called gifts were actually lost on me after all? Maybe I couldn't rise to the occasion? Parably put, maybe I was poor soil?

I set down my scone and tried again, looking right at my

friend. "Rache, maybe I'm wrong? Or maybe I'm not strong enough?" There, I finally said it, or rather, asked it.

"Caro," Rachel said reassuringly, "we all have these fears at some time or another."

"Well, if I'm honest, I'm not always so sure about this marriage," I told her flatly. "Look, at this point I'm way more concerned about my commitment than God's."

"If you mean, where is the promised peace, all that constant love and joy? Or where are the answers? Then I understand," she replied warmly. "It's the typical morning-after scenario, Caro. We all go through it to some degree. And as if that's not enough"—she yawned for effect—"Christians often grow world-weary themselves, even God weary. We get 'used to Him'; we become pretty chuffed with ourselves and our better-than-others supposed stance, our righteous worship, all our perfect acts. It's a hard habit to crack—especially for an overachiever—that over-achieving means nothing in His eyes. And *grace* is even harder. Accepting it is one thing, but really believing it and living it out—yeah, living in it—is not. The cross reminds us of all this. A much-needed humbling *memento mori* among all the lilies, if you will."

"It stinks," I said.

"Yeah, in-betweens often do. When we're really called to have patience, when we're really left to rely on faith. No wonder Jesus visits hell between the crucifixion and the resurrection. In a sense, so do we. But remember, Caro"—Rachel half-grinned as she poured the tea—"it's Friday (actually today, it's Saturday), but Sunday's a-comin'."

I went to remove my spoon from my cup, to get it out of the way, but Rachel stopped my hand.

"Keep the spoon in the cup," she insisted. So I did, resting it against the rim as I watched the brown steaming liquid cover the intricate flower pattern of the china.

"Keeping the spoon in the cup keeps the china from cracking under the heat," she explained. I looked up at her, surprised. "The metal of the spoon becomes a conductor, protecting the delicate china from the extremes in temperature."

"Interesting!" I marveled at Rachel; she always knew this stuff.

"You need to keep your spoon in the cup, Caro," she said gently, "especially when things get hot. God lifts us up, but He also grounds us. Fear will get into the cracks; fear, ultimately, is what breaks us apart. Jesus' constant refrain is to not be afraid. Whenever the angels appear, they tell you not to fear."

I interrupted. "I used to think it'd be amazing to be visited by an angel, but now I'm not so sure."

"Caro, think of what you sang, just yesterday. Of this grace, so amazing. Of how you cannot be plucked from His hand."

"I know, Rache. I'm beginning to realize just how much I love hymns." I sighed. "But what about when hymns don't cut it? What to do when it gets really difficult, both with the world and with God?"

"Keep your spoon in your cup, and you won't crack," Rachel reminded me as she passed the sugar.

The train ride out of Oxford to Regina's crumbling, rambling farmhouse did not take long, but it felt as though we had entered an entirely different world by the time we arrived. Bumpy fields met our feet as soon as we descended from the platform; the air smelled honey-fresh and hummed with insects, birds, life. There was no traffic, not even a traffic light. The tiny rural village seemed straight out of a George Eliot or Elizabeth Gaskell novel: a pretty place with a rector who might nod by the fire; old maids in bonnets, gossiping; a suitor climbing the hill with a wildflower bouquet.

I stayed in her late husband's study. It had been his favorite room, a retreat, in this bustling, busy house full of children and farm animals. Literally. The geese and ducks still wandered through the rustic kitchen that reminded me of those I had seen in Provence or Tuscany, with lavender drying beside herbs and hanging baskets of fresh vegetables. Regina used the study now as a guest room, complete with a pull-out cot. She did not keep it as a morbid shrine to her husband's memory; rather, she had updated it over the years. She used his old mahogany desk for her own work now. Completely lined with books and overlooking the brightest part of the garden, the room was cheery and serious at the same time, much like Regina, I thought. Only the heavy velvet curtains looked dingy and old-fashioned, which surprised me when I considered how meticulous Regina was about aesthetic details.

It was only when I went to close the curtains that I realized why they had not been replaced. At exactly the spot where you reach to pull them across the window, the fabric was worn in palm-sized patches. The curtains had grown almost threadbare in this spot from years of her husband pulling them open every morning, closed every night. Regina told me she liked this "flaw" in the otherwise renovated room. "It reminds me of his ritual," she said.

I ran my fingers down the curtains, feeling the richness of the velvet and then the want of it in the patches. God's reinstating of the old, tired, and frayed—treasures only apparent when seen with new eyes.

That Easter Eve Regina brought me a simple but delicious meal—an omelet made with eggs fresh from her own chickens and a glass of mulberry wine made by her neighbor. To this day I have not eaten such a sumptuous dish. I had not enjoyed mulberries since my sister and I stole them as children from the umbrella-like tree next door. I now understood all too well Augustine's thievery of pears.

Undisturbed by the pressures of college, I took a long, hot bath (pure decadence for any student living in a dorm) in a massive, pre-water-efficient tub and then slipped on the warmed pajamas Regina left out for me, wrapped around a hot water bottle tucked between my sheets.

I decided to read a little before bed and scanned the books along the wall—an overabundance of choice, and painful to choose just one. But my eyes eventually fell on a beautifully bound copy with the gold letters of the author engraved along its spine.

I randomly opened up Dostoevsky's *The Brothers Karamazov*, remarking that it was one of the original editions of the earliest translations into English—that's just what kind of nerd I can be. I shivered with delight at the find.

Until I saw where I was in the story: "Why have you come to disturb us?"

Jesus, who had come back to earth, stood on trial. The Grand Inquisitor, a grisly old man who represented the church, flung his accusation: "Why have you come to disturb us?"

I set Dostoyevsky down. The only way to set Dostoyevsky down, I think, is with a thud.

I needed to get some sleep, and Dostoyevsky, contrary to the

suggestion by the length of his novels, was not a choice conducive to relaxing me into sleep.

Who else, among these dear friends? Who else might be a
pleasant embrace before bed?

Ahhh, and then I saw him, also leafed in gold: Rilke. Just his
name moves over your tongue like a silken ribbon through your
fingers. I opened him hungrily. He did not disappoint.

"Perhaps everything terrible is in its deepest being something
helpless that wants help from us."[2]

I looked up at the worn patches, so apparent now that
the curtains were closed against the night. Fear lies at the
unexamined core of who we are. Faith grows from the surpassing
of fear in spite of its presence. It is not a denial of fear, but rather
a "working" from fear, so that faith, by its very process itself,
acknowledges the fear and in fact uses it to engulf the fear itself,
transforming it into the most powerful, rather than debilitating,
force there is: *love*.

A soft knock at my door.

"It's late," I heard Regina call from outside. "I saw your light
on. Is there anything I can bring you?"

I opened the door and welcomed her in.

"A little light reading?" she joked, nudging aside my gilded
authors with her hip as she sat on the bed, patting for me to sit
next to her.

"Regina," I asked as I sat next to her, "why is conversion so
hard? Actually, it wasn't that hard, in retrospect. It's the postcon-
version that is." I looked at her plaintively. "*Why*?" I whined, my
voice sounding like a child's.

She pulled me close to her, and I settled my head on her
shoulder. This dear woman, who smelled like her garden: honey

and earth and lily of the valley. Who smelled like my grandmother, swathed in butterflies.

"I will tell you what I told my own children when they faced the same questions, despite growing up in the faith, or maybe because of growing up in the faith, as they should," she said with her little laugh. "Grace is indeed a gift, but it doesn't give everything away. On the precipice of a question, there is nothing to lose and nothing to fear. When doubt gets turned inside out, all the fear pours out. It really is as the saying goes: when you work from faith, either you will step forward onto something solid, or you will be given wings."

"I feel as if I still, in spite of grace, fall so short," I said, leaning into her.

"Grace takes a lifetime to really grasp," Regina responded. "And then some. In fact, most of us don't ever 'get it' fully, I think." She stood up, taking the books and setting them back on the shelf. "But even the crumbs from His table are enough." She sighed as she lovingly brushed the spine of Viktor Frankl's *Man's Search for Meaning*. "Caro, hopefully your time at Oxford will ignite a lifelong cultivation of self-discernment resulting in social service, whether it be to a single child, or a nation full of people. Your education here has included your conversion, or, put better, your conversion has marked the beginning of your real education. Your time here has not only honed your intellect, but hopefully it has contributed to the shaping of your spirit, so that as you now walk off your 'ledge of familiarity,' you will also be able to walk with those you meet every day, ranging from their own issues to grave suffering and social injustice. It's like sharing your last crumb of bread when starving in a concentration camp." She turned to look at me keenly. "People assume that our dignity only lies in our choices, in what we think we so powerfully will and wield. But it can reside in our reactions, too, in our decisions about how to respond."

She walked over to me and opened the drawer of the bedside table.

"But here is what I recommend you read now, to relax and get a good night's sleep." She passed me a gossip magazine. I marveled that my hostess, such an established scholar and one of the only senior women of an Oxford college, had these lying about her home.

Regina noticed the slight look of surprise on my face. "Hey," she said, "don't equate being 'in the world and not of it' with sticking your head in the sand. I like knowing what Hollywood is up to. Isn't that just the American version of our monarchy anyway?" She smirked. "At the very least, it always works in making me drowsy."

She tucked me in, lowering the light.

"Get a good night's sleep, Caro. You have been working so hard for so long. Rest now." She kissed my forehead. Standing up and grinning, she added, "*Now* being the operative word. My young and, let's just say, very loud grandchildren will be here bright and early, and once they are, you'll know it. I thought we could all walk together through the meadow to Easter service."

"Sounds lovely." I smiled.

"Good. There'll be a light tea waiting for you, if you'd like, before we go. But if I don't see you, I won't wake you until it's almost time to leave. We'll plan on eating the big celebratory breakfast after service, so don't feel rushed. Just relax. Tomorrow will be your first Easter as a Christian, Caro! This is a time of celebration. I encourage you to soak it all in: the service, the company, the food, the meaning. Everything! Do it consciously and with care. Pause. Rest. Reflect. Don't underestimate the power and importance of celebration. It should be our perpetual way of life—we shouldn't be folks too rushed to say hello, or too beaten to bless, but a people recalling joy." Regina's voice lowered, growing even more comforting in the dim room. "Caro, for Christians Easter is the ultimate reward of patience, of waiting for the resurrection and the fulfillment of the promise of everlasting life—indeed a sweetness to the soul."

"Thanks so much, Regina, and you're right," I said from my cozy cocoon, wrapped in comforters against the late-night chill of an old farmhouse. I felt my chest loosen; its usual tenseness had grown so familiar that the lack of it made me feel uncomfortable. That adrenaline addiction to overscheduling, overdemands, overperformance, overeverything felt normal.

"This is almost as good as getting to be home," I sighed.

"Caro, you *are* home, perfectly home, and you *know it* this time."

Regina blew me a kiss, and then closed the door gently behind her.

❧

I slept soundly that night. Feeling rested and restored, I luxuriated in the downy bed, listening to the silvered tinkling sounds of children laughing in the garden and teacups rattling against saucers in the kitchen. The smell of just-baked bread filled the air, and the thought of fresh cream butter melting on a slice enticed me to get up. I put my hands in the worn patches of the heavy curtains and pulled them open. Unspeakably bright sunshine flooded the much-loved room so tenderly prepared for me.

My first Easter morning.

TWENTY-FIVE

TIDE OUT: DO I HAVE TO
BE A LOUD CHRISTIAN?

> *Much Madness is divinest Sense—*
> *To a discerning Eye—*
> *Much Sense—the starkest Madness—*
> *'Tis the Majority*
> *In this, as All, prevail—*
> *Assent—and you are sane—*
> *Demur,—you're straightway dangerous—*
> *And handled with a Chain—*[1]
>
> —EMILY DICKINSON

A gift for you from Wales," Regina announced as she poured my tea into a beautiful handmade mug glazed with sheens of brown and green. It changed color in relation to its position in the light. I'm very particular about mugs: I can taste how it influences my drink. I loved this one right away.

We were seated in her covered porch, watching the children hunt for any previously overlooked Easter eggs. Though nippy when we walked to church that morning through fields that crunched with frost under our feet, the day had now grown quite warm. It was not until I settled back on the brightly flowered couch and turned the mug around that I noticed the delicate Celtic cross carved into the other side.

"I liked it," Regina chirped, "because the cross shows outwardly if you hold it with your left hand, and inwardly if you use your right." Giving me a stealthy glance, she added, "So you can direct it wherever you'd like, whenever you'd like."

I shifted a bit uncomfortably on the gladioli. "Is it wise to let people know you are one of *them*?" I heard myself say, more nervously than I wished to let on.

"If you mean someone who drinks from the cup of the cross, then yes," she said matter-of-factly, passing me an array of pastries. Earlier we enjoyed a grand feast for brunch. I did not think I could possibly eat again for a week. But at the sight of these treats for tea, my second "dessert" stomach, as always, did not fail me. Luckily Regina delighted at my appetite and refilled the plate before I could mutter an embarrassed apology. Students are like termites; if you have them over, they will eat up everything in your home, leaving only a trail of sawdustlike crumbs. I was no exception.

"And I have news for you"—she chuckled as I ate—"very good news. You *are* them. Yep, now *them* is *you*, dear girl."

The shadows were falling along the garden; soon it would be time to leave. Regina's son Daniel offered to drive me into

Oxford so I would not have to catch the only train on a chilly holiday evening.

I carefully placed my mug in my school bag, nestling it between the pages of *Paradise Lost* to keep it safe on the way back to college. "Thanks for everything, Regina," I said as I leaned in to hug her good-bye. "I will always remember your generosity."

"Not mine, *His.*" She hugged me back. "And don't forget to remember."

Daniel went ahead to chase away the chickens roosting on the car before starting it up. I made my way down the little uneven lane to the main road, where he would pull up.

"Preach the gospel at all times." Regina waved from the doorway. "And when necessary, use words."

I hesitated, always hooked by a good quotation.

"St. Francis of Assisi," she said, rewarding my pause. "A good medieval saint," she could not help adding with a smile.

I nodded, smiling back as I lifted the latch and slipped through the narrow gate.

Ruggedly handsome, Daniel chatted merrily as we rode along in the little silver Peugeot. A film director, he lived in Los Angeles with his wife, an accomplished actress, but they liked to spend time with family in Britain whenever possible. They were expecting their first child this summer, and his flagrant excitement endeared him to me right away. All of Regina's children were fascinating, fun people and thoughtful, committed Christians. I asked him what it was like to be a believer in his line of work.

"It's a lot easier than being a Christian in LA," he quipped.

"But seriously, Dan—"

"But seriously, my dear," he replied, "I listen to a lot of Pink Floyd."

"Pink Floyd?"

"Yes, Pink Floyd. Entirely a closeted Christian rock band, if I ever heard one," he proclaimed.

I was beginning to see, and be unnerved by, how everything seemed to work to the glory of God. But *Pink Floyd*?

Daniel looked amused at my confusion. Accustomed now to driving on the right-hand side of the road for most of the year, he veered the car back to the left and then explained, "Jesus brings the most radical message there is into any society at any time: you are beloved; you are worth a price that only the God of the universe could pay. You are not merely a brick in the wall. People like to contend that Christianity is a form of mind control, a panopticon for political purposes, an opiate for the masses. But if they *read what Jesus actually has to say*, and not the regurgitated socially inaccurate garbage . . ."

He stopped to concentrate on the exit off the roundabout.

"Hey, do you have time to see something wonderful before I drop you off?" he asked as we entered the city center. Weaving back and forth, he kept fighting to remember to drive on the left.

"Sure!" I exclaimed. I had already seen two of his films and was a big fan, so I was certain whatever he had in mind would be a treat.

He took a quick turn up Worcester Street and cut across Little Clarendon through St. Giles, pulling up in front of Keble College.

Keble College? I thought somewhat disappointedly. What could be of interest to a fast-paced, tattooed film director (with a cool nose piercing nonetheless) at the sedately dignified Keble College?

Always the gentleman, Daniel swept around the car in time to open my door. "Mom and Dad often took us here as kids," he explained as he directed me through the lodge, waving at the night porter as one would at an old friend. "Feels a bit like a second home. Did you know that Keble owns the most impressive collection of illuminated medieval manuscripts, second only to the Bodleian?"

"Ah, the bane of being the offspring of historians." I smiled.

"Yeah," he joked back, "most kids get to go to the fair, or even Disneyland, while our parents' notion of a good time consisted of visiting historical sites and documents. But they still made it fun. That's probably why I ended up interested in films too." He smirked. "Films make history—only better."

I grinned back.

Daniel led me through the quad along a back walk toward the college chapel. By now we almost had to feel our way because it had become so dark. Once in the chapel, we stood, in contrast, shrouded in that other kind of darkness of the indoors at night. The cool, quiet air settled around us like a secret.

"Look, there it is," Daniel breathed.

I looked, but I did not see anything, probably because my eyes had not yet adjusted to all the different kinds of darknesses. I squinted and waited, but still nothing came into view.

"See what?" I finally had to ask.

"*The Light of the World!*" Daniel's awe rebounded off the chapel space like a coin tossed in a well.

"The what . . . ?" I had no idea what he was talking about.

"*The Light of the World!*" he repeated, pushing me in front of him.

There, tucked in an unobtrusive corner, a painting did indeed glow out of the darkness. It showed the traditional but riveting figure of Jesus on a lone landscape, standing at a door overgrown with weeds. He raises one hand, about to knock, while in the other he holds a bright lantern.

"His gaze is mesmerizing," I whispered, sensing the awe of the portrait too. "I feel as though He is looking right at me, right *through* me."

"Yes," Daniel agreed. "He looks directly at the viewer, and yet I've never quite been able to pin His expression—patient? Discerning? Not judgmental. Hmm, it's not quite any one of those, but how else to put it?" Daniel struggled for the right words, then shrugged. "As though He is *there*."

We stood side by side, looking back at this description-eluding Him.

"I thought you might like it," Daniel finally said, "because it dates from your era of interest. Mid-nineteenth century. William Holman Hunt painted it as an allegory of Revelation 3:20, 'Behold, I stand at the door and knock; if any man hear my voice, and open the door, I will come in to him, and will sup with him, and he with me.' It's also reminiscent of such passages as 'Seek and you shall find,' as Matthew 7:1 tells us."

"It's haunting," I confessed. "Thank you for thinking to show it to me."

"Often when I have been in a dark place in my life, this picture comes to me." Daniel spoke with surprising seriousness. I was used to his being perpetually jocund. Successful, attractive, at ease in any group—it never occurred to me that Daniel could face any "darkness" at all.

"We all struggle, regardless of what we believe," Daniel spoke uncannily into my thoughts. "But it's what we believe that determines the outcome of the struggle."

I nodded, slowly understanding.

"Hunt believed he painted this by divine command," Daniel continued. "Cool or crazy? I love 'em both." He chuckled. "Whatever the reason, it's a life-changing piece of art."

As we turned to leave, one small detail of the painting caught my eye.

"Daniel!" I almost cried, "Wait! Something is missing . . ."

I walked up closer to the painting, not trusting my eyes in the gloom. I inspected it carefully.

"Yes, wait . . . It's just as I thought." I caught his arm. "Look, there's a mistake."

"Carolyn, this is a masterpiece. As with all masterpieces, there are no 'mistakes.'" Daniel smiled.

"But I tell you, Hunt made a mistake!" I turned back to point at the door in the painting. "Look, the handle is missing. How will Jesus ever open the door?"

A chain of candlelight dotted up behind Daniel. The choir-boys were beginning to light the pews and altar, in preparation for Easter Sunday Evensong. Soon the chapel would be full.

Daniel took my hand, leading me out the side door so as not to disturb those arriving for the service. Once out amid the buildings around the smaller quad, a keyhole of clear night sky opened above us.

"Hunt did not forget anything, Caro. No, in fact he remembered." Daniel jingled his keys as we walked back to the car. I stole a sideways glance at him, bewildered. Daniel kept walking, looking straight ahead.

"The door can only be opened from the inside," he said.

TWENTY-SIX

TIDE IN: DANCE LIKE A FISH

The only God worth believing in is a dancing God.
—FRIEDRICH NIETZSCHE

Grasping Blake's beautiful illumination of a tiger by its tail, I pulled the postcard out of my box.

> Tyger! Tyger! burning bright
> In the forests of the night,
> What immortal hand or eye
> Could frame thy fearful symmetry?[1]

As I turned it over, I recognized the distinct handwriting at once. She wrote that to say that she would be at her sister's this week and would I like to get together for what I might find a "curious little walk"?

Dr. Restell was one of my former professors from Canada; British by birth, she often traveled back to see family and friends, as well as do research, at Oxford and Cambridge. She had become an esteemed full professor but never married, having come from the generation of women who had to choose, usually, between a spouse and a career. Her specialty was Old English, but she owned one of those massive intellects that almost frightens with its ability and which effortlessly knits everything together.

On the outside she appeared a somewhat homely lady, stooped with age and years of study. Unknowing freshmen often avoided her classes because she had a reputation for being a harsh grader. Moreover, some lacked the patience to weather what seemed to be an initial pedantic tedium to her courses. But if you were patient and applied yourself, you were richly rewarded, not only with an appreciation of Old English (no small feat), but also with getting to intimately enjoy Dr. Restell's contagious joy for learning and for life. Simply put, she was great fun. She waited until you used up all of your words, and then she tended to speak slowly and deliberately, almost monotonously, until she began to pick up speed. And then, before you knew it, you were in front of a live wire, all animation and energy. Her senior courses filled to overflowing. I couldn't wait to see her again.

> When the stars threw down their spears,
> And water'd heaven with their tears,
> Did he smile his work to see?
> Did he who made the Lamb make thee?[2]

Studying Blake's image, I noticed that his tiger appears to be smiling as it creeps below the text:

Tyger! Tyger! burning bright
In the forests of the night,
What immortal hand or eye
Dare frame thy fearful symmetry?[3]

We met for lunch at the Bird and Babe, appropriate for a classics and Old English scholar with a passion for Tolkien. She ordered each of us a "lager and lime," or beer with a splash of lime cordial. Usually considered a gentlewoman's drink, the refreshing combination takes the edge off the beer.

"I heard from a few colleagues that you were entertaining becoming a Christian." She looked at me from her matching armchair by the fire.

I cringed. "Wow, word sure travels quickly," I said sardonically.

"Yes, the Word sure does," she replied, giving me a wink.

"I never knew that you were a Christian, Dr. Rest—I mean, Elizabeth," I said. I found it difficult to call cherished teachers by their first names. It always seemed to me as if these respected figures sprang forth, perfectly formed, from the forehead of Jove, surnames and titles intact.

"Yes, especially difficult to be in my line of work and not face the question eventually, and," she added with a smile, "I suspect for you too."

I nodded, answering her subsequent questions about my recent conversion.

"Well, it's wonderful to share it with you now so openly, now that you believe and are equipped to handle the truth." She clinked her glass to mine.

"I would hope that you could have always trusted me to do that," I said, a little hurt.

"Oh, Caro, please, I don't mean that in a condescending way. It's not you. It's, well, academia. Start crowing about being a Christian, especially on a public campus, and you get, well, crucified." She smiled wryly. "Add being a woman *and* being a confessed Christian, and *wham*, you have a recipe for all sorts of chaos that might not serve your students prudently in the end. Sometimes subtlety works far better."

"I met Dr. Dayton and Dr. McCraghy for tea when I was home for Christmas, and we got into a heated discussion of what I had been learning while at Oxford." I tried to act nonchalant, but then the dam burst forth. "I've always admired them, all of you . . . You were all so good to me back there. I wanted to share with them what I was starting to think through, what I was starting to feel, about God. Not just God in the abstract or philosophical sense, but in terms of having a personal relationship with Him. Really knowing and being and resting in such a thing."

"How did they react to this sincere sharing of your search?" Dr. Restell asked gently.

"Dr. Dayton warned me that God was a projection of humanity's imagination. Or, to put it more precisely, an ephemeral act of wish fulfillment of our collective unconscious, at best," I said haltingly.

"Go on." Dr. Restell took a dainty sip of her lager and lime.

"He was rather upset and warned me that my whole academic career would be in jeopardy if I jumped on *that* bandwagon. He claimed I would never be taken seriously at an institution of higher learning, especially in our postmodernist age. He then relented a bit and seemed gentler, saying he only wanted to protect me. His partner is a psychoanalyst, and he felt that I was trying to use religion to fix my 'father complex.'"

"Reminds me of two of my closest friends—one's a writer, the other a psychiatrist," the pub waiter interjected as he set down our fish and chips. "I love them to pieces, but I can't relax enough in their company to really enjoy a meal, especially when they're together."

We nodded our thanks; then Dr. Restell returned to me. "I see," she remarked but then did not say anything else. She took another sip of her drink, saying, "And Dr. McCraghy?"

"He just seemed sort of shocked at first, and then sort of sad."

"Really? Why did you sense that?" she asked.

"He admitted that he had 'tried religion' once, but when the chips are down, God doesn't really show up." I thought of Dr. McCraghy's painfully earnest teaching of *Waiting for Godot*.[4] I watched Dr. Restell closely. These were longtime colleagues of hers with whom I knew her to be on good terms.

"And you feel badly about these reactions?" she asked.

I did not have an answer; I had not thought of why I felt disappointment, or sadness, or hurt at these reactions. Objectively my own response should have been, well, *objective*.

"Is it because you want them to believe too?" Dr. Restell leveled at me.

I reeled back. "Yes. No. Well, of course I want them to have the same relief, healing, peace, joy . . . but I don't want to hammer on their individuality. And I don't need their affirmation. Well, I'd like it. Oh, I just don't know," I stammered. So much for tea and talking of trivial things.

"Yes," Dr. Restell sighed, "unfortunately, 'evangelizing' or 'conversion' or the like often conjures up Inquisitionist images of being racked on a wheel or stuck all over with pins."

I grinned in agreement.

"And yet the urgency of Christ's message is very real, both for our present lives and for our lives ever after," she stated. "Academia, for instance, like any other political institution, becomes such a hotbed of contention because, I think, people don't like the notion of *revealed* truth being given as much weight, or even more than *discovered* truth. Then try to explain things like being moved by a Holy Spirit, and you've got quite a mess."

We sat together, eating our pub fare in silence. As Dr. Restell cleared her plate, she dabbed the corner of her mouth with her napkin, saying, "Ah, nothing like a good meal with a good friend to set the heart to what matters. Our conversation reminds me of a little poem that I put to memory after discovering one of my professors had been a Christian too. He shared it with me then, and I'll share it with you now:

> If only the good were clever,
> If only the clever were good,
> The world would be better than ever
> We thought that it possibly could.
> But, alas, it is seldom or never
> That either behave as they should:
> For the good are so harsh to the clever,
> The clever so rude to the good.[5]

"That's exactly how I see it at times," I agreed heartily. "Who wrote it?"

"Elizabeth Wordsworth, the great-niece of William Wordsworth. A woman of much intellect and influence, she founded two Oxford colleges for women, and yet she wrote under a male pseudonym. A shame? Yes, of course in many ways, yes. But a greater shame if she hadn't written or been published at all. The world is the world is the world, from age to age to age: how to survive in it but not be of it? As her great-uncle wrote, 'The world is too much with us . . .'"

"'We have given our hearts away, a sordid boon . . .'" I replied from Wordsworth's poem, lost in thought.

"The instructions are there; He provides us with practical advice, Caro," Dr. Restell said as she stacked our plates. "As Matthew 10:16 says, 'Wise as serpents but innocent as doves.' The Lord should have mentioned chameleons too. Not that the truth needs us, but sometimes we do need to adapt to our environments, to be savvy enough to live it effectively."

"How difficult to be a serpentine dove!" I lamented.

"And how perfectly beautiful!" Dr. Restell marveled, as she stood up and put on a bright red slicker.

"Well, then," she said, passing me my old grey raincoat, "if it's not too damp for you, let's venture back out before we lose our daylight completely. We'd better step lively."

❦

"There it is, the Martyrs' Memorial." She swept her arm toward St. Giles's busy intersection, where a shaft of stone surrounded by three statues rose up from the surrounding bustle. Dr. Restell explained how, in the sixteenth century, Thomas Cranmer, archbishop of Canterbury; Nicholas Ridley, bishop of London; and Hugh Latimer, bishop of Worcester, were put on trial for

Protestant heresies when the Catholic Queen Mary came into power. A commission of Oxford and Cambridge divines found them guilty, sentencing them to be burned at the stake.

"What a strange place for a memorial," I remarked. "I mean, you're likely yourself to get killed by a bus or a bicycle if you cross over to examine it."

"Well, for one, it commemorates the actual spot where these poor unfortunates were set on fire," Dr. Restell responded. "Also I think it highlights very effectively the nature of cruelty, and of suffering, and of death, as when Auden composed his poem '*Musée des Beaux Arts*' upon considering Breughel's painting on the fall of Icarus—that such things happen in the everyday, right under our noses, amidst the busyness of other things, as does believing."

There it was again, my habit of separating spirituality from any reality, of insisting that relevance and reverence were necessarily strangers—quiet, contained, formal, and removed from one another—rather than intersecting intimates, also alive amid the busy, loud, mundane, and chaotic.

"For generations of students popular legend had it that the monument was in fact the spire of a submerged church," Dr. Restell continued, probably lecturing a bit now out of habit. "Regardless, its existence in the midst of all this hubbub does cause one pause. It does make one question what one believes, or"—she shrugged—"does *not* believe, for that matter."

I nodded as she spoke, for it was already having that effect on me.

"Latimer and Ridley were burned first on October 16, 1555. Latimer famously addressed his condemned mate: 'Be of good comfort, Master Ridley, and play the man. We shall this day light such a candle, by God's grace, in England, as I trust shall never be put out.' A familiar phrase now," she noted.

I turned to Dr. Restell and asked, "Why does religion have to get so ugly, even among sects of practically the same creed?"

"I don't know, but it was happening from the start in Christianity. The disciples were bickering in Jesus' very presence, and then, not long after the resurrection, Paul's letters already speak of dissension amidst the early church. God bless them. A proliferation of committees always has that effect. Just look at academia . . . Oh, I must behave. That's another tour someday," she laughed.

"Christian persecution was a dramatic part of early church history," Dr. Restell continued as we sat together, huddled against the dampness, on a bench outside Balliol College. "Some argue that the life, death, and resurrection of Jesus Christ was a man-made hoax conspired by a group of disciples. But that doesn't hold any water if weighed against the legacy of martyrdom. Eleven of the twelve apostles, and many of the other early disciples, died for their adherence to this story. I guess even Judas the betrayer did, in his own way, come to think of it. That's pretty dramatic."

"Why is it so dramatic?" I asked. "After all, lots of fanatics have died to defend a religious belief."

"Because people don't die for a lie." Dr. Restell looked at me. "Just consider human nature throughout history. No conspiracy can be maintained when life or liberty is at stake. Dying for a belief is one thing, but numerous eyewitnesses dying for a known *lie* is quite another."

I tapped my feet to the rhythm of my train of thought. The drizzle waned, so Dr. Restell pulled her umbrella closed and set it against the bench.

"St. Jerome wrote that Peter was crucified upside down, at his own request, because he claimed he was unworthy to be crucified in the same manner as his Lord," Dr. Restell stated softly.

Wow, I thought. *That's coming a long way from betraying Jesus thrice before the cock crowed twice.*

"Paul, himself a persecutor of Christians before his own sudden picaresque conversion, if you remember, suffered in the first persecution under Nero. But his presence was so dramatic in the face of martyrdom"—she looked up at the memorial—"that the authorities removed him to a private place for execution."

"Lucky him. Which disciple was spared?" I asked.

"Well, if you can call it that." Dr. Restell sighed. "It was John, the 'beloved disciple.' Around 74 AD he was ordered to Rome, where history confirms that he was cast into a cauldron of boiling oil. He escaped without injury, by the way. Maybe he was spared a bit longer for good reason, since it was in exile where he wrote the book of Revelation. He was the only apostle who escaped a violent death. Many of these letters, many of these testimonies, are given from prison, from places of persecution. They still spoke this truth, even when faced with much suffering and pain."

Shame burned my cheeks as I thought of my hesitation to share the truth, especially with those I cared for and from such relative safety.

Dr. Restell looked back at me. She must have read my red, for she said simply, "I would give my life for you to have this truth. To be amazed by His grace, healed by it, and have your life renewed in Him. To live and to die assured in this comfort and joy. Our tears wiped away and all set right. Forever."

I looked at her, not sure what to say.

"That's what you *would* say, what you *want* to say, isn't it?" She returned my gaze.

My eyes welled up and my throat grew tight.

"The memorial says it for you." She took my hand as she stood up. "Come, cross with me."

⚬⚬⚬⚬⚬

We meandered down St. Giles, window-shopping and popping into nooklike bookstores all the way down to Carfax. "Are you still interested in taking that walk?" she asked once we reached the High.

"Of course I am; you have me intrigued!" I replied eagerly.

She pointed her umbrella up the High. "Well then, let's step lively," she repeated as she took my arm. I felt as if I were embarking on an adventure with an extremely erudite Mary Poppins.

"Is academia really that antagonistic an environment?" I asked with dismay. We were panting up the long, slow grade of Ifley Hill toward the outskirts of Oxford into Headington. Actually I was the one panting. My older companion fared fine. I stopped to look at the river as an excuse to catch my breath, but then I had to hurry on to keep up with yet another wise and tireless professor.

"Yes." She tapped her umbrella to her pace. "Well, for instance, when they hire for diversity, everyone is quick to tick the skin-color box, and the gender-orientation box, but never the spirituality box. Advisory boards don't go around saying, 'Well now, we have enough Jews and Hindus; better throw an Evangelical into the mix.' I have a lot of issues with what defines true *diversity*. But that's neither here nor there; it's not the purpose of this walk."

"What is the purpose, then?" I asked.

"To see that the extraordinary abides in the ordinary, all around us, every day. If you know where to look, how to look, it's all diverse but connected. I'm sure the Romantic in you will like that one." She smiled. She then poked a spot nearby with her umbrella. Astonished, I spied something, which just a moment ago passed unnoticed: the sign of a fish carved into the pavement.

"See! There's one! Hee hee!" the sweet old lady cried with glee. "You'll soon see the fish are everywhere. That's the point."

"Of what?" I ventured, a bit taken aback by her youthful jubilance.

"The walk! This journey by faith, Caro." She smiled. "Ye are not alone! Ye are never alone!" She grabbed my hands. In her raincoat set against the overcast dusk, she marked a red sail in a grey sea. Raising her hands she exclaimed, quoting Matthew 28:20, "'Surely I am with you always, until the very end of the age!'" Her joy was infectious. I laughed, too, and hugged her back.

We spent the rest of the afternoon walking throughout Oxfordshire, wandering side streets and following previously unnoticed paths. All along the way Dr. Restell used her umbrella to point out the same sign, a simple fish, carved onto a step or a porch or the edge of a walkway. Sometimes it was hidden under brush or the overhang of a fence or wall; sometimes it was in plain sight, at the end of a lane or by the street. Some of them were so weathered as to be barely detectable, but they were there. I had never noticed any of them before. Once we began finding them, however, it was as though we could not stop.

"Why are these here?" I asked, more curious than ever.

"Back when the town was under pagan rule, Christians put the sign of the fish on their property to signal kinship with other Christian travelers. During times of persecution the symbols marked a place of refuge for those who believed. Christians have continued to add them throughout the years to sign community. Neat, eh?" She winked as she spoke in her Canadian-British accent. "Even now persecution still takes place around the globe, Caro, and first-world countries are no exception. They experience less overt forms, of course, but still sinister."

Thinking of my own prejudices, I began to have an inkling.

After dinner at Dr. Restell's sister's house in Headington, we caught a concert at the Holywell music room. There is always something to do or see in Oxford at the drop of a hat. The "menu" was literally printed in the various postings throughout town, and many events were free or very affordable. Stop to make a phone call in a bright red booth, and the next thing you knew, you changed your evening plans based on an advertisement stuck to the glass, even if you had just used your last pence for the call. That evening's production indeed proved to be the perfect dessert. You had to be made of stone not to tap your foot. Bagpipes and dancers: what gluttonous pleasure! Like being on a marvelously romantic date in a Scottish bookstore. As we left the hall, I hummed Sydney Carter's catchy hymn from the concert:

Dance, then, wherever you may be,
I am the Lord of the Dance, said He,

And I'll lead you all, wherever you may be,
And I'll lead you all in the Dance, said He.[6]

"Thanks for a lovely time, Dr. Restell," I said as we walked arm in arm, navigating the cobblestones.

"Elizabeth," she corrected me.

"Yes, Elizabeth." I smiled. "I especially loved the 'fish walk.' A good name for it, for being in the world and yet not of it. For braving the elements for what is elemental."

I declined her kind offer to give me a lift, wishing instead to meander back to college beneath the now clear night sky open above me like a Van Gogh painting, an oceanic swirl of stars visible above domes. The thirteenth-century Persian poet Rumi's lines floated over the ages: "Ecstatic love is an ocean, and the Milky Way is a flake of foam floating on it." The city lay dark and still. With all those fish about, however, I felt far from swimming into the deep alone. We hugged our farewell.

"Dr. Rest—I mean, Elizabeth," I said, studying her aged and—I noticed for the first time—truly exquisite face. "How *do* I walk like a fish?"

Her eyes gleamed in the streetlight. "Not walk, dear one. *Dance!*"

TRINITY TERM

TWENTY-SEVEN

CHURCH GOING

A serious house on serious earth it is,
In whose blent air all our compulsions meet,
Are recognised, and robed as destinies.
And that much never can be obsolete,
Since someone will forever be surprising
A hunger in himself to be more serious,
And gravitating with it to this ground,
Which, he once heard, was proper to grow wise in,
If only that so many dead lie round.[1]

—PHILIP LARKIN

*T*ap. *Tap. Tap.*
    The dream dissipated. I rolled over, chasing after it.
Knock. Knock. Knock.

If I pull my comforter up just so . . .

Bang! Bang! Bang!

My eyes shot open. The alarm clock gave me an accusing look, betraying me with its silence. I had overslept! It was so easy to do on a leisurely Sunday morning without the confines of tutorials or the calling of the reading rooms. I fumbled out of bed, grabbing my robe as I reached for the door.

A proper "lie in," as the Brits called it, happened rarely: most mornings you could count on your scout to knock you up, nice and early.

I better explain that one, given what flashed before my mind the first time I heard the phrase. For the Brits, *knocking you up* merely means "waking you up"; unlike in North American jargon, it owns no connotations of conception whatsoever. You can see how for a foreigner things can get lost in translation, even from English to English. For instance, Edward told me how the bursar surprised him with a visit once, causing him to madly stash a few birds under his bed. I sat there, wondering how on earth Edward managed to do that. And were they the delicate mourning doves regularly perched out back or homely pigeons from the alley? And what did he care if the bursar knew he had birds in his room anyway? I mulled that one over until I finally learned that *bird* was British slang for "girl," as "chick" is for Americans.

At Oxford, a *scout* was someone who came to clean your college room most weekday mornings. It could be a very strange experience for North American "democratic" students, used to living quite comfortably in their dorm filth. I did notice, however, that many of my fellow students, including my neighbor from Spain, thought nothing of such regular domestic help; in fact, they were quite used to it back home, for either cultural or financial reasons, or both.

I thought the world of my scout, Althea, although she had a tendency to hit the streak of rooms in my staircase with the crack of dawn. "Cleanliness is closest to godliness," she used to sing in her Austrian accent. I usually responded with an "ugh" before crawling back under my pillows.

"Caro, hurry up or we're going to be late!" I heard Linnea's voice strain through the door.

I apologized profusely as I let in her and Rachel. I threw on a few clothes, sticking my hair clumsily in a clip as I brushed my teeth and grabbed my jacket.

"Ready!" I pronounced. They both stared at me.

"What is it?" I asked. "Surely the Lord doesn't care what we look like at church."

"No," Rachel stammered, "but I think the guy seated behind you might get more out of the service than he bargained for this morning."

Linnea giggled.

I looked down. Sure enough, in my haste, the back of my skirt got tucked into my panties.

"Nice knickers, by the way," Rachel said as she helped straighten me out.

"Only the best on the Sabbath." I winked as I sashayed over to get my shoes.

❦

"Relax." Rachel put her hand on my arm as we stood in the pew, preparing to sing the next hymn.

"I can't help it. I feel so, well, so . . ."

"Idiotic?" Linnea finished my sentence.

"Yeah. Thanks." I frowned at her.

Attending church always made me feel so incompetent. When the pastor announced the Scripture reading, everyone around me seemed to open their Bibles to the correct page on the first try. Meanwhile, I would feign nonchalance while breaking a sweat, flipping through the Old and New Testaments as though creating a cartoon, all the time painfully aware of how much noise those tissue-paper pages make in the silence before the reading. Which book of the Bible followed which? What was the funky name of that prophet again? You mean, like Microsoft programs, more than one "version" exists of Samuel, Kings, Chronicles, Corinthians, Thessalonians, Timothy, Peter *and* John? Finally, in embarrassed frustration, I would have to resort to the table of contents. And by then, the reading would be over.

"This is the Word of God."

Wait, I just found the passage!

"Thanks be to God."

Oh, man!

"Amen."

Then there was the singing.

Oh yes—or, oh no—the singing.

I am one of those folks who, unfortunately, *likes* to sing, but cannot do it well. It's a terrible combination, as unrequited love is a terrible combination. My performances should be limited to a shower stall. A very private shower stall at that.

So I would rein myself in as the hymns started up, but lo and behold, I would end up losing myself in the beauty of the music, and before you knew it, I was making a not-so-joyful noise unto the Lord.

And then, because I did not grow up singing these songs,

if the lyrics failed to project on the screen, or if I did not get to the hymnal in time, I was stuck making them up. It reminded me of how the Canadian national anthem gets sung. Throw English *and* French versions into the mix, and you end up with one long monotonous mumble at the beginning of every hockey game.

To make matters worse, there was the timing and the notes to take into account. Painfully often my voice rose as the lone insertion in a pause, an awkward "over" into what should have not been "lapped."

Some people fear the sermons in church; I fear the silences.

As if the lack of biblical knowledge and of singing abilities were not enough, there was always the church etiquette to keep one reeling. When to stand? When to sit? When to politely drink the little communion cup or chew the wafer? When to applaud, and when to praise? To tithe by cash or check? To opt for a tax deduction, which means usually passing along the collection plate like a great wooden puck? Or to put something tangible in but have it lost to Caesar?

Phew! And I wasn't even Catholic.

It was time for the New Testament reading.

I gave up. I just did not have it in me—that mad scramble to find whatever number of John and to be the lone miscreant identifiable by the after-rustle.

I looked at everyone around me, worshipping so capably, singing so beautifully, flipping their Bibles open so artfully—all that confidence and familiarity taken for granted. Participating in a crowded church with the ease of a talented figure skater on an open rink.

Rachel must have heard me sigh, because she leaned in, saying, "Caro, it's okay."

"It's not okay," I lamented back. "Rachel, I have no idea what I'm doing. I'm so far behind."

"Behind what?" she asked.

I thought of my own behind, exposed by my hiked-up skirt. It seemed a sort of metaphor for me at church. I, who did not have an upbringing steeped in Sunday school or trained in the timing of genuflection. I, who did not know all the words to all the hymns, who did not know if Jacob came before Joseph, who could not keep the regions where Jesus traveled straight, who could not name all the disciples without pause. What's a *psalm*, and what's a *proverb*? Who wrote what? Who had which vision?

I, of the Great Deficiency.

I, the Exposed Church Bum.

I tried to tell Rachel but stopped. What was the use? She was one of those steeped Christians. She was strong tea; I was weak.

"Church can be intimidating"—she smiled—"but only because you haven't fully grasped grace. Once you really get that, you'll see that nothing, not even church, intimidates you any longer, or at least for very long or with any real resonance."

Hey, I thought, *she does get it!* But then I thought again, *She probably gets it because she is so well steeped. I, however, am doomed to never get it, or get most of it. To never "catch up."* I decided to risk telling her that.

"Caro!" She almost laughed out loud in the service, but then realized that I did not laugh with her. I noticed that Linnea was listening intently too. "Caro," Rachel said again, this time gently, "of course God wants our faith to season as we grow into it. And nothing takes the place of hard-earned, hard-prayed, and hard-lived wisdom. But it's not as if you're a side of beef, only making the cut if you are marinated accordingly."

"Bad image," I whispered back.

"I know you're from a cow town, well, at least sort of," she said, laughing. "So work with me here."

Memories of cow tipping did, in all fairness, low into my mind.

The pastor started reading from 1 John 4:12, saying, "If we love one another, God lives in us and his love is made complete in us."

"Here," Rachel said kindly as she set her open Bible across both our laps. I breathed a sigh of relief. We stood up together. Rachel threaded her arm through mine and hugged it tight. Linnea smiled at me.

In spite of not knowing all the words, in spite of being out of tune, I sang.

***

"For me," Rachel explained at the coffee hour after service, "I chose St. Ebbe's as my home church because the gospel was taught with all due respect and care, and yet it was apparent that the congregation was having fun. The sermons were not just about love and peace, like dotting your *i*'s with hearts whenever you wrote. There existed an appropriate emphasis, I thought, on much of the hard stuff, like sin and consequence, accountability, the relevance of spiritual discipline, and the rules needed to direct the flow of traffic, so to speak, to optimize all that life has to offer. But there was plenty of room for celebration too."

She took a sip of her coffee. "To put it simply, I guess, it's because I found that the people here, for the most part, take the gospel seriously without taking themselves too seriously."

None of the snacks laid out appealed, I inwardly complained. But then, empty paper plate in hand, it suddenly occurred to me that perhaps I had been so picky in trying to find the "right fit" in a church because I wanted church to fill *me*? Yes, if I were honest, I wanted to be thus *serviced*.

"Churches are far from perfect, as fallible institutions, consisting of fallible people, in a fallible world," Rachel conceded. "But when they do work, there is nothing like them. There is no greater high than experiencing the love of God in action among His people, for His people, and for the world."

It occurred to me, too, that, like Aesop's famed tale of pleasing the masses, the same can be said of those attending church. There is no way of pleasing all of the people all of the time.

People go to church, get disappointed, and go back out. Church *going*. This great impulse in ourselves is to visit church, to want to *go to* church, and yet church is disappearing from our lives. Why?

I thought of my mom, who has always held that she prefers Mass in Latin. It's so beautiful, I agree, but no one can understand it. Different generations flock to different service styles. Old folks are mortified at an electric guitar shuddering out "Amazing Grace," or the kid with long hair pounding out a psalm on the drums. Young folks fed a steady diet of television, video games, and special effects complain that church is not hip enough, not cool enough, because the entertainment does not come fast or furious enough. Married folks don't attend because they cannot agree on which denomination to choose. A Presbyterian at a Baptist service might be disappointed by the swallow of grape juice from the communion cup, preferring instead a fine oak-barrel aged port. A Baptist might be disappointed at the Presbyterian being satisfied with only a sprinkling of baptism water (let alone on an infant's head).

One of my friends was taken aback when she saw that the communion host consisted of crushed saltines. "Why didn't they just bless some goldfish crackers from the nursery and pass those around?" she sniffed. *Hmmm*, I thought, *not a bad idea, actually. I like the cheese-nip to goldfish, and it'd be symbolic as well as kind of cute.*

Other complaints rumble on and on, like a cement truck full of preferences. Church administrations spin countless plates to keep the mix of demands from setting. Tennessee Ernie Ford's deep voice rolled through my head: "Sixteen tons and what do you get?"[2] A church full of options but no one happy yet.

No wonder churches were spent.

<hr/>

After returning to college I decided to sit down at my desk and make up my own church shopping list. Strangely that old diurnal paradox raised its head again.

As I listed (quite self-congratulatorily, thank you very much) my social justice awarenesses, followed by my developing theological stances, followed by my service predilections, followed by my architectural preferences, followed by my . . .

Something suddenly became very clear as I went back over the list, reviewing things. Everything mattered, and yet nothing did, except the Great Truth. So when I struck items from the page one by one, only one thing was left.

Yes, all else canceled around it raised into relief the remaining item, the only item with the power, in turn, to cancel out the absurdity of merely growing "another day older and deeper in debt."[3] The only item that filled up—essentially overcame—what I had given up on as insurmountable: My Great Deficiency.

Church, it became clear, should "service" first and foremost one thing: Christ.

It seemed to me that where we gather thus in Him, there fulfilling fellowship blooms.

TWENTY-EIGHT

LOOKING FOR THE
LOCH NESS MONSTER

But Mousie, thou art no thy lane,
In proving foresight may be vain:
The best laid schemes o' mice an' men
Gang aft agley,
An' lea'e us nought but grief an' pain,
For promis'd joy!
Still thou are blest, compared wi' me!
The present only toucheth thee:
But och! I backward cast my e'e,
On prospects drear!
An' forward, tho' I canna see,
I guess an' fear![1]

—ROBERT BURNS

331

I have nothing to wear!" Her wail reached me across the arrival crowds before her hug. After scrimping and saving together for her airfare, our train tickets, and a modest lodging budget, my sister arrived at Heathrow Airport in a whirlwind of drama: her luggage lost, she was in a panic about being prepared for her first big trip overseas. "Essentials" for my sister involves coordinating accessories. Travel-tossed, Kelly looked gorgeous nonetheless with her thick mane of hair crowning a gymnast figure. My sister is one of those women who would look good in a paper bag. It would be nauseating, if she was not so much fun.

We laughed the entire train ride up to Inverness, drinking hot chocolate and eating cookies while threading north, hodgepodging schedules together because of the various train strikes. The picturesque hills of England rolled behind us; before us, the sublime, moody mountains of Scotland loomed. We talked the entire way as only sisters can, relishing every moment together.

But we both knew that the real reason for our trip was to hunt down the Loch Ness monster! Yep, the supposedly fictitious monster that lurks deep in the lochs of Northern Scotland. The entire concept strangely riveted my otherwise pragmatic sister.

We checked in at a local bed-and-breakfast late that night, stuffing ourselves with pizza from a pub, followed by chocolate-caramel shortbread and endless cups of tea. In the morning we awoke to bagpipes playing outside our window. We walked into town and got in the queue (or how the Brits refer to a "line") for the tour bus to take us to the Loch Ness Monster museum and guided tour of the lake. Yep, again, there is indeed such a museum, an entire collection devoted to the study of this elusive creature. My sister could not wait.

Conscious of her hair in the misty morning, Kelly asked the bus driver whether there were any umbrellas to be had.

"Luv," he replied matter-of-factly, "if you donnae like the weather, wait a minute."

Sure enough, the sun broke through by the time we reached the museum. We joined the gaggle of tourists pouring out onto the meadow by the waiting boat. Various posters at the site read,

A REWARD OF 1000 POUNDS
FOR VERIFIABLE PROOF OF THE
LOCH NESS MONSTER

Kelly's jaw dropped. "Did you see that? Actual money, and a lot of it, too, for evidence of something that doesn't even exist."

"If it doesn't exist, why were you so excited to come here?" I teased her.

"Well, of course it doesn't exist. But if it does, I'll find it, and I'll make a fortune proving so," she replied, undeterred.

If anyone could spot such an evasive sea monster, let alone draw it out, it would be my sirenesque sister.

We climbed onto the weathered deck of a rickety cruiser. I suspect, like most countries, Scotland maintains a love-hate relationship with tourists. Let's just say I did not feel too confident in the boat. Kel, however, loved every minute. Noting my discomfort, she began humming "The Wreck of the Edmund Fitzgerald." I whacked her with the tourist pamphlet.

Kelly spent the entire cruise with her eyes fixed on the water.

"It's so murky," she complained. "How can anybody *see* anything?" she asked the tour guide. Dollar signs reflected in her eyes as she continued to scan the loch.

"Yeah, it's all the peat. It makes the water appear almost black," the guide explained.

"I was so sure we'd see it." Kelly cuddled the little stuffed sea monster she had bought at the museum.

"You had your retirement entirely planned, eh?" I laughed.

"Seriously, I'd like to ask it a few questions," she persisted.

"Like what? It's a monster, Kel, not 'Puff, the Magic Dragon.'" I started crooning Peter, Paul, and Mary. I couldn't help myself.

Ignoring my singing (no easy feat), she began: "Questions like, why have you gone around scaring people for centuries? Why do you live in such inaccessibility? Why do you let people doubt your existence? Just how powerful are you? And what is it you do all day?" She pretended to address her stuffed sea monster, which did resemble more of a friendly dragon than a leviathan.

"Good questions." I laughed again, but then stopped and looked at her. She wasn't laughing.

"What's up, Kel?" I asked gently.

"Who is this God, this God you were looking for? Or who you said is looking for you?" She tossed me her little dragon. "Now that you have found each other, now what?"

"I'm still figuring that one out," I replied, catching her toss. "I've started going to church . . ."

"No, no, that's not what I mean. Lots of people go to church." She shook her head. "I mean, I want to know Him, too, I think, but I'm afraid. I'm afraid of what I will discover. About Him. About me."

"Yeah, me too," I confessed.

"And what's worse? Or better? To discover He *is* there? Or to discover He's *not*? And then there's the fact that there is no reward for that search . . ." Her voice grew soft.

"Well, that's debatable." I smiled at her.

"True." She smiled back. Then she grew serious again. "Carolyn, I want a better life."

"Who doesn't?"

"But you don't understand. You've left home. You've left it all. And you know what you want to be, where you want to go, what you want to do. You have it so together. You are so, well, *free*. I am trying to deal all alone with Mom and Dad and school and Jason and with, well, everything . . ." she petered off.

"I know. It's messy." I sighed.

"Yeah. Did I ever tell you that when I was very little, I dreamt of Jason saving me from a burning house?" Kelly mentioned. I loved my sister's boyfriend, Jason, like a brother, and with all the adoration and annoyance that comes along with loving a brilliant, stubborn, sweet, highly organized younger brother. We had known each other since childhood, he and my sister secretly sharing a mutual crush. He moved away; then we did. Unexpectedly reunited as teenagers, their love, still there, now publicly tumbled forth. My fondness for Jason had long been a rare certitude, given that no one was good enough for my sister. But he was.

"What about hell?" Kelly suddenly shot across the bow at me.

"What about it?" I tried dodging one question with another. I knew what she was asking; it plagued me too. A monster of a question. A monster-shaped question mark. A proudly arched neck poised over murky waters. The rest submerged in obscurity.

"Well," I began, "I think—"

"Despair must be hell," Kelly interjected thoughtfully. She often finishes my sentences.

"Yes, I believe forgetting about God, whether one chooses to or has failed to be reminded, must be hell."

"And so must deciding to become a believer, when those

you love don't believe yet, or never will," she said, looking directly at me.

I took a breath, and then said all I felt I could say: "Kel, sometimes I feel that the waters of my soul are as dark as these peat-infested waters. That the monsters lurking there are of my own making."

I leaned over and touched the water from the side of our boat. Ripples spread out from my fingertips. Resting in the boat, I thought of Father Pierre Teilhard de Chardin's plea:

> I pray, O Master,
> That the flames of hell
> May not touch me
> Or any of those whom I love,
> And even that they may never touch anyone.
> (And I know, my God,
> that you will forgive this bold prayer.)[2]

How can heaven be heaven without those I love most in it? What if this question plagues God too? And yet what if He's already answered it for us?

"Everyone who calls on the name of the LORD will be saved" (Joel 2:32).

Every one.

TWENTY-NINE

MISS GEORGIA

> *Whenas in silks my Julia goes,*
> *Then, then, methinks, how sweetly flows*
> *That liquefaction of her clothes.*
> *Next, when I cast mine eyes and see*
> *That brave vibration each way free;*
> *O how that glittering taketh me!*[1]
>
> —ROBERT HERRICK

It was a seemingly ordinary day, like any other day in term. In the cramped common graduate kitchen, I hunched over my simmering pot of the student diet staple, stirring salt into the water for my instant ramen noodles. Gavin balanced on the windowsill of the tiny, shared kitchen, reading a newspaper. A gourmand, Gavin muttered without looking up, "You really should pick up some sea salt instead of using that pathetic table salt. And you shouldn't stir it so much, or it will take longer to boil. Remember, 'A watched pot never boils.'"

"A watched pot never boils *over*," I sniffed back, handing him one of my mom's proverbs. Gavin peered at me over the fashion section and then rattled his paper in indignation. I stuck my tongue out at him once his face set behind the paper.

"I saw that," he said without lifting the paper.

"What?" I pretended innocence.

"It's one of my superhuman powers, my X-ray vision," he said, keeping a serious face.

"Thank goodness I don't own that one." I smirked at him. "I'm still trying to get your Tasmanian Devil out of my mind."

Gavin jumped off the windowsill with a flourish. "Come on," he said as he tried to sweep me up in a waltz, "just admit it. You're hot for me."

"Gavin," I said, trying to return to my needy noodles, "you're gay."

"Yes, but that doesn't preclude your being hot for me."

"True. Okay, I will admit there is a certain ease about being in your presence."

"All women need a gay man. It's like having a courtly lover. All the attention with none of the strings, gorgeous." He nuzzled into my shoulder. I let him do it; he did just call me gorgeous, after all. "It's a sort of relief, I think, at not being pursued," he whispered into my ear.

"Like an object of prey," I laughed. "True. It's always easy cooking for you, because I know you don't expect dessert, if you know what I mean."

"Speaking of dessert . . ." Gavin's voice trailed off. I sprinkled the packaged seasoning into the pot and then looked up from my noodles, curious as to the cause of his sudden silence.

When I looked over at Gavin's face, it was frozen, like a Renaissance angel's in admiration. He was staring at the doorway behind me.

That's when I first saw her. Or I should say, when I first *heard* her. Jingling caught my ear, and I turned my head toward the sound.

She stood tall, blonde, and magnificent. Everything about her seemed larger-than-life, except her weight, which was like sand distributed perfectly throughout a thin hourglass. Big hair. Big earrings. Big dimples. Big, white, wealthy American teeth. Big Louis Vuitton purse. Forget smuggling a Chihuahua; the bag could have housed a police dog. Mile-long legs emerged from a Chanel minidress, culminating in four-inch-high Manolo Blahniks.

Gavin and I stood together, gaping at this wonder of nature. At the bling of it all.

She extended a hand doused in rings at the end of a perfectly toned arm; three large, gold bangles jangled as she announced in a drawl that dripped honey, "You must be Carolyn. Caro, if I may? I've heard all about you!"

I moaned inwardly. Was I really that easily identifiable? Feeling more dismayed than complimented at this warm greeting from a stranger, I felt suddenly self-consciously unshowered, in my broth-splattered ratty T-shirt and my torn, old sweats.

Her big earrings clinked in the silence as she looked down at my bare feet and chipped toenail polish. She cleared her throat politely as her gaze returned to my face. She smiled brightly.

Gavin stepped forward and thrust his hand into one of her outstretched, waiting ones, introducing himself. More jingling and jangling. He knocked me out of my stupor with an elbow to my spine.

I pitched forward. "Hello," I managed to mutter.

Then the peach dropped.

Oh, I thought. *This is* her. *This is who TDH mentioned in passing.* The blind date who was flying out to meet him. The absolutely perfectly accomplished godly virgin from that first fateful e-mail, I imagined. Regardless, TDH had told me that his and this beauty queen's parents had since become good friends, and they were up to a little matchmaking.

Alas, this was her—Miss Georgia—in all her Southern glory . . . to my Northern discomfort.

I nervously patted my greasy ponytail. Did I put on deodorant after staying up all night to finish that paper? I could not remember.

"Caro!" My name traveled toward me on a waft of expensive perfume. Modern stilettos dimpled the ancient wooden floor as she reached to embrace me like a long-lost friend. Instinctively I tucked in my toes.

Nope, forgot the deodorant, I thought despondently as I raised my arms to hug her back.

❦

Miss Georgia joined us, politely refusing the delicious bowl of ramen noodles I offered her. I sat and simmered with my own bowl as she and Gavin hit it off. Gavin pulled out a chair for her (something he had never done for me in dozens of meals together), and she parked her haute couture nicely at the table. He poured her a glass of wine (one from his own collection, not one from the graduate stock made up of the 50p sale at Odd

Bins) and then started asking her a million questions about her public relations job, her pageant duties, her book signings, and her television appearances.

"How *do* you manage it all?" he cooed, leaning on one elbow and gazing at her like a lovesick poodle.

"Well, I'll admit," she purred back, "it surely does get a bit hectic here and there. Why, just last week I barely had a smidgen of time to myself, what with completing the marathon and then traveling with my father to speak to the troops."

I tried to stifle my choking. I did not want a noodle to come out of my nose. That had happened before whenever my sister got me to laughing too hard while eating soup.

Miss Georgia talked about her father's heroic actions in war and his utter devotion to their family. She talked about her mother's own modeling career, followed now by her invincible efforts for veterans and related talk show appearances. She talked about her sister's marriage to a leading athlete and her excitement over becoming an auntie soon. She talked about how much she was looking forward to spending time with TDH, who she thought was "the cutest boy ever" and getting to sightsee Oxford with him (in high heels, nonetheless). She talked about this being her first trip to England.

She talked and she talked and she talked.

Apparently she was quite the pageant winner. I could see Gavin salivating at getting all the details.

Please, Gavin, I begged to myself, *please don't ask her . . .*

But Gavin dropped the gavel anyway.

"What did you do for the talent section?" He leaned in, gently pushing against her.

"Oh, y'all don't wanna hear about it," she playfully pushed back.

"Yes, oh please. Do tell!" Gavin blinked his doe eyes back at her, captivated. "Which of your many talents did you choose to showcase? I can only imagine how difficult it was to select from such an array!"

"Well, my goodness, aren't you just the sweetest thaaaannngg!" she honeyed on him. Gavin shuddered with delight. I was afraid he might just roll over on the table and ask her to rub his belly. He did look ready to climb into that Louis Vuitton and go home with her.

"Well," she started teasingly, "if you insist. I know this might sound silly . . ."

"No, no. Try me. Carolyn, aren't you dying to know?" Gavin took each of our hands in his and held them up together over the table. With a mouth full of noodles, I managed a nod.

Miss Georgia paused for dramatic effect.

"I sang 'The Star Spangled Banner'!" she squealed with delight.

"No!" Gavin dropped my hand and took up her other free one. For someone who boasted X-ray vision, I was surprised he could be so obtuse.

"I swear!" She put their hands over her heart. "Every American's favorite, and no new words to memorize. Kind of a sneaky choice." She winked.

"How . . ." Gavin struggled to find the right word.

"Patriotic," I slurped through my soup.

Gavin stood up with zeal. "Oh, God bless you!" He pulled her to her feet and hugged her passionately. Then he sat back down and wiped a tear from his eye.

Miss Georgia looked at her TAG Heuer. "My, my. Talking with y'all friendly folk here, I lost track of the time. I'm supposed to meet that good-lookin' host of mine. Have either of you seen 'im? I was hoping to see 'im in the lodge, but a nice man sitting at the desk there in a funny little hat directed me up to his room. I tried to follow his directions as best I could, but I'm afraid I'm lost." She blinked her made-up green eyes at me, all the wider with questioning.

"His room is right across the hall," I said, pointing the way.

"Oh, goody!" She giggled. "I did arrive a bit earlier than anticipated, so I suppose I will just go knock and surprise him. Or, how do the Brits put it . . . shall I go *knock him up*?" She giggled again. Gavin laughed excessively. Those antennae on his *gaydar* seemed pretty bent to me.

She stood up, all a-tinkling.

"Oh, must you go?" Gavin pulled her chair back and stood up with her.

"You heard her, Gavin." I smiled tightly. "She has plans for the afternoon, and we'd best not hold her back any longer." I stepped aside in the tiny kitchen to let her pass, quoting Jane Austen: "You have delighted us long enough," I sang out sweetly, convinced more than ever that dead authors really do make the best friends.

"Lovely to meet y'all." She smiled as she clickitty clacked by. A moment later I heard her knock on TDH's door, followed by his voice in delighted (alas, much too delighted) response. I waited until I heard the door shut and, sadly, lock.

"I thought you were supposed to be gay," I hissed at Gavin.

"I'm gay, Caro, not dead. Besides, that makes me all the more the connoisseur," Gavin shot back. Then he whistled. "My, my, she *is* something, isn't she?"

"Yes," I had to admit. Why was I so ticked at my universe having been disturbed by this peach?

"That was quite the sightseeing getup," I commented. I wanted to add, *I hope she twists her ankle on a wayward cobble-stone*, but I refrained.

Gavin perched back on the windowsill, ruminating. "Stilettos throw your hips forward." He rubbed his chin with his hand. "A throwback to evolutionary gesticulation."

I threw him a confused look, but he continued.

"Look! Here! I am tilting toward you. I have childbearing hips! I am fertile, hear me roar!"

"Gavin, as usual, I have no idea what you're talking about."

"Who would have guessed?" Gavin started chuckling. "I always thought of him as such a quiet theology student, but I guess still waters do run deep."

"Whatever do you mean?" I finally took the bait.

"Miss Star Spangled has on her banner, and it *ain't* just con-geniality she's going for, Caro. She means business." He put his hand on his hip and thrust it at me. "Girlllll," he drawled, "she's here to catch a husband."

Gavin looked at me kindly, as though he could see into me. I twisted uncomfortably on my seat, feeling a bunch of emotions that weren't, well, very *Christian*. I began to wonder if Gavin owned X-ray vision after all.

"Are you serious?" I finally asked feebly.

"Stiletto serious." He put his arm around me, without a care that I had not showered.

Something deep inside me shuddered, and it was not the ramen noodles.

THIRTY

BALD IN THE
LAND OF BIG HAIR

> *I made my song a coat*
> *Covered with embroideries*
> *Out of old mythologies*
> *From heel to throat;*
> *But the fools caught it,*
> *Wore it in the world's eyes*
> *As though they'd wrought it.*
> *Song, let them take it,*
> *For there's more enterprise*
> *In walking naked.*[1]
>
> —WILLIAM BUTLER YEATS

So"—Linnea began with that curious lilt in her voice she always has when she's about to embark on some juicy campus gossip—"have you heard the latest about Dr. Condorston?"

Weaving through the crowd, I shook my head. Although I had not heard, I was sure it had to do with "inappropriate behavior" of some kind with an adoring undergraduate.

"It seems he suffered some sort of breakdown," she said.

"What?" Surely I could not have heard her correctly over the jubilant street noise. It was May Morning. For centuries members of both town and gown throng to High Street and Magdalen Bridge to listen to the choristers sing from the top of Magdalen tower after the bells chime six in the morning. Dancers and street performers tumbled through the crowds. Children arrayed in flowers paraded about with walking sticks and homemade wreaths. By now the revelers were beginning to disperse to champagne breakfasts, punting, and picnics. Linnea and I decided to pick up breakfast sandwiches and head behind Merton College, where we could rest against the city wall and watch many of the continued celebrations in Christ Church meadow and along the Cherwell.

She repeated herself louder.

I stopped in my tracks; as a result, a stampede of students with champagne glasses rushed past me, like rapids around a flooded tree.

"It was a meltdown, or whatever you might call it," Linnea threw over her shoulder as she continued to thread her way ahead. "Apparently he stopped dead in the middle of his lecture last week, shaking his head and mumbling over and over again about how he couldn't 'do this anymore,' and then he walked out. Just like that. His thesis students are pretty panicked. My housemate is one of them. They're scared to death at being left high and dry before their defense."

"Where is he now?" I managed to break free, following Linnea's flowing and flowered hair as a beacon. Linnea always dressed dramatically and relevantly for an occasion, like an actress for a part. Today she looked like a Grecian statue draped in Midsummer Eve attire: in a billowing dress of verdant silk and capped with a mass of blossoms, she floated amid the crowd like a solstice vision.

"He's living on a farm out in the middle of nowhere. He apparently resigned his position, at least for a while, claiming he wants to live off the land, alone with just his wife and kids, for a while. To sort things out. To find himself." We stood at the intersection with the masses stopped as if by a dam, waiting for the light to change.

"Rumor also has it," Linnea continued as we began walking again, "that he's writing a treatise against postmodernism and its unraveling of meaning."

"Really?" I could barely believe it. On second thought—I smiled to myself—perhaps I should exclaim, *Absolutely!*

A bicycle whipped by, so close it almost clipped Linnea's dress in its spokes. "Hey, watch out for the goddess!" a tipsy undergraduate roared from behind us as the cyclist dinged his bell in apology.

"Thank you." Linnea looked back at her defender demurely. He continued to follow us, puppy-eyed.

Poor thing, I thought. But I was used to Linnea acquiring admirers as a child does pretty marbles; I would be surprised if there was not an entire train of glass allies behind us by the time we reached Merton.

Linnea continued to rattle on about other Oxford gossip;

there was always plenty. I tried listening, but soon she must have noticed my distraction.

"Caro, what is it?" she asked as we waited in the queue for our sandwiches.

"Oh, I'm just tired of gossip, I guess." I shrugged. Linnea seemed affronted, so I hurried on. "Oh, Linnea, it's nothing personal. It's just that I've already had enough of an earful, and an eyeful, come to think of it, for one day." I then told her about how Althea had knocked me up even earlier than the crack of dawn this morning. I didn't mind her starting the vacuum that much, given that I wanted to get up anyway to join friends at the Magdalen tower singing. But it was what she said as she emptied my garbage that made me bolt straight up in bed.

"Well, have a look right there, why don't you?" Althea marveled. "There's that tall, good-looking American lad, turned out early and seeming very dapper, too, if I may say so! It must be that beauty of the bird who's perched on his arm."

I almost stuck my foot in the dust bin on my sprint to the window.

There, down below in Magpie Lane . . . my heart dropped at the sight. TDH walking arm in arm with Miss Georgia, her laughter punctuating whatever it was he was saying to her, and saying to her quite animatedly. Her smart summer dress accented her tanned, athletic body; her hair flawlessly upswept to reveal the nape of her graceful neck. The click of Jimmy Choos echoed on the cobblestones.

"They seem to be having a lovely time during her visit," Althea called out cheerily as she cleaned the bathroom. "I heard through the grapevine that it may be quite serious. It seems their parents set them up . . . She obviously traveled quite a distance to come meet him." Scouring out the toilet, she started singing "It Had to Be You," flipping in and out of German, Austrian, and English.

Pressed against the glass, I tried to move but couldn't. Sitting like a cormorant on my window ledge, high above these happy two, I watched them below, unaware. A Miltonic satanic voyeur who wanted to care less, but who could not help caring: "Sight hateful, sight tormenting! Thus these two / Imparadised in one another's arms."[2]

It was the sight of TDH that pained me the most. Actually it was the sight of his new sweater. His chiseled shoulders rippled like a tiger's through the expensive fabric.

Something welled up in me that worried me greatly. I could not tell if that something was the new sweater, or her perfection, or the sight of them together, or the sight of them together so obviously enjoying each other's company, or if it was all of these things. Or if that something was the worry itself.

"He never wears anything new!" I almost yelled at Althea, thinking of how TDH could barely afford groceries. Prompted by compassion for a grumbling stomach while studying, I had taken him a bagful from the market once, as a friendly gesture, out of my own scholarship budget.

"He rarely matches his socks!" One of my first convincing signs that even though he lived next to Gavin and they cooked together in their staircase kitchen, TDH (to Gavin's great disappointment) was not gay.

"Well, they certainly look lovely this May Morning!" Althea remarked in her von Trapp singsong voice.

If this guy did not mean anything to me romantically, if we were not more than friends, why did the sight of him with this *perfect Christian girl* bother me so?

Suddenly, I felt like a cigarette butt squashed under the dirty heel of life.

Fa, a long, long way to run, I thought sadly.

⁂

"You did what?" Linnea practically shrieked as she unwrapped her sandwich.

We were sitting with our backs against the sun-warmed wall outside Merton College. A picturesque array of blossoms, cows, and drunk undergraduates spread out before us in the Meadow.

"I lent her my hair dryer. She came to my room, asking to borrow my hair dryer, since she had forgotten to pack a volt exchanger. So I gave her mine."

"You gave the enemy *ammunition*?" Linnea asked again, in reproachful disbelief.

"I lent her my hair dryer and trusted in the providence of God," I replied with mustered holy confidence.

Linnea glanced at the punters on the Cherwell and then back at me. "Caro, you might want to remember that old Russian proverb . . ."

"Which one?" I asked with a mouth full of ham and cheese.

She passed me a napkin. "Pray to God, but keep rowing to shore."

⁂

A few weeks after I became a Christian, Linnea and I sat in this exact spot, memorizing Keats while discussing preparations for our massive spring papers on Wordsworth and Coleridge.

"What are two such lovely ladies doing out here," a deep voice rose from behind, "adding to the beauty of a spring day, and yet heads bowed and backs bent over books, books, and more books?" In the blink of an eye, TDH swung down from the wall, sprinkling wildflowers at our feet. "Mad handfuls, not bouquets, girls!" he laughed. Irritated at my concentration being interrupted by flattery, I resumed my studying. Linnea, however, collected the flowers and began weaving them into my hair.

"Come on, I have an idea!" TDH roared with glee, pulling Linnea to her feet.

I sat there, looking up at them. "What on earth . . . ?" I gasped, once I fully comprehended what he was wearing. There stood TDH, dressed head to foot in punting attire from the last century. White pin-striped suit complete with a crisp bow tie, and yes, even a gentleman's straw hat.

"Don't ask." He put a finger to his lips. With TDH I was slowly learning not to ask. He had all sorts of tricks up his striped sleeve.

With much poking and prodding, the two of them finally convinced me to pack up my work. I wandered behind them as they ran ahead down the path like excited children, their feet crackling on the gravel.

TDH pointed to a little boat docked expectantly nearby, and said, "Come on, get in!"

"Oh, look!" Linnea squealed with delight, and she climbed over the side. "Caro, he's thought of everything! There's even champagne, strawberries, and cream in here!"

The boat rocked dangerously with Linnea's enthusiasm.

I arched my brows at TDH as I climbed deftly in, grateful for all that canoeing experience as a Canadian. "What are you up to?" I leveled at him. "You know it's almost finals time for spring papers." I scolded him as if he were some errant child, hiding my real distrust under a pedantic charade.

"It's spring!" he sang. "Time to celebrate all that is beautiful, all that is to the glory of God! All that is *Love!*" He drew out the last syllable with a French accent, invoking the cartoon skunk Pepé Le Pew. "Besides, we haven't properly commemorated your conversion yet. Hence the champagne," he said as he popped it open, pouring our glasses to overflowing. "To Caro's new life in Christ!" He clinked our glasses, downed his drink, and then pushed us off with his pole from shore.

Linnea giggled. "Amen," she said, adding, "Gee, maybe I should become a Christian too."

"Worth some thought." TDH winked at her.

We spent the afternoon making lazy circles in the peaceful water, sharing poetry and discussing things great and small—an afternoon of glorious everythings and nothings.

TDH did all the hard work, maneuvering the pole while balancing in the boat, thus allowing us ladies to luxuriate in our flower-wreathed, lazy languor. Drifting past numerous colleges and fields, we experienced more of the beauty of a quintessential "Oxford day" than if we had spent it in our static studying. As we passed other happy punters, we shouted our favorite lines from Keats across the water in poetic greeting. TDH read a poem he brought specifically for Linnea about Petrarch's dark-haired love; he then presented an anonymous one for me on a golden-haired lady. We floated along in high spirits.

"Ah, *la belle dame sans merci*," he said to me, again in his Pepé Le Pew voice. Linnea laughed and looked away. He then repeated Keats's words, directly at me, softly, seriously.

My heart stopped in spite of myself. My initial, "I have been half in love with easeful Death," becoming "That I might drink, and leave the world unseen, / And with thee fade away into the forest dim."[3]

> *Was it a vision, or a waking dream?*
> *Fled is that music: Do I wake or sleep?*[4]

"I'm moving this weekend," I told her as we made our way back to college. It had all happened quite to my surprise. St. Peter's, another Oxford college, offered me a position as a welfare officer with some undergraduate teaching for the fall. My dorm room contract at Oriel would run out by the end of Trinity term, and my new room in St. Peter's wouldn't be ready until Michaelmas. Fortunately, for the interim, St. Peter's provided me with temporary lodging in a large and beautiful house shared with one other Junior Research Fellow just outside the central bustle of the city on St. Margaret's Road. I liked walking from one world into another along Woodstock and Banbury Roads, passing from the stony colleges and busy shops out to the quieter, more residential neighborhoods of majestic old houses.

"Yes, so?" Linnea said distractedly. She was trying to decide whether to stop for dessert or not.

"I haven't seen him. He hasn't even offered any help. In fact I don't even know if he's noticed I'm going. Linnea, I doubt he's noticed *anything* since she's been here," I whined, drawing out the final complaint most pathetically.

Linnea replied very rationally. "I'm sure he's busy, with finals, his parents in town, yes, even this girl visiting. He probably feels pressured to entertain her, regardless of how he feels about her. Have you outright asked him for his help?"

"I would die first," I cried dramatically. "He knows I'm moving; I told him so. He should be able to *infer* that I could use the help."

"Aren't like, oh, another fifteen or so men helping you?" Linnea inquired coyly.

"That's just a fact of life, if you're a woman at a place like Oxford," I insisted. "And those guys are all lovely, and thoughtful, and good friends. But it's just so annoying, that, well . . ."

"That all of them offered, except that one you wanted most to care?" Linnea finished my sentence.

I did not say anything. I hate it when she does that. She is like my sister that way.

"Why don't you two just admit you're in love with each other?" Her question flattened me.

"What?" I stammered.

"Seriously. It's so obvious. And so pathetic. And so darling. And so, well, *romantic* . . ." She sighed.

"I am *not* in love with him, Linnea," I argued. "He's so, well, so *different* from me. Besides, while I respect him, and he has helped me immensely in my spiritual walk, he drives me crazy."

"Why?" She gave me a playful push. "Because he's not afraid of you? Because he's gentle and kind, but he doesn't bow down to your usual alienating escapades?"

"Well, now, isn't that the pot calling the kettle black?" I shot back.

"But I have an excuse," Linnea sniffed, adjusting the flowers in her hair in a shop window. "I'm still doing it because I haven't found a man who can deflect it yet. Nor deflect it so gracefully, and with such sincere care for the source." She gave my image a playful glance.

Then she peered closer into the window. "Hey!" she called out. "Look!" She responded to a reflection behind her reflection. "Listen!" She swung around.

Linnea pointed across the High, waving wildly in return at another figure waving wildly. I squinted. TDH came into view, leaning dangerously out of his window above the little map shop.

"He's trying to get your attention, Caro." Linnea grabbed my hand, forcing me to raise it and wave back. "Come on, toss the man a crumb."

"Linnea, I don't want to hear what he has to say." I turned to her. "If he didn't have time for me when *she* was here, then I don't have any time for him at all."

I feigned the impossibility of not being able to hear TDH's thunderous American accent across the busy street. But that didn't work for long, as Linnea obviously could hear him well enough that she had no trouble responding.

She stood at the edge of the curb, asking him with loud innocence over the traffic how his visit with Miss Georgia went. I felt my face go hot, and turned back to the shop window, pretending to study something of great interest on sale. Unfortunately, it was men's clothing. In the reflection I saw TDH lean out even more precariously, yelling at Linnea how Miss Georgia had left very early that morning for the airport, so he accompanied her to the bus terminal before the festivities began. He seemed annoyingly jovial.

"Come on, Caro." She tugged at me. "Say *something* to him. He's obviously so happy to see you!"

"Yeah, now that one bird has flown out of town, he's ready

for the next," I said glumly. "No way! Tell him I have a sore throat and can't yell."

TDH shouted that his parents were still in town, and would I like to join them for dinner tonight? I shrugged and told Linnea to tell him that I had plans the rest of the week. She yelled back that I would be delighted. I hit her arm, hard.

"Leave Caro a message in the lodge as to the details," Linnea directed, giving him a final wave. TDH's face lit up as he pulled himself back into the window. A moment later a man and a woman, presumably his parents, peered out the open window, waving with delight. I recognized their faces from the photo. They looked so kind and so genuinely friendly that I felt my heart twinge at wanting to meet them. I wondered, *Maybe there is some way I can dine with them, without him? Or would that be too awkward?*

Linnea kissed both my cheeks as she left me outside Oriel. "Have fun tonight!" she chirped, all artlessness.

On my way into the lodge, I bumped into Philip, who, of all people, appeared startlingly sober on May Morning.

"Wow, who's the Southern babe paying theology-man a visit?" he asked, looking at me shrewdly. I informed him that she was a former Miss Georgia.

"I really love your peaches, wanna shake your tree," Philip sang in falsetto as he picked up his mail. I hit him hard on the arm too.

The porter chuckled behind me. "Yes, luv, did you hear that this Miss Georgia blew a fuse and put the entire MCR block in darkness? Seems she was using a hair dryer and—"

"Did she get to style her hair?" I interrupted.

"What, miss?" He looked confused.

"Her hair. Did you notice if her hair looked nice or not?" I was silently hoping that the hair dryer had blown *before* rather than *after* she had finished styling her hair.

"I didn't really notice, luv." He smiled dreamily. "She's such a stunner it wouldn't matter."

I sighed.

"Besides, can't say I was looking much at her hair anyway." He grinned with his tongue in his cheek.

Bah, humbug, I thought. *So much for Christian charity.*

There was her lifelong faith. And her perfect family and pedigree. And then her looks. And then her wardrobe. And then her poise, and pageant banners, and her knowledge of American politics. And then, that hair.

Oh yeah, and one more thing. Actually, two. I looked down at my chest.

So much for a level playing field, I thought miserably.

It was like looking into the feminine form of TDH's face. Her eyes the same color, dancing with the same light. I reached over the papadums, or Indian appetizer wafers, to shake her hand.

"We've been so excited to meet you." TDH's mother smiled warmly.

Wow, I thought, *she's even more beautiful than Miss Georgia*.

Indeed, her deep-blue outfit, which brought out her dark hair and eyes, was accented elegantly with just the right kind and amount of jewelry. She appeared class personified. This first impression was only confirmed when she opened her mouth.

"Come," she called out warmly, patting the chair next to her.

"Sit and rest. Sounds like it's been quite a season for you, and we can't wait to hear all about it!"

For the rest of the meal, she barely spoke of herself; her questions were all about me. More than offering polite attention, she obviously shone with genuine interest in others. I gut-liked her. And I instantly knew that my own mom, a fellow classy lady, would gut-like her too.

TDH had taken the liberty of ordering appetizers; we all shared a love of Indian food, which is terrifically authentic and plentiful in England. So deciding to meet at Jamal's restaurant was easy. I warned him I would probably run late, having to walk all the way into the Jericho district of town after my tutorial.

"You gotta love these names," I commented as I hurried to set down my schoolbag while TDH's father took my coat. *Imagine having dinner in a restaurant in* Jericho *with the man most influential in my conversion, and the ones responsible for his impact,* I mused to myself. *Talk about the rippling out of legacy!* "I just came from New College," I said to the table. "It's a funny name once you realize it happens to date from the fourteenth century."

"Only in Oxford." TDH's father laughed. "I suppose it was new at some point, or at least, *new* in Oxford terms."

He pulled the expectant chair out for me, helping to seat me at the table. Even more impressive in person than in his family portrait, he made me feel as if I was in the presence of some genteel lion. I remember distinctly at the time thinking that, if I had to choose a literary character to compare him to (a game I often play in my head), it would be Aslan, the hero from Lewis's *The Lion, the Witch and the Wardrobe.* He moved with a quiet majesty; a powerful current seemed to run below his composed surface. He spoke with a voice that reminded me of my brother's—deep and resonating—a voice that held one's attention without over-powering it.

I could see instantly how TDH was his son. Although TDH resembled his mother more in physical appearance, the two men had the same effect on a room: commanding and yet comforting. I immediately gut-liked his father too.

I thought of how my sister, during her visit, ran into TDH in the back quad at college. She and I were returning, loaded high with goodies from a nearby bakery to enjoy with tea. She turned the corner ahead of me and saw a tall, dark, good-looking man just as he saw her. That was the very first time they met. Kelly later told me that when their eyes clicked, she felt a rush as though she knew him from long, long ago. Her precise word was "recognized." When I caught up, I introduced her to TDH; they hugged right away, getting along like a house on fire. I stood back, studying both of them, these two who despised small talk, immediately talking ardently together, apparently clueless to my staring presence, immersed in their own quick-bloom conversation.

Later, as we spread out our tea, Kelly put aside the most beautiful of our little cakes as a gift for TDH to enjoy with his parents, who would be arriving shortly. "There's something about him . . ." Her voice trailed off. "I don't know . . . He's just *good*."

I had to agree with her there.

Now, after having learned more about them over an intimate dinner, and feeling so sun-warmed in the dark restaurant by how they treated me and spoke of him, it was clear that his parents were *good* too.

His father had grown up in the Christian faith but faced a spiritual crisis in Vietnam (who wouldn't?). A former Green Beret, the man witnessed and endured suffering far beyond what most of us could ever imagine. I asked him how such an experience with war did not end up alienating him from God.

"Well," he began, "I'm sure you're familiar with the old adage, 'Man's extremity is God's opportunity'?"

I nodded.

"That applies to extreme joy as well as to extreme pain, physical or emotional, I think. Take away either, the joy or the pain, and you'd be doing religion out of its very best chance, and church out of what it does best," he said softly, lost briefly in thought.

"But surely you didn't have church out in the killing fields," I remarked. "Where is God when you're dodging snipers in the jungle?" I could not help the rise of my own bitterness.

"Caro," he replied kindly, "I hope it's okay if we call you that, by the way."

I nodded again happily. He said my name in a manner that I found myself wishing I had grown up hearing a father's voice say.

"Caro, suffering and violence have the capacity to compress things into an airtight decision. Literally airtight—keeping you from breathing—until you make the choice. Will you join the dark, or fight for the light? That's the warrior's greatest question. And just ignoring it, or hoping it will go away, or lingering without your boots on . . . well, indecision *is* decision too. Apathy is often the darkest option of all."

I thought of Yeats.

"Right then and there," he continued, taking his wife's hand, "I decided to become a pastor. To minister."

"It came as a bit of a surprise for me," TDH's mom admitted. "After all, he had this promising military career. I was delighted, but I wasn't quite sure how we were going to make it through seminary."

"Yeah," I agreed, laughing and ribbing TDH, "given how much being a theology student pays."

"And it doesn't stop there," TDH replied, in turn ribbing his dad. "Being a pastor doesn't pay much either. It's as though they take the lack of worldly affirmation a bit too literally in church affairs."

"I know, I know." His father returned the good humor. "Hence, why we ate so many peas."

"And smelt," his mother added. "Freezers full of those tiny little fish that neighbors donated to us in the overflow of the season." She crinkled her pretty nose at the memory.

"Bless you, Mom," TDH said warmly. "There you were, making it all work at home on very little, while Dad was starting the church from ground zero."

"Good harvesters, you are." I smiled at them. "Think of these amazing boys you raised too," I added with genuine admiration of TDH and what I had heard him share of his brothers.

"Yes, with God's grace, they turned out okay." His dad smirked.

"I sure love my boys," his mom sang out.

I observed these two people, who clearly loved each other, their sons, their family, their church, their lives, their country, their God. Their delight was infectious. They could barely believe God's blessing at allowing them even the means now to afford plane tickets to come visit their son on his great adventure abroad, let alone eat at a beautiful restaurant. They had come a long way from starting a church out of nothing in a living room. Though they patched together food and clothes for their three sons, they never fell short on presence or principle. The church grew into a successful, large ministry. Both of them eventually became accomplished writers and speakers. Raised secure and happy, their sons now flew like arrows of God's love, straight for full impact on a world much in need of it. I had to admire God's humor at its finest, that I got to sit at their table.

But then I looked down at my hands. I had not expected so many hurdles from *within* the faith. Was it not supposed to be getting easier now somehow? Instead I found not only going to church, but even being among Christians, and such *perfect* Christians, amplifying this feeling of inadequacy.

I have so many insecurities and shortcomings in terms of my faith, I thought as I chewed my *peshwari naan*, the sweet mixture of raisins and nuts lost on my tongue. Life offers so many excuses for shame. I looked up at TDH's parents, enjoying their meal with relish, laughing, and talking with their son; all of them so . . . *there*. Hypothetically speaking, of course, I allowed myself the dangerous thought, just for a moment—*I would never be good enough for their son. I lack the Christian dowry*, I told myself, *in all aspects. I'm good company*, I rationalized, *but I would never be good enough* family.

As we waited for dessert, I announced, "What a delight this dinner has been," adding, with complete sincerity, if not a little wistfulness, "you are all, well, so *perfect*."

TDH's mom put her hand over my hand. TDH's eyes shone at me from her face. "My goodness, no one's perfect, Caro. And certainly not us! But at least we know what is."

His father smiled. "The pleasure, my dear, has been all ours."

I studied them carefully. *His father is way too normal, and well, even attractive, to be a pastor*. I smirked to myself. *And while his hair is perfect, it's not shellacked into immobility*. I had to concede that this man, this *pastor*, had really seen life; he had been tried and tested and not found wanting.

His mom did not have the supercoiffed hair that I expected as a prerequisite for being a pastor's wife either, nor did she drip Christianese. Rather she clearly took pride in herself as a woman of God, as well as in her family and in serving, intelligently as well as heartfully, to the tune of an eternal investment. This wife supported her husband's call to poverty and pastoring. This mother, alone in a foreign country with her husband away on military duty, uncertain of his return, made tapes of him reading stories so that her son would know his father's voice. This woman happily made endless loaves of French toast on game day mornings and embedded in her sons a love for their God, and thereby, a deep respect for others, especially women. This woman now looked at me with the kind shrewdness of a mother whose grown son has invited a girl to dinner. And, I suspected, looked right through me. And yet this woman could still put her hand on mine.

Next to the Christians I had been getting to know at Oxford—in fact, next to Jesus—it was pathetically obvious that I did not have big hair. I did not even have a small ponytail. In fact I felt very, *very* bald.

Later Hannah gifted me with a poignant and funny true story by Joni Rodgers about her living with cancer *and* faith as a wife and mother. Her book's title, *Bald in the Land of Big Hair*, is hilarious and apt, since the story meaningfully chronicles her hair loss due to chemotherapy while living in Texas, of all places, the "home" of big hair. One of her many wonderful images particularly stays with me. She rightfully rants about her problem with the phrase used when someone dies of cancer, that he or she "lost the fight." "Lost?" she replies vehemently. This is not about "failure" as the world tends to see it. How can anyone "lose," fighting something as insidious as a disease, something so symptomatic of our fallen world? You might as well accuse someone of not dodging a bullet in time. From her strengthened identity in this God who works His grace even through cancer, she shows us that the ultimate coming home for those who believe in what this grace entails is far from "losing." *Lost*, rather, is remaining ashamed in the persistently loving face of grace. *Lost* means not knowing your way home.[5]

We stood up to go, giving hugs and feeling as if we had known each other for ages. I thanked them for the treat of dinner, on which they insisted. They had a show to catch, trying to cram in as much as possible on their visit without overbearing their son, but as it was growing dark, they offered to drive me home. I assured them, however, that I needed to run some errands before shops closed.

I picked up a few odds and ends along Little Clarendon Street, and then a new hair dryer in the department store at Northgate. On the way back I passed under the Bridge of Sighs, named for the *Ponte dei Sospiri* in Venice. Beautifully crafted, it cleverly links the two parts of Hertford College together over a small street. Looking up, I remembered when I had fully expected Christians to be naive and unrealistic. I certainly did not expect them to come out of Vietnam. Or Boring, Oregon, for that matter. And what I really did not expect to discover was just how *realistic* they are, while striving for the *idealistic*. Now I understood that there is an art to honesty. And there is nothing naive about cultivating a pure heart.

Talking with TDH's father cemented other ways I was getting to know folks in ministry. I initially thought pastors just married and buried. But now I began to realize that they weathered the trenches. Drinking, drugs, disorders, divorce, debt, despair—they saw it all, and yet they aimed, in spite of their own struggles, to remain confidants of the darkest secrets, upholders of families, hubs of social wheels. All the spokes circled around them madly, while they learned to be still. To be present. To give both momentum and stability. A lot like parenting, I imagined. I had never before equated shepherding with love, or soldiering with pastoring.

I used to think, *What does a priest or a nun really know about life, sworn to chastity and cloistered with their free meals?* Then I saw how they ministered to the dying and the sick, the forgotten and neglected. How they touched the untouchables, whatever a society deemed those to be. They walked a far braver walk than that of self-indulgence. Our culture wants to ignore death, pretend it does not happen. We want to live forever, and live that way without, very literally, the weight or weakness or wrinkles of wisdom.

The really crazy thing was that these Christians loved doing this loving. *L'amour de Dieu est folie.* They derived joy from doing it. They conveyed joy in doing it. Even from states of exhaustion that must happen for them often, busy folks with busy lives tried to help others not succumb to the opiate of busyness. They tried to build community, tried to ease a death or support a birth. With *enthusiasm*, in its etymological sense: to be "filled by the presence of God."

Sure, we all had our struggles. But in general these Christians seemed to function along a common denominator that, well, surprised me. Like spoons in the cup, they excelled at conductivity. Like a bridge spanning poles, they crossed over to others and embraced. They loved the world so at odds with them, as they trusted themselves to be loved. Or, at the very least, they *tried*.

And the really committed ones did not even rely on trying, not even on their willing. Sometimes they were forced to dredge up what they could from a seemingly dry well, with no accolades or affirmation outside of God's. But that sufficed. And it was more than I could say about the majority of those I had met who did not claim any belief at all.

Mark and Michael walked up, having just left the King's Arms pub lovingly referred to as the "K.A." by locals.

"Hey, Caro!" Michael called out. "Can we go back and buy you a pint?"

I told them I was full from dinner; at the mention of TDH, and then of his parents, Mark and Michael shared a knowing look.

"What does *that* mean?" I asked them.

"Nothing," Mark answered obtusely. "So why are you standing here staring up at a bridge?"

"Funny you should ask," I smirked. "I was just thinking about how bridges remind me of Christians, and then here come two of my theology friends."

"Glad to be of service." Michael bowed low.

"Don't you have an architectural degree or something?" I turned to Mark. He had almost every type of experience I could imagine.

"Yeah, did a little dabbling in it after college the first time." He smiled. "Why?"

"What's up with bridges?" I asked. "Just how do they function?"

"Well, you need to understand the arch. An arch is a structure that spans a space while supporting weight," Mark offered. I tried remembering my art history class, but things got fuzzy.

"It makes the weight bearable and crossing even possible."

Mark peered at me. "Are you unpacking some sort of life meta-phor again?"

"Yes, bad habit of mine," I admitted.

They looked at each other again.

Then all three of us looked up at the bridge together, admir-ing its beauty and capacity. *This is where the Holy Spirit comes in*, I realized. *Breathed in and among us, it does the heavy lifting of this world.*[6]

Passersby began to crane their necks, too, wondering at what we were looking.

"Will they see what I see?" Michael asked.

"Will they hear what I hear?" Mark sang back, with a smirk.

They put their arms around each other and started singing, in all earnestness, with the kind of force that only strong male voices in perfect harmony can produce:

> A star, a star, dancing in the night
> With a tail as big as a kite!

I stood there, mouth open but nothing coming out. They, how-ever, kept singing. I had to laugh at how much they were enjoying themselves. Their voices grew, and as they grew, so did the sing-ers' obvious delight. These men were sober, I marveled. And yet, they were intoxicated by something else, something transmittable and more compelling than just random music belted out in an everyday street.

> A song, a song, high above the trees
> With a voice as big as the sea!

By now, a few passersby tossed us odd looks. Christmas in May? But a few gathered around.

> Said the king to the people everywhere,
> "Listen to what I say
> Pray for peace people everywhere
> Listen to what I say . . ."[7]

Soon those who were not sidestepping us were singing with us in the growing dusk. To my surprise, by dark there were more singers than sidesteppers.

Oh, to be bold! To tell those we love, not just strangers at a table, of the glory of God. To go out in the street and sing your heart out, embraced by the beautiful, breathtaking, indescribable Bridge of Sighs.

I hugged M&M good-bye before heading toward Holywell Street. A small crowd still lingered, haloed in the streetlamps' glow, laughing and talking to each other. Most likely, now all were in better spirits after singing unexpectedly with strangers than when they first came down the street, focused, like me, on tasks and errands and inadequacies.

I walked quickly the other way, pounding out my thoughts to my pace. I was trying, but this Christian thing was not easy. And yet we are called, with ample reward, to be bold in the land of big hair.

And in the land of little hair. And in the land of no hair.

Bridged and bridging. Over this land.

Everywhere.

THIRTY-ONE

MARY AND ME

If
you want
the Virgin will come walking down the road
pregnant with the holy,
and say,
"I need shelter for the night, please take me inside
    your heart,
my time is so close."
Then, under the roof of your soul, you will witness
    the sublime
intimacy, the divine, the Christ
taking birth
forever . . . [1]

                                    —St. John of the Cross

For some reason, I felt more comfortable talking to Mary about this.

About being a flawed woman.

About being a woman who tried but was found wanting.

I had many Catholic friends now at Oxford, and no doubt we would enjoy each other's company, alongside all sorts of denominations, at the final table. Personally, I found myself leaning toward a nondenominational church home, and yet, I could understand Catholicism's attraction to ritual and the reverence for saints, especially the amazing appeal of Mary, the mother of Jesus. Why even the Beatles sang about her.

I sat alone in St. Mary's Church the night after Miss Georgia left. The prayer candles flickered on the tiered holders at the side of the altar. Ever since I started coming here, I always lit my candle on the lowest rung. Somehow the lowest rung seemed to be where I belonged.

Earlier that morning I found Gavin's note in the kitchen when I reached for the milk. In jest he had switched *peaches* for *plums* in William Carlos Williams's confession:

> I have eaten
> the peaches
> that were in
> the icebox
>
> and which
> you were probably
> saving
> for breakfast

Forgive me
they were delicious
so sweet
and so cold[2]

Wanting to laugh and cry, I stood there in my ratty old pajamas, exposed to the bracing refrigerator air.

My bowl, empty.

Something about the insertion of the perceived "perfection" of Miss Georgia into my own little tattered self-esteem threw all of my want into relief. Next to her I felt insignificant. Even though I knew this was petty, I could not shake feeling somehow unworthy. It was not anything she purposely said or even did. The irony, actually, was that she seemed genuinely lovely. She even left me a thank-you note for the loan of my apocalyptic hair dryer, offering to pay for the replacement. And I am sure if I walked a day in her high-heeled shoes, I would gain insight into her struggles too. In fact, I would probably find I had more than one sister with perfect hair. We all have pain and anxieties; it is all relative. Everything matters and nothing does.

The truth was that all these demons lived within me—shame, guilt, feelings of inadequacy, fear—regardless of the existence of Miss Georgia. Rather Miss Georgia, with her big earrings and big hair and big impact on TDH, provided a momentous catalyst in my life. My fledgling faith that tentatively began to validate my true value crashed with my most insistent ways of undermining that value. Enter Miss Georgia into the equation, and *bang!* There sat I, dazed as the smoke cleared, in torn clothing and singed identity, not *really* accepting what grace was trying to give me. Not *really* buying that I had been bought. Not *really* getting the *real*: that I was valued, loved, esteemed, already and in spite of me, beyond measure.

Not really.

Often the darkest things within ourselves become the keys by which we open ourselves to God, to His healing, and to a better comprehension of grace (full comprehension, I think, is beyond us at present).

Yes, Miss Georgia's loaded presence threw my perceived inadequacies as a woman in my face. These took the form of largely cultural pressures dictated by status, class, money, a good figure (all of which Miss Georgia had, and then some). They piqued my craving for a deep, lifelong faith, a stable home, a grounded history, so many "things" I did not have. Talk about coveting my neighbor—envy, pride, bitterness—all of the sins that our ancestors so astutely named came up in rotation. Such age-old lists exist for a reason, roots reaching deeper than the frost.

I envied her relationship with her loving and heroic father. I imagined her enjoying coherent mother-daughter evening outings without wincing at the cost. I longed, simply, for family meals all together, with no ghosts at the table. In the recesses of my soul, if I were to admit it, I envied these things most of all—more than any pageant banner or perfect hair day, more than even the shoes to match every outfit.

How my friends who grew up in Christian homes took their gifts of faith from their parents for granted! How prayer came as second nature, an obvious problem-solver or comfort or alternative to panic, anxiety, and fear. They took for granted the powerful pause of grace before meals. How oblivious they could seem to the precious and effective armor they had been given: to have the gift of faith from your childhood, to lean into it and grow into it . . . to even have the luxury to rebel against it.

Mourning came in like a wave I did not know how to surf. Mourning for a lifetime lost in not having had a faith. Mourning for all the things that wounded, for all the things that I thought I deserved.

Miss Georgia, and all she represented, did not just stir my want; she blew it out of the blender!

Yes, I forgot to leave my spoon in the cup, and it cracked. Badly. And so the fear seeped in.

I looked at the statue of Mary, and she looked back. As I sat there, just the two of us, it occurred to me: all for which she had labored.

Firsthand she had known the greatest joy there was—the birth of the Lord of all creation! And she had known the greatest sorrow—His death. She had cradled His newborn body and His lifeless one; she bore witness to His resurrected one. The virgin birth, as for all of us, the first birth from innocence through the narrow gate of flesh and bone. Then a conscious rebirth, from experience, this gate now of the spirit, still narrow. Familiar but new. A breaking of the waters in birth and rebirth. A full circle in baptism.

I reached over, gently touching the roses at Mary's feet.

Yes. The most submissive, the most powerful of words.

Whenever I begin to complain about being a woman, my friend Angie, a fellow scholarship student and a devout Catholic with Puerto Rican roots, likes to remind me, "This is a problem for your culture, not mine. My femininity is not an issue for me; it is a gift from God. The problem lies with how the world deals with my femininity, not with how I was made in God's image, out of His pleasure. What God created was good."

Then Angie would usually feed me something wonderful, saying kindly, "You poor, skinny, white women lack God through community—you are starving, literally, for so many things. Live in the Hispanic part of town, and you'll never go hungry, for food or anything else. We are far from immune to sin and the pressures of culture, but because we live in intimate relationship with each other and with the saints, we understand the community of intercession. We are not afraid to ask or to receive, to take or to give freely. Remember, Caro, true oppression comes from everyone else but God."

"Grace, the name of a girl," U2 later sang. And the name of a thought that changed the world.

Mary, fellow woman, indeed our lady. Speaking still so powerfully now, regardless of the centuries between us. This virgin who gave me my "mojo," who gave me my God groove for which I had been built. It was mine for the taking. For the true taking back.

Grace means you get to light your candle on the top rung. So that is what I did for the first time ever, that night. And that is where I have lit it ever since, even when I am tempted not to.

Feeling lighter, I practically danced out of St. Mary's into the soft night without a soul in sight. The song "Natural Woman" naturally bubbled forth. As I hummed, I marveled at how two such different women on the "outside," Aretha Franklin and Carole King, could sing the same song so amazingly from the inside. I also marveled at how *loaded* the words rang now. Swinging around it like the needle on a compass, I crooned at the streetlamp.

Everything! I thought of how Dr. Sterling danced from his wheelchair. *Why not*? I thought, and began belting it out, complete with backup echoes.

Suddenly, a familiar voice called out from the Oriel window across the empty street. "Caro! Caro!"

I froze, slipping into the habit of embarrassment. But the joy won out, and I laughed as TDH yelled down to wait, that he would join me shortly. I watched him disappear, followed by the light going off in his room.

"'Cause you make me feel like a natural woman," I whispered back to the empty window.[3]

TDH rushed over to me, dodging a lone cab that honked angrily at him. "I was up late studying and thought I heard something, and then, I saw you . . . dancing? What are you doing, coming out of St. Mary's at this hour, crazy girl?"

I beamed at him.

"Crazy. Natural. Wonderful. Whatever." He smiled at me. Oh, that smile.

Wait, I thought, growing irritated.

I could not rag on him, of course, in front of his parents, so it all tumbled out now. "Where have you been? I haven't seen you in ages. I've barely seen you since . . ." I stopped before finishing, "*she* came to visit." My annoyance hung in the air. He looked at me, all sincerity.

"So tell me what you've been up to?" he put his arm around my shoulder.

I swear I planned to tell him the courteous bare minimum.

But in the face of that persistent smile, in the curve of that arm, more and more came out until I bared all that had happened to my soul with Mary that night. My lows exposed right there on the High. Everything, barring specific reference to Miss Georgia, of course. I still had some pride stuck like gum to the bottom of my soul.

TDH swept me up with his eyes. "I'm so happy that you are starting to get it, to really get it!" he said gleefully. "Grace *is* amazing. This Christian stuff is not all gloom and doom, not all martyred saints with sour faces, see?" He poked at me playfully.

"Yes, I see," I admitted. "Joy is the Christian's secret weapon. No one else has it in such abundance. With such *blessed assurance.*" I laughed, lowering my voice an octave in playful sanctimonious emphasis of the final two words. A habitual joke of TDH's that I now lobbed back at him.

"Do you want to see something amazing?" TDH took my hand eagerly.

"It's late," I replied, the old trepidation coming back at enjoying his company too much. "I should be getting back . . . I have a paper due tomorrow."

"Oh, come on. It won't take long." He pulled on my arm, luring me back across the street to St. Mary's.

"But I just came from there," I said, hesitating.

"Ah yes, of course I know that, but I bet you haven't seen it in quite this light!" TDH continued to pull on my arm. I relented and we snuck like church mice through the side door.

I followed him to the far side of the altar, through a previously unnoticed arch, and then up the first part of a dark, steep staircase.

"Do you think we should be doing this?" I fretted, getting more nervous with every step.

"Of course. This is a self-guided tour. They hold them all day. The only difference now is that it's night." Staying one step ahead of me, he squeezed my hand.

We rounded a few more windings, and then I stopped.

"What is it?" he asked, turning around. I could barely make out his features in the shadows.

"I don't think we should go." I leaned against the wall. "There isn't a railing," I hedged.

"Of course there isn't a railing," TDH laughed. "No codes to meet in, like, the eleventh century."

"Very funny. I'm serious, I don't know if we should go any farther."

"Are you scared?" he challenged me. Man, he knew my buttons.

I chafed at the tossed gauntlet. "No, of course not. It's just that . . ."

"Well, come on, then." He took my hand again.

I tried not to look down into the shadows, into the gaping gyre of the stairwell. I tried not to think of Dante. Of Hitchcock. Of my fear of heights.

Perhaps one's Moro simply morphs into vertigo? I wondered.

TDH must have sensed my hesitation, maybe even my impending nausea.

"Trust me," he said calmly. He wrapped my arm all the way up to the shoulder firmly against his chest. I leaned on him as we continued up the steepest part. It got very, very dark. So dark I tried not to think of Milton either. And then, suddenly, a portal of starlight opened in front of us: the blackest sky I had ever seen spotted with a million points of light. It looked as if someone had taken a board of black felt, held it against the sun, and then poked holes in it. It reminded me of the toy "Lite Brite" I played with as a child, where you insert the glass pegs in a screen, and when you turn it on, the dots glow as whatever you "drew." I loved to sleep with the scene plugged in; it felt like Christmas.

"Wow! It's beautiful!" I sighed as we came up over the summit of the staircase.

"Wait," TDH said, steadying me by my arm as I came up behind him. "You haven't seen it all yet. Close your eyes."

"Are you crazy?"

"What do you care? Anyway, it's already dark." He smirked.

I stood stock-still.

"Don't worry," he said, reassuringly. "I have you."

I closed my eyes. He took both my hands and led me out of the stuffy tower; the fresh air immediately felt cooler. The floor, too, changed under my feet. Instead of the smooth, worn stone stairs, my steps now hollowed on wooden planks.

"Okay—open!" TDH exclaimed, still holding my hands.

I opened my eyes and found myself on a wooden parapet with a fragile railing encircling the highest spire of the church. It was like standing on a precipice. Now I could see how the ground rivaled the sky, for far below lights spread out in various patterns, emanating from the city center like a great fractal into the surrounding hamlets. It looked like someone had spilled a bag of sparkling diamonds across a jeweler's touchstone. Not ironic points of light, but iconic. Nature and man, reflecting. I felt a rush of affection for this elegant city of dreaming spires, all stone and lights like a Langston Hughes poem.

We each stand alone at the same precipice; Regina was right. We can lean into the human fear, acknowledge it, and move through it to the larger vision, or we can remain crumpled by it, crumble to it. I had been more sharp than rough, I would say, around the edges. And yet, through His grace, here I towered, all the height with none of the vertigo, a sparkling diamond in this everlasting crown placed so that I could appreciate the other diamonds. Admiring the work of His hands.

So here was the dignity and the health and the freedom of it: I was not responsible in this very first and important step for anyone else but me. Just as, except God, no one else can be born or die for you, no one else can believe or choose for you either. Nor can you believe or choose for anyone else. I knew that, like everything and everyone else in the world, I was broken far beyond my ability to repair myself. And others' brokenness was not the issue here. Mine was. For once, as it is for each of us, it was completely and unabashedly about me. About taking care of my business first. Between God and me. No excuses. No distractions. No more lies from a self-proclaimed place of ignorance or justification, white or darkest dark, or otherwise.

Paradoxically, once that's squared away, it's not about me.

"The really amazing thing about grace is that it takes you even beyond the top rung," TDH said gently, so as not to disturb the night divine.

"And how," I breathed, as we stood there together at the top of that very tall tower, gazing, bewildered, and bejeweled.

THIRTY-TWO

PAROUSIA

And Odysseus took his time,
turning the bow, tapping it, every inch,
for borings that termites might have made
while the master of the weapon was abroad . . . .
But the man skilled in all ways of contending,
effortlessly in one motion strung the bow.
Then slid his right hand down the cord and plucked it,
so the taut gut vibrating hummed and sang
a swallow's note . . . [1]

—HOMER

It was a blustery day, the wind rattled the Bodleian windows distractingly all morning while I studied. After lunch at the King's Arms, Edward offered to walk me to my afternoon tutorial. We started out along Broad Street, deciding together to stroll

Cornmarket back to the High. We agreed it would be more conducive for people-watching that way.

We paused in front of Blackwell's, the famous bookstore, surveying best-selling titles in the front window.

"Doesn't it just amaze you how enduring the Bible is?" Edward's comment surprised me.

"I mean, look," he said, pointing at an array of books set on tiny perches. "Here we are, on the brink of the millennium, and something as old as the Bible is a best seller. The Bible! Look at all these editions."

I nodded in agreement, adding, "Maybe it's because we're on the brink of a millennium." There were student Bibles and study Bibles. Bibles in conservative black and Bibles in neon green. Bibles in pastels for her and denims for him. Bibles in large print and pocket-size Bibles.

"Look." Edward pointed again. "That's my personal favorite."

I squinted at a book in the display with a distinct white, black, and yellow cover: *An Idiot's Guide to the Bible*. I leaned in closer, trying to make out the subtitle: *A User-Friendly Translation in Modern-Day English, with Explanatory Notes Even You Can Understand*.

Accessible passages for the lowly worm came to mind.

"It's perfect for you!" I laughed, as I nudged him with my arm. "I especially like that it's user-friendly. Now I know what to get you for your birthday."

Pretending to pull an arrow from his chest, Edward staggered back and feigned being hurt.

"But seriously," I said, "I know I could use one."

Edward shot me a wary look.

I didn't look directly at him but watched our reflection in the window instead. I took a breath.

"Edward, I've become a Christian."

"What does *that* mean?" I could not quite tell what he was thinking from his tone.

"I've handed my life over to Christ." I decided to be bold (well, as bold as one could be talking to a reflection once removed). "I want to know God and to grow in Him. Edward, I don't have all the answers, and I don't really know how much they all matter. But I do know one thing: I need His grace and I want His love."

I studied his reflection for any response. He stood very still. He did not say anything for some time. Passersby streamed endlessly behind our static pose. Two people, side by side, not looking at each other, but communicating, or trying to, through a reflection.

Finally Edward took a step back from me. I was relieved at the movement but then saddened at its direction. I braced myself.

"Oh, don't go there," he pleaded strangely.

"Where?" my eyes said as I turned to him. Now he insisted on addressing the window, however, so I turned back, putting my hands in my pockets.

"Jesus." I felt him cringe next to me. "Gee, that gets under my skin."

"Why?" I asked his reflection.

"You know what I mean," it responded.

"No, I don't." I shrugged.

"Yes, you do. Don't play coy with me," it grumbled.

"You, Edward, accusing me of playing coy?" I smiled coyly.

"You were one of *us* not that long ago. Now you're one of *them*. One of those . . ." He searched for the right words.

"Jesus freaks?" I offered.

"Yeah. Surely you can remember what it's like to be a normal person," he said agitated.

"I didn't ever think you were so 'normal,' Edward."

"Come on. You know what I mean."

"No, I don't. Nonbelievers accuse believers of using lingo and Christianese, but now that I'm a Christian, I can see that nonbelievers are guilty of the exact same thing, if not more so— falling back on canned phrases and retorts that are not thought through. Cultural regurgitations or cop-outs." I tried not to get defensive, but language was intimate territory for me.

"And you Christians have it together, huh? With your centuries of persecuting others, causing wars, inflicting empty clichés," Edward was gesticulating wildly at the window now. People inside as well as outside of the store started giving us alarmed looks. I took his arm and looked steadfastly at him, finally.

"Let's keep walking," I urged, "or I'll be late."

The strolling grounded us. We both backed off a little. I let some time go by, as we browsed successive shop windows, trying to act as if what we were talking of was as trivial as any item for sale. I smiled a little to myself. Edward's charming but brooding exterior belied an idealist, if you got to know him. I have found idealists to be some of the most poignant unbelievers, because their craving for what they are arguing against is so painfully apparent.

"Edward," I finally ventured, "I have lamented the pain caused by so-called organized religion too. Who doesn't? There is a dark side to anything institutionalized, no matter how well-intentioned, just as there is a dark side to each of us, no matter how good we believe ourselves to be. Systems are made of people, and people are sinners." I thought of Rachel's words about church.

He visibly winced at the "s" word. In solidarity I hugged his arm tighter and continued.

"Edward, I've been giving it a lot of thought. It seems to me that the clichés are only empty if they are divided from their conscious meaning. But if not, they are meaningful beyond words, which is why they're clichés."

"Oh, we are separated by a great gulf indeed, Caro. Houston, we have a problem. Ground control to Major Tom." Edward coned his hands to his mouth. "Caro, come back to being normal, please?!"

"Edward, what is *normal*?" I lobbed back at him. "To be 'average' only works, if it works at all, for so long. Then what? Living in despair? In denial? In bitterness or shock or anger at where it all *went*? Without any honest or real connection with anyone ever? Living for the short-term fix? Living afraid of dying? Living without any ultimate meaning?"

"Oh, now, now, don't go running off into those circles," he chided. "You don't need Jesus to have meaning."

"Give me one alternative that does," I asked him point-blank.

"You don't need God to be good," he hedged.

"For all of your philosophy, are you so sure?" I studied him. "Humans are full of conditions. We can only be good to a point, and that point is almost always defined by what is comfortable to us. As Lewis put it so well, 'Pilate was merciful until it became risky.' But God's love is unconditional; His grace is all encompassing and indiscriminate, if we only choose to accept it."

"I give myself meaning." Edward pulled himself up defensively. "I am a perfectly good standard of goodness." I could not believe he managed that one with a straight face. But then I thought of Ben, who did. Followed by so many others, including myself, all very straight-faced.

"Oh, that's a good one. There's a dependable source." I finally could not help laughing.

"Hey, no better source than *moi*," Edward partly joked back.

"Okay, Miss Piggy," I snorted at him. "You're definitely above average when it comes to being chuffed with yourself."

"All this evangelism makes me want to hum 'The Devil Came Down to Georgia,'" he complained as he dug around for his cigarettes.

"Not such a bad thing." I shrugged.

"Of course it is." Edward bummed a matchbook from a street musician, handing him a cigarette in return. Cigarette in mouth, he grumbled, "Anything country and western is."

"I love country and western," I said protectively.

Twiddling his cigarette and moving his brows in his best Groucho Marx impersonation, Edward crooned, "If I said you had a beautiful body, would you hold it against me?"[2]

Well, who wouldn't be disarmed by the Bellamy Brothers, I thought?

I could see the wheels turning in Edward's mind, though calculating who knows what.

So I sang in response, "But daddy always told me, 'Don't make small talk.' He said, 'Come on out and say what's on your mind.'"[3]

Edward smiled, in spite of himself. "Sweet Caroline, you don't count. You love everything. Your brother was a famous disc jockey, your mom a beautiful singer—you grew up appreciating all music. Besides, you're Canadian. You guys produced Shania Twain." Edward sighed as we turned up the High. He finally got his cigarette to light in the windy street and then casually leaned back for shelter against an, oh, thousand-year-old wall.

I chose to ignore him. I liked Shania Twain too.

"He wins because he plays his heart out," I stated.

"Who?"

"The guy who beats the devil," I said in frustration.

"What are you talking about?" Edward peered at me through the smoke curling around him.

"In 'The Devil Came Down to Georgia'!" I cried. "Everyone loves that song, even snobs like you who are actually closet country-and-western fans. Come on, admit it: you love it because the fiddler who plays his heart out beats the devil at his own game."

Edward blew a smoke ring at me.

"Are you playing your heart out, Edward?" I asked him directly.

Now it was his turn to play dumb. "I don't know what you mean." He puffed another ring, continuing to hold his mouth in an open *O* of mock surprise.

"Are you singing your heart out? In your life here, now, and always? At the end of your days, will you have loved well, knowing you're loved so well?" I leaned in to him now, despite the smoke.

Edward did not make a face this time. In fact he turned away.

A few moments later he turned back, having refueled his ammunition.

I waited; I knew what it was like to have to reload.

"Why Christianity?" Edward finally asked. "Why not choose from a plethora of religions? A little religious roulette?"

"Name another religion where an omnipotent, omniscient, and good God becomes human and dwells among us and dies for us. Name another religion that operates according to resurrection, and to grace."

He did not answer. He took out a second cigarette.

I continued, "Don't you ever wonder what it's all for? Don't you think you'll get to the end of your life, look back on it, and regardless of what you've built for yourself—if you're lucky enough to have even achieved that—it won't quite seem enough? Haven't you ever had a strange 'What is it all for?' feeling as you flip past an obituary? What about when it's *yours*?"

"Okay, okay, Ebenezer Scrooge, I see your point, but . . ."

I leaned in further. "Don't you want to learn all the secrets?" I whispered near his ear. "See only what you love most about the world—dear relationships, beauty, virtue, art, music, a good steaming cup of coffee—magnified? And what you despise—illness, crime, tears, pain, injustice—eliminated?"

"Does that include country-and-western music?" he interjected.

I gave him my patented "Caro Scolding Glare," then continued. "And the same about yourself—the best illuminated, the worst washed away? To experience joy beyond words, relationship beyond comprehension, love that fills you to overflowing and that levels you, prostrate, in awe and thanks, while it raises you up, higher than any 'high' we can conceive of here?"

"Well, when you make it sound like that . . ." Edward lit a third cigarette. He chain-smoked when anxious. Now the cigarettes were flying out of his back pocket, almost smoking before being lit.

I pressed on regardless because, as with all my friends, I loved him.

"But it is like that. And more." He was looking at me so intently the words caught in my throat, just for a moment. I thought of Moses' speech impediment in the face of so much truth. Suddenly they tumbled out, clear as diamonds on a bed of coal. "Edward, don't you want everything to have meaning here? And then, when it comes to the unavoidable, and once you've wiped aside all the yucky human elements, don't you want to be actually *happy* to die?"

Edward skewered me with his eyes as he continued to puff. "Who on earth is happy to die?" He looked down, adding, "My mother certainly wasn't."

"No one is going to deny that dying sucks, Edward." I reached out, putting my hand on his arm. "In fact, that's much of the point."

Edward gave me a wistful smile, a sort of pushed-and-pulled look. I recognized it; I had been there. I sometimes still visited, but it wasn't home. "Yeah," he sighed smokily. He looked as if he wanted to say a lot more, but he didn't.

I took his hand in mine. "Edward, knowing Jesus doesn't preclude suffering on this side of heaven. It doesn't stop one from killing oneself, necessarily, or from living a life of pain. But the reality is that when we live *and* die in faith, we get to be with God. *With God, Edward.* Just stop and try being present with the utter reality that after death, because of grace, we enjoy restored familiarity with all we love most, including this mighty but intimate King."

He smiled again, a little less wistfully.

By now a thick wall of smoke had built up between us, out of reach of the wind, our backs against the wall. The haze stung my eyes, but Edward ignored it. Slowly his smile faded.

"Whenever you weirdos speak of the King, it only conjures up Elvis for me." He dropped my hand. "And I'll tell you what, Caro," he said as he flicked the ash off his cigarette, "the king left the building a long time ago."

"Eddie," I said, "I know, it's a really tough one to wrap our heads around, especially as the plane is going down or the tests come back positive or the bullet enters the bone. Or maybe that's when it's easier? I don't know. But now that I'm on the other side, so to speak, one thing is for certain: I don't know how anyone can live, let alone die, without faith."

He gave an almost imperceptible nod, so I continued, tiptoeing truthfully through the tulips, "It grounds our identity in a world that vies to define us by a million worthless things. Edward, I find it's a heady thing, indeed a hearty thing, to know (at times, to battle to know) that The Fear—our fear of death—to which we can trace all other fears—has been debunked, disempowered."

"*De-feared.*" He grinned.

I grinned back and took his hand in mine again. He didn't resist. I held it up to my heart. "This faith gives the tools to make it through; it is the only true source of hope and peace and perspective in the face of our mortality."

He dropped the cigarette from his other hand and ground it under his heel. I felt, intuitively, something move within him. He pulled my hand, holding his, toward his chest.

For a moment Edward stopped. He stopped smoking. He stopped wincing. He stopped talking. I felt his hand in mine, so human, so like my own and yet with its very own fingerprint.

Dear friend! Come too! My heart pleaded. But I respected his silence with my own. We stood there, still as joined statues, with the wind blowing tiny tornadoes of debris around our feet.

He spoke slowly, looking past me, in search of something neither of us could see. "I want to die very old and in my sleep, Caro. That way I'll never wake; that way I'll never know the difference.

To ease into nothingness. To not find out with my dying breath that I have been tricked, and it is all nothing but a cruel deception, a myth of the world."

"Or to wake in death and find it's true." Something in my voice brought his eyes to my face. "So true it blinds the eyes. And you have wasted your life, wasted your death. Regret and despair your deathbed fellows, Edward," I said softly.

He dropped my hand. Again. "Either way, I don't want to know. Don't you get it, Caro? *I don't want to know.*"

Now the tennis ball in the game of hurt feelings smacked into my court. My turn to step back. Fighting the urge, however, I stepped closer.

"Oh, luv," Edward said quickly as he wrapped his arm around my waist and whisked me into the steady pedestrian stream on the sidewalk. "I don't mind sleeping with such bedfellows. They demand nothing of me. Not even a cigarette." He smiled.

"I wouldn't be so sure." But my words were lost amid the noise of jostling tourists.

We walked by a poster featuring a lecture on Nikos Kazantzakis, the eminent twentieth-century Greek writer and philosopher. Edward rushed on, but I lingered. Below the writer's picture, his prayer:

> I am a bow in your hands, Lord.
> Draw me, lest I rot.
> Do not overdraw me, Lord. I shall break.
> Overdraw me, Lord, and who cares if I break![4]

We continued together to Oriel College, where I gave him a quick hug before continuing up the High for my tutorial on Keats. As I leaned in, I whispered, "Eddie, adultery of any kind gets old after a while." Then I gave him a wink. "I doubt anyone is happy to actually keep it up forever." He chuckled.

I ran down the block to University College, hearing the bell toll and hoping Dr. Parker had not locked the door to his office yet, barring all latecomers. Once at the lodge, I glanced back down the street. Edward was still standing there beneath Oriel's coat of arms, smoking, looking after me. I blew him a kiss and then passed through the arch.

THIRTY-THREE

ALL JOY REMINDS

People need to be reminded more often than they need to be instructed.[1]

—SAMUEL JOHNSON

A rush of hot air punctuated our conversation every few minutes. For once it came from an outside source rather than from the Rhodes scholar in our group. The basket swayed beneath me as we began to rise slowly but steadily over the main quad.

As a tradition Oxford colleges rotated hosting elaborate celebrations called "balls" at the end of spring term when the weather fared best. These balls were sophisticated affairs, often planned years in advance by student committees, and offering an array of indoor and outdoor events on the hosting college's premises. Attendance was limited to college members and confirmed guests, and tickets, though far from inexpensive, were in high demand. But the experience is priceless.

Usually a theme dictates the production, which usually spans an entire day, night, and following day. You might visit an underwater enchanted world of Atlantis, or an exotic foray into the Arabian nights. Or you might enter the magic realm of an Arthurian legend, or the science fiction projection of a utopian world. Everything spanned a lavish range, from the food, the decorations, the music, and the endless offerings of things to do. Such revelry came as a welcome relief to the stresses of intense study, and an exclamation mark to Trinity Term before dispersing into the long summer vacation. Oxford demands hard work, but it also knows how to celebrate in style.

Linnea invited me as her guest to the Worcester ball, this year's theme being "Around the World in Eighty Days." Thus I found myself holding on for dear life to the edges of a basket dangling precariously from a hot air balloon.

Dress for Oxford balls involves black tie, with a twist. Attendees dress very formally (tuxedos for men, long ball gowns for women) but often with a nod to the theme, if possible. Our group, as Linnea's guests, consisted of Dorian, Mark and Michael (M&M), and Linnea's housemate, Celeste. With their theology examinations just around the corner, TDH and Rachel were too stressed-out to join us, and Hannah was out of town.

Linnea, as always, looked her part to perfection. In deference to Jules Verne's 1873 classic adventure novel, she wore a period dress of ivory lace, complete with long gloves and feathers in her hair. Her father owned almost an entire American city; it would be an understatement to say that Linnea's wardrobe was immense. Generous to a fault, Linnea bought a round of tickets for her friends. When she saw my concern at what to wear, she even offered to purchase a vintage gown for me. I declined, however, feeling confident that with a few strategic strokes of a needle, I could transform a former bridesmaid's dress (which, ironically, I thought would never see the light of day again) into something quite apropos. Thankfully, I did; I even heard the porter announce with an admiring wink when I entered the grounds, "My luv, now *that's* a ball gown!"

It is hard not to feel like a princess in such an environment. Decked out in elegant evening wear, surrounded by a bevy of adoring men in adorable bow ties, served exotic foods and whisked from one grand event to another, every woman present rode on a lavish wave of adulation, from the moment she received her gardenia corsage upon arrival, to the moment the doorman, sweeping his hat to the floor in her presence, bid her farewell. Intoxicating indeed. And that is even before the champagne and cordials. And *then*, as if you were not swept up enough, there comes the dancing: modern, disco, ballroom, baroque—whatever your heart desired, whatever your partner could tolerate.

I swallowed back my fear, soon forgetting it entirely as the park came into view. Now with optimum height attained, the bursts of hot air stopped. The silk billowed noiselessly above us travelers, nestled beneath this gentle expanse as though under some great downy wing. I could see the torches dancing along the winding paths, marking the way to various events in the different college buildings, through the growing twilight.

It seemed a shame to descend. The basket landed with an apologetic thump.

Later, somewhere between watching a snake charmer and getting my fortune told, I began to succumb to the sensory overload.

"I'm ready to call it a night, friends." I smiled weakly at my group. "Or maybe I should say, 'call it a morning.'" M&M were sharing a hookah, or a Middle Eastern water pipe, so-called because the tobacco smoke is cooled over a water filter. They were passing it back and forth over Celeste, who lay asleep with her head in Mark's lap. Linnea and Dorian were deeply engaged in an intense conversation, as always. We were all barefoot after hours of dancing.

"I'll walk you home," Dorian offered. I hated to pry him away from Linnea, but she and Celeste were going to crash in college with some friends after the ball soon anyway. It was still dark enough, and I had grown tired enough, to think it best to accept. We put our shoes back on and then set out for my new house. The predawn air nestled about us, sweet and still. We could not have asked for better weather for the event; we had wandered in and out of doors with almost no perception of a temperature change all night.

Dorian and I meandered along, talking over all the delicious details of the ball. I noticed that, although the streets were empty, he walked between the traffic and me. At first I chalked this up to how he must want to favor his arm with his remaining hand. But then I felt how he maneuvered around me, so that he always came between the idea of traffic and me, with the grace of a dancer leading his partner with such subtlety you barely feel you are being led. You just *respond*, as a woman, and it feels natural.

We walked in this mutual respect along Beaumont Street, rounding the corner at the Randolph Hotel. I smiled to myself, enjoying it, instead of calling him on it.

After the rush of rehashing the ball, we continued in silence, both lost in our thoughts. A man in a crumpled tuxedo and a woman in a makeshift princess dress, we crossed over at the Martyrs' Memorial, remembering.

"Dorian?" I finally asked.

"Yes, my princess," he crooned, remembering how I had told him I felt this way all night.

"How long have you been a Christian?"

"Well, let's see." He looked at his watch, and we both laughed. "About twelve years now."

"Does it get any easier?" I could smell the heady perfume of my gardenia corsage whenever I turned to look at him.

"Yes and no," he said thoughtfully. "Yes, in that I feel Scripture becoming more and more powerful in my life on a daily basis. Yes, in that developing fellowship seems more natural now. But in moments of weakness, no, in that I don't have all the answers to which I still find myself feeling entitled."

I sighed. My feet hurt badly. I did not realize just how far up Woodstock Road I had to travel now that I lived in college housing on St. Margaret's Road.

"Like everyone else, Caro, I, too, lived with longing. I still do. But now I recognize, to use Blaise Pascal's image, the void is God-shaped. I know of that for which I long, and it makes the longing more bearable, and strangely, more beautiful because the promise of fulfillment lies beyond the deficiency of my wildest dreams." He squeezed my hand. "Caro, the Love is so great that it weaves in and out of my line of vision: I am too human, too myopic, to keep it in focus for long. But the glimpses assure me it's there."

Dorian looked concerned at my pained face. "Don't worry, Dori," I explained, pointing down at my feet. "It's these soles, not the other."

He offered to carry me. I knew he was serious, and I knew he would, but I also knew we had a long way yet. So I removed my shoes. Dorian did, too, in solidarity, and then steered me to the street-side strip of grass, the dew cooling my burning feet. We crossed Canterbury Street, two barefoot pilgrims at dawn, proceeding in silence until Dorian raised his handless arm, turning it to and fro as though examining a hand that was still there.

"I became a Christian as the result of this loss," he said. "Tragedy or opportunity? The lines get blurred on this side of heaven. Perhaps the tragedy lies in not seizing the opportunities. I have the gift of my conversion story. You have your own too. Peter or Paul, we all fall in one camp or the other." He smiled as he wrapped his arm back around me. "Perhaps, for you, the letters that will come after your name when you finish your studies here will 'remind.'"

"Yes." I smiled back. "You know, Dori, I finally began to realize that I could do all the thinking in the world, all the research of a lifetime, drill all the questions great and small, and I would still fall short of the perfect, airtight answer to the meaning of life and the essence of faith. I could set my wits to yours and emerge easily riddled with rhetorical bullets. But what then? A great clashing of swords? Someone else will always have a better argument, a stronger intellect, a sharper tongue, a quicker mind. Someone else will always ace the debate, prevail in the argument, win the jury. Someone else will always have—"

"Better game?" Dori interjected.

"Yeah." I laughed with him. "But I see now it's not that kind of 'winning,' not that kind of 'conviction.'"

Dorian nodded. "Caro, God knows each of us so well and for so long—since before the beginning of time—that He knows what best touches our hearts. And"—he gave me a wink—"our heels."

Surrounded now in birdsong, I considered how God laid His truth bare when I could do just battle, turning my deepest hurt— the fact that I would have traded every accomplishment for a close relationship with my father—into, miraculously, somehow even deeper healing. I thought about telling Dorian this, but I didn't. There was no need.

After a while, Dorian spoke. "As I've discovered, Caro, if you look back on your life, you'll see His hand in it, and over you. You'll begin to see with new eyes all the times that were subtle as well as flagrant opportunities to know Him."

"True, and yet why did I not come to know Him until this year?" I asked.

"Only God knows." Dorian chuckled. "But maybe that's not the question. Maybe the real question at stake is, why did He keep trying?"

As we turned onto St. Margaret's Road, I closed my eyes, resting on Dorian's arm, on the absence that brought him such presence. How differently things had turned out from what I initially expected to gain from Oxford University, the symbolic pinnacle of the "educational experience." As I aimed to become a teacher, God made me a student. My spirit as a questioner does not affront Him; rather, it reflects Him, and honors Him, and pulls me toward Him.

Through our gifts and weaknesses, our strengths and short-comings, He works in each life thus. In His own life, death, resurrection, and teachings, Jesus reminds us of our decision to accept, build, serve, or deny this most fundamental of all relationships—this belief that is the fine line between Nothingness and All.

Dorian's gait kept me accountable to the ground, and his arm supported me over any bumps. Sustained thus, I was able to soak in The Trust. My heart lifted with the birdsong. I felt the rising sun warming my face. The scent of roses mingled with the honeysuckle from the hedges along the road. My sore, tired feet luxuriated in the soft, cool grass.

I opened my eyes.

And I was home.

THIRTY-FOUR

TRINITY SUNDAY,
TRINITY TERM

There lives the dearest freshness deep down things;
And though the last lights off the black West went
Oh, morning, at the brown brink eastward, springs—
Because the Holy Ghost over the bent
World broods with warm breast and with ah!
    bright wings.[1]

—GERARD MANLEY HOPKINS

Have you ever emerged out of clear water face-first on a sunny day? Your eyes *open*? If not, I highly recommend it. Something elemental happens as the water bends to air, as you gaze into the azure sky through a pane of sea glass. This rebirthing into the inverted world.

The image stays with you forever.

It will with me.

***

"Are you completely nutters?" Hannah shouted over the music, almost missing a curve in the road as she looked to see if my face was serious. "Who on earth gets dunked fully clothed in a river in late spring?"

I had just finished explaining what would happen at my baptism service the next Sunday. Passing through Thomas Hardy territory, soon we would come to a rest in Matthew Arnold's subject matter. The drive into the county of Kent was a lovely respite from final exams and papers. We talked as we blared U2 throughout the gentle countryside.

Dover Beach came into view. An ebb and flow of land, as well as sea. The setting of Matthew Arnold's poetic calling, "Ah, love, let us be true / To one another!"[2]

After our hike we started on our way back to Hannah's little family cottage along the dirt path edging a heady precipice. Because the cliffs run right up against the water, what beach exists remains largely inaccessible. The rugged terrain made it necessary to concentrate.

"I do not understand this God of yours, who demands such crazy things of you." Hannah broke the silence, almost at the cost of her stumbling.

"He doesn't demand anything, Hannah. That's the thing," I said to the back of my dear friend. "I do this of my own free will as an act of profession." I looked down at the ocean rolling beneath us, still humming U2 in my head. I wished I could take off my shoes and wade in the elusive but beckoning water.

"That just makes you extra crazy." Hannah leaned down to pick up a white rock with crystal-like specks. She turned it over in her hand and then stuffed it in her pocket.

I smiled. Hannah loved collecting things whenever she went on walks. Baskets and bowls filled with nature treasures dotted her home. This extraordinary hoarding of the ordinary was one of the many things I loved about her.

She took the rock back out of her pocket, giving it a second look. "When I was little I thought these were jewels . . . literally." She laughed at the memory.

I loved Hannah's laugh. No demure, restrained chuckle for her; rather a deep, hearty, unabashed laugh, often hysterically improper and always dangerously infectious.

"I did too. Hey, I understand the imaginative reasoning of kids." I laughed myself. "It makes complete sense to think of these as jewels, don't you think?"

Yes, jade. It exists along the beaches of the Great Lakes, and you can find it if you know where to look for it. "Look!" I would cry out with glee to my sister whenever we found one of these "sea jewels," or weathered pieces of glass tossed on shore. "Oh, it's *wonderful*," she would always breathe.

"Yeah, I also had an imaginary friend." Hannah's giggle interrupted my thoughts.

"In school I played with a kid who had an imaginary *foe*," I replied. "I always thought that was pretty clever. Someone he could compete against, and blame for things."

Hannah laughed again. Then she passed me the glittering rock so I could admire it too. "See how it gets even more beautiful in the direct light?"

"Much like sea glass," I told her. "Just a piece of broken glass that's been weathered by the waves. Nothing that special," I considered, "until it has suffered and been buffered."

"Yes," Hannah murmured thoughtfully, "a piece of glass at the beach, dangerous rubbish that would normally just cut your foot. But exposed to the ebb and flow, it becomes something precious. The ordinary becomes extraordinary. 'To see the world in a grain of sand,'" she added, quoting Blake.

It is utter delight to be friends with other Romantics. It is also safe enough to share with them Psalm 66.

"What do you miss most about home?" Hannah asked me, looking out toward France. "Besides people, of course," she clarified.

My ballet school and our own little cottage sprang simultaneously to mind, having remained the two stable poles in the midst of often swirling waters. The first consisted of a stately mansion converted into dance studios, the lot brimming with violets every spring. The century-old dilapidated cottage, by contrast, sat lopsidedly in a gully across from Lake Erie. A tiny box with two bedrooms separated from the main area by curtains, not doors, it had a galley kitchen that lived up to its name, sloping so badly you felt a bit seasick whenever you cooked. But how we loved that little cottage and its humble but sufficient retreat.

"Oh, where to start?" I sighed.

"Besides places, too, or . . . smells," she laughed. "Quickly, Caro, name three *things*." Like my sister, Hannah enjoyed such games.

"Well, if I had to answer in a flash, I guess I'd say . . . fireflies at dusk, the sound of robust crickets at night, and . . ." I glanced down longingly at the unattainable beach. "Sea glass glinting in the sun."

"Caro, dear one, perhaps you're not so crazy after all."

Hannah gave me a cherishing look. "Well, my sea-tossed sister, either way I'll be there for you. I'll be there at your baptism."

"Thanks, Hannah. Thanks so much! That means a lot to me."

"Besides, you're going to need someone to hold your towel and then buy you a pint to warm you up," she said as she hooked her arm through mine, steering us through the tall grass to her old but upright cottage.

My baptism happened to fall on Trinity Sunday of Trinity Term. A small band of us, all different but bound now by a common faith, met at Pennyfarthing Place outside St. Ebbe's Church after morning service. Because we were a fairly inconspicuous crew, no one would have guessed from the outside that the Lord moved with us, leading the dance. Shortly we would undergo baptism in the Thames River, referred to as the "Isis" around Oxford. Given the impending immersion, I was grateful for a warm and rainless day. Our affable pastor led us along Turn Again Lane, across Greyfriars onto Paradise Street, then up the Botley Road. From this vantage point, Oxford lay behind us, just as in Matthew Arnold's famous lines: "And that sweet city with her dreaming spires, / She needs not June for beauty's heightening."[3]

While pleasant, especially on such a fresh and quintessential English summer morn, the pilgrimage was not for the faint of heart. Once beyond Oxford we hiked Port Meadow, turning onto Binsey Lane, threading toward the river. I carried my change of clothes in one hand and my towel in the other. Hannah had not attended the church service, but as I neared the banks of the river, I spotted her waving. A small crowd had gathered there to welcome us. Instinctively I scanned for TDH until I remembered, with a shot of disappointment, that he'd had to travel for a job interview. But I did spot one, two, and then several friends, emerging to congratulate me. I was surprised to discover that most bore gifts.

Dr. Restell's sister waited patiently to gift me with a boxed paint set from their recent trip to Japan. A bicycle bell jingled, and along came Regina, riding as spryly as a ten-year-old girl, waving madly and blowing kisses. She pulled up, overflowing with gifts made by her grandchildren, and an academic *Women's Bible Handbook* from herself. I showed her my Celtic cross mug, which I had brought along to enjoy my tea in later along the river.

Rachel came up, smilingly handing me two books: the first, Isak Dinsen's *Out of Africa*, one of her personal favorites; the other, a small Bible in English and Hungarian, my mother's language. I looked at her in surprise; she embraced me warmly, saying, "To honor the knitting of your old and your new heritage." I thanked her in Hungarian.

Dorian gave me a shawl in vibrant purple that his mother had made especially for me. "The color of baptism and of kings," he reminded me, "and of princesses in certain ball gowns too." He winked.

"I'll wear it as soon as I shower off the Thames," I joked, trying to laugh to keep from crying.

Linnea gave me a set of scented handmade candles. "These only work on the top rung," she forewarned.

Mark and Michael each gave me a bottle of wine; one vintage, the other with the current year, marking my baptism. "To remember miracles by," they explained, laughing.

And then, to my surprise, Edward appeared from the crowd. "I had to see this with my own eyes," he said as I moved toward him. "Sorry I didn't bring you anything. I didn't know gifts were expected," he added uncomfortably.

"I didn't know gifts were coming either," I laughed, "or I might have done this a lot earlier."

He smiled, a little more at ease.

"Hey," I added, "your presence, even just your curiosity, is gift enough." I hugged him. He gave me, in return, the sweetest kiss on my cheek.

"Remember, my gift is your restorative pint," Hannah said as she came up behind Edward.

"Do I get one too?" Edward spun around to tickle Hannah. "For moral support?"

"Wouldn't that be *amoral*, in your case, Eddie? Or *immoral*?" She smirked.

"Touché, Flaming June." Edward seemed in the best spirits I had ever seen him.

Gathered by the river, we sang a few hymns, simply but sincerely. A bridge of song through all of time and then beyond; the notes, to my great relief, eternally in tune. Our pastor prayed a blessing over us and a commitment. Then each of us to be baptized gave a public profession of faith. I admitted and repented of my sins, asked God for forgiveness, so as to be washed and given a new life in Christ, and promised to live my life as a testimony to my faith.

Without hesitation, I entered the waters.

❧

Long shadows fell with the day, dappling the patio dark and light. Quite the party followed the baptisms as we all poured from the river onto the patio of the famous pub, aptly named for a fish and frequented by Lewis Carroll and C. S. Lewis. Featured, too, in Colin Dexter's Inspector Morse series, as Hannah, a devout fan of detective fiction, reminded me. Hannah, my socially outgoing and yet spiritually reserved friend. The last one to leave, she placed a tiny box into my hand.

"I thought my first official drink as a baptized Christian was your gift," I scolded her.

"You can open it after I go," she said with uncharacteristic shyness as she unlocked her bicycle.

"Thanks, in advance," I said, hugging her tight.

"Caro, I won't promise anything," Hannah said when we pulled away, weighing her words carefully, "but I figure if you can do something this crazy, and yet be someone I admire so much, maybe there's something to it." She climbed on her bike, shifting her weight from side to side. "I want the same, well, *thing* that you have. But I'm just not there . . . *yet*."

I nodded my understanding. Hannah began pedaling along the gravel back toward town, picking up pace against the growing gloom. She gave one final wave, calling over her shoulder, "I want! I want!"

Smiling at her deliberate farewell, I sat back down on the old bench by the river, alone but not lonely, watching Hannah's figure struggle for control on a wobbling bicycle down the uneven path, eventually disappearing behind the black poplars. Hannah's thesis featured Blake; I figured it would not take long before the *want* caught up with her.

I took my little unopened box and set it on the wood table grooved with centuries of pub use and ringed with glasses that had drowned sorrows and toasted joys. I looked at my gift, its surprise yet hidden inside.

When my tea came, I poured the steaming liquid into my strategic mug, cross facing me tonight, and made sure to keep in the spoon. Settling back, I watched the last glow fade along Binsey Lane as I sipped my tea along with the memory of my day. Night reigned by the time I finished the pot; I picked up the little box and took off the lid. On its underside, I recognized Milton's lines in Hannah's hand:

> And fast by hanging in a golden chain
> This pendent world, in bigness as a star
> Of smallest magnitude close by the moon.[4]

Inside something glittered against the dark. I held the opened box up to the candlelight now at my table. A beautiful piece of sea glass winked at me. Only when I took it in my hand did I realize it was attached to a fine silver chain. "You refined us like silver" (Ps. 66:10). I remembered our day together at the beach. I drew it out carefully, admiring how the sea jewel's brilliant blues and greens shimmered in suspension against the red and orange flame. My breath caught at its seeming fragility, at its bright and bold beauty.

How can we be so small, and so significant?

Yes.

Boxes and boxes of paradoxes! Open them all up, and therein glistens the gift of truth.

SUMMER SUNRISE

THIRTY-FIVE

ST. MARGARET'S ROAD

*Here is my secret. It is very simple: It is only with
the heart that one can see rightly; what is essential is
invisible to the eye.*[1]

—ANTOINE DE SAINT-EXUPÉRY

Sitting on my bedroom window seat, bathed in the glow of
the streetlamp, I kept rereading the same passage of the book
open on my lap. Soon I would formally transfer my affiliation
from Oriel College to St. Peter's College as I continued my studies while holding a student advisory position. Little did I suspect
then all that St. Peter's actually had in store for me.

In the interim there was something special about this quaint
tree-lined street named for St. Margaret. Perhaps it was because
my life had been circumscribed by Margarets. My mother and her
dearest friend, my godmother, or *Keresztmama*, were born one

day apart; they have been "soul sisters" ever since. My mother's eldest sister, who died from cancer when I was very young, I later came to realize was one of the few "religious" people I knew from my youth. She had visited just after she lost her hair from chemotherapy. Though disease ravaged her body, she seemed at peace. Growing up we celebrated my adored maternal grandmother's birthday on 14 February. I thought this was her actual birthday until she informed me when I was older that it was only symbolic because her birth records had been lost. *Margaret.* The name I think of when I look at a butterfly. The wings beat at each syllable: open, closed, open.

The address of my new college housing reminded me of what Dorian said—that when we do look back, we can see how God not only provides opportunities, but that He *provides.*

My mind wandered to TDH, wondering what he was up to, where life would take him. I had not seen him much over the past few weeks. He remained busy with exams and job interviews, and I was less of a feature about college now that I had moved. He would be leaving Oxford permanently tomorrow, his romance with England drawing to a close; mine in many ways just beginning.

Oxford tradition states that students wear a white carnation for the first exam, a red carnation for the last, and a pink for exams in between. *Dianthus*, the botanical name for carnation, means "divine flower"—an apt boutonniere for the university crest. TDH had looked dashing in his academic gown and red carnation, getting sprayed in champagne (another tradition) on the High outside the examination schools. Exhausted from completing his crushing exams, he still shone with exuberance as he told me he would be taking a position in Washington, D.C. I felt anything but exuberant, though I managed to congratulate him. That was the last time I had seen him, a few days ago. *Now*, I thought sadly, *the last time I might ever see him.*

Startled by the sudden horn blare outside my window, *Out of Africa* slipped from my lap. The loud honking continued, incessant and demanding. My housemate yelled, "Shut up!" from downstairs. I peered outside, but it had grown too dark to make out who was in the car below, idling impatiently in our driveway.

A strong American voice filled the night, resounding against my window: "Caro!"

With all the exhilaration of the night before Christmas, I threw open the sash. "You're crazy!" I yelled down to him. "Why are you doing all that honking?"

"I wanted to make sure I got your attention." He leaned out of the driver's window into the light of the streetlamp. "It worked, didn't it?" He grinned. Cheeky monkey. *"Cheeky" must be his middle name*, I thought. *T. Cheeky. D. Cheeky. H.*

"I just settled in for the evening." I shrugged.

"I have to return the car when I go back to the airport early in the morning," he called up.

Oh yeah, I remembered. He rented it with his parents to chauffeur Miss Georgia around town, keeping it after their trip to use up the lease. This would be the first time he offered *me* a ride, just before returning it, nonetheless.

"I'm in my pajamas," I called out.

"Throw something on," he replied, undeterred. "Come on, Caro," he pleaded. "One last ride together?"

I glanced over at my plum ball gown, still hanging on the back of my closet door.

Why not? I thought, and threw it on.

In the spirit of outdoor summer productions of Shakespeare, St. Hugh's College across the street was putting on *Much Ado About Nothing*. Every night for the past two weeks, the actors' voices had reverberated throughout the street. Since the evenings were warm now, I often left my window open. By the final performance, I ended up just about memorizing the entire play.

"A vision in purple," he whistled as he came around to open the passenger's door for me. "My lady Lydia," he bowed.

As I climbed into the car, I heard Leonato's line from Shakespeare's comedy: "Well, niece, I hope to see you one day fitted with a husband."

"You can't just sweep in and out of my life like Superman, you know," I said to TDH as he slid back into the driver's seat. He actually bore an uncanny resemblance to Superman, but that was beside the point.

He gave me a confused look.

"I haven't seen you for ages; you haven't given me the time of day. I moved out of college, and you barely noticed. Now here you are, leaving tomorrow, and . . ." I looked down at my bare feet against the floor mats, thinking of how often *her* shoes had rested there. The Hermès sandals with matching handbag came to mind first.

Gee, this grace thing takes a long time to actually soak in. I caught myself aware that my toes felt frosty.

"I don't need any man to save me," I said anyway.

"What are you talking about? Besides, you've already been saved," TDH chuckled.

"True." I allowed him that much.

"Though you don't always act like it," he said, starting the car.

"So not true!"

"Yes it is."

"No it's not."

"Yes it is."

TDH thrust the car into reverse. I sat there, arms crossed, watching the raindrops start to hit the windshield. I recognized the slow build. Soon it would be pouring, English-style.

We backed into the night, driving past St. Hugh's College's Shakespearean shoutings.

The Volkswagen bug crawled along as we aimed toward nowhere in particular. After living an ambulatory life as a student in an accessible city, riding in a car had both an invigorating and a lulling effect. I relaxed a little into my seat, thrilling to the very distinct opening notes of U2's "Pride (In the Name of Love)." The lyrics resonated with more meaning than ever before.

How the music has led me and followed me! As has the dance.

We talked of trivial things: our new opportunities, our plans for the summer, our friends and families. And we talked of deep things, related to the same topics, diving and surfacing with ease and enjoyment.

During one of our happy silences, I thought of that electric *something*, that quality that defied description, shared by TDH and his father. Dinesen's words rose up in my mind, freshly read:

Pride is faith in the idea that God had when He made us. A proud man is conscious of the idea, and aspires to realize it. He does not strive towards a happiness, or comfort which may be irrelevant to God's idea of him. His success is the idea of God, successfully carried through, and he is in love with his destiny.[2]

"That's it!" I exclaimed out loud, feeling as though I had finally properly scratched a longtime itch.

"That's what?" TDH responded, a bit taken aback at the wheel.

"Oh, nothing," I said, "and everything."

❦

Reclining my seat into a more casual angle, I managed to ask him with an air of objective politeness how his visit with Miss Georgia went.

"Do you really want to know?" TDH answered, squinting through the rain.

Csupa fül vagyok, or, basically, "I'm all ears," I said to myself in Hungarian, as when my mom discussed confidential matters in front of us with my godmother. I thought it best to guard my thoughts as much as possible from TDH—thinking in another language seemed extra safe.

"If you'd like to tell me," I shrugged while nonchalantly looking out the window, but my entire being now, indeed, one giant ear.

"Hmmm, let's see. How to put it . . ." TDH drawled out, perhaps unconsciously, as he made a slow turn around a rain-flooded corner.

I sat, on pins and needles, feeling the rush of the water beneath the car's carriage.

"I guess you could say . . ."

I closed my eyes, waiting for the drop of the ax.

"Well . . ."

I peered out at him from under one lid, ever so slightly.

"I don't think I was quite her cup of tea," he grinned. "Besides, she's a nice breeze, but she's no stiff gale." He looked dead at me . . . with those eyes.

We continued to drive, sometimes talking, sometimes not, for the entire length of the CD. "It's getting late, and you have an early flight to catch," I reminded TDH when the music stopped. Hesitantly he agreed and turned onto St. Margaret's Road, also now empty of noise. The play most likely had been rained out. I realized one reason I liked TDH so much was because it was as easy to be silent with him as it was to talk.

We gave our valedictions, promising to stay in touch. The usual things people say when they have no idea what the future holds, but need to say something, anything. TDH ducked out in the rain, passing through the headlights and then emerging from the darkness to open the door for me. In that moment, I fully recognized the treasure he was. He represented a race of men I did not dare believe existed. He was indeed heroic, with all the right kind of pride that entailed. Although I was entirely capable, he slew my dragons. Yes, I was grateful to him for saving my life, for sharing the secret with me so boldly.

All this rose within me, turned within me, as I turned toward him. But I said nothing.

"We always have e-mail." We laughed, our embrace rushed by the downpour. He slipped me an envelope, then held his hands over mine: "All relationships remind, Caro."

Standing, my hands in his, I felt, indeed, very reminded.

Then he added, "A question mark is a good metaphor for the Christian life. Trusting even when it's hard. Appreciating the mystery and being surprised by the joy." He gave my hands one last squeeze.

I raced up to my porch. In a moment, he would be gone.

Viszontlátásra, kedvelt.

"Good-bye, my love."

Wait.

"Wait!" The realization crashed through my voice now breaking the silence, calling out from the steps. I wanted to tell him how I felt. I needed him to know what I just realized. What a delight it would be!

Throwing the door back open, I raced out, still barefoot in my ball gown. His car, however, was no longer in view. I looked to my right toward Woodstock Road, and then to my left toward Banbury. I decided to take Banbury.

I should have taken Woodstock.

I should have gone right, toward St. Margaret's Church. Toward its treacle well, the medieval connotation of *treacle* being "healing waters." Toward the well Lewis Carroll depicted three times in *Alice in Wonderland*. I should have followed the path marked by centuries of pilgrimages: the well famed for curing the blind.

Hindsight is twenty-twenty. Or is it?

My pace was fast at first, as though I could outrun the rain. But then I slowed—first to the inevitability of getting drenched, but then to the acceptance of the car's disappearance. Woodstock stretched before me, vacant as an empty lot.

I came to a breathless halt outside Wycliffe Hall. A couple stood very close together at a side door. When suddenly, out of the silence,

> Over the cobbles, a horse clattered and clashed in the
> dark courtyard.

I froze, quite literally, in my sodden dress.

> Tlot-tlot; tlot-tlot! Had they heard it? The horse-hoofs
> ringing clear;
> Tlot-tlot, tlot-tlot, in the distance? Were they deaf that
> they did not hear?

Genteel knight or apocalyptic rider? My mind raced.

> Tlot-tlot, in the frosty silence! Tlot-tlot, in the echoing
> night!
> Nearer he came and nearer! Her face was like a light!
> Her eyes grew wide for a moment; she drew one last
> deep breath . . . [3]

Then a voice shattered the lamplight, "Are you all right, miss?"

Turning around, I came face to muzzle with a massive steed. I half-expected to see Alfred Noyes's Highwayman of my mind's ravings, but as I raised my gaze, a mounted police officer, or "bobby," as they are affectionately referred to in Britain, gave me a nod.

Oscar Wilde compared getting published to standing at a cross-road with one's pants down. Publishing and love are both risky endeavors it would seem. For similarly I would compare the slow quickening of falling in love with standing there, alone, pounded by rain on a dark street, soaked to the skin in elegant attire, a disheveled mess, barefoot and out of breath. Exposed. Apprehended. And about to be charged with some sort of misdemeanor.

I stared at my feet, wiggling them in the gutter water, realizing, unlike Miss Georgia's I was certain, that my toenails were not even polished.

The officer coughed politely.

"Miss?" he repeated.

Even in the dark I could see that he was not going away until I gave him an answer.

"I'm fine, I'm fine." I waved my hand in irritation. "Just chasing a man, that's all."

The horse was not the only one who snorted at me.

"Well, then," this equestrian defender of the public's safety asked, "may I give you a ride home?"

At first I thought he was kidding, but when I looked back up and keenly peered into his face, he appeared serious. Holding the reins in one hand, he leaned down and offered his other hand to me.

My initial reaction was to reject the gloved open palm—a habit of mine even when I am not in dire straits.

My mouth instinctively started to say no, my tongue already against the roof of my mouth. But then I stopped.

The horse anxiously pranced in place.

I was cold. Dreadfully cold. And tired. Dreadfully tired. And my feet hurt, badly.

It was much easier leading my dragon home from horseback, I thought, as I held on to the bobby's yellow rain cape. We were traveling at quite a clip. "Let's hope that's the end of any chasing now, miss," the officer quipped as he helped me down. "Be sure to get some rest."

My housemate let me in, since I left in a rush without my key. Though it was very late, and I resembled a drowned bridesmaid of a rat, in typical Brit fashion she did not betray any surprise. Nor was she amused.

"Well, let's get you into the bath before you catch your death of cold." She started up the stairs. "Come on, Catherine Earnshaw. Or would you prefer Elizabeth Bennet?" she asked over her shoulder.

"Bennet is better." I smiled, trailing behind her.

I ran a steaming bath, taking care to crack the window a little so as to allow the vapor to escape, or else the fanless room would be unbearably muggy by morning. A spoon for the cup of my tub.

The body-length mirror on the back of the bathroom door reflected a sad picture. There I stooped, a bedraggled, soggy mess. TDH would be flying far, far away about the time I completed my bath and slipped into sleep, I reflected.

I peeled off the silken purple as though shedding a second skin. Naked now, I pulled back my shoulders and stood up straight. Though shivering, I realized I had never been so happy or so at peace. My goose bumps were of the best kind.

Excited about this burgeoning relationship, this one with

God before all others, I was also at peace with loving TDH while letting him go.

As I sank down, the foam rose up to my chin. The bubbly beard made me feel happy and wise at the same time. Taking care not to further saturate the ink beyond deciphering, I opened the envelope TDH passed me in the rain. A single character, very large and drawn by hand, inquired boldly:

Alone in the bath, I chuckled out loud. Then I crossed the query with careful folds, placing it inside my Bible resting on the counter, choosing 1 Corinthians. I could almost find the New Testament book by feel now—a new old friend.

I settled back into the antique claw-foot tub, immersing myself in the relaxing waters of an abundant bath. Another perk of a house so lovingly prepared for me.

It's okay to live the unanswered questions, I thought as I soaked luxuriously by candlelight, listening to the rain pulse on the roof through the open window and feeling the cool night air mix with the hot steam while watching the mist reflect in a halo around the flame. *Storm conditions*, I mused. *And rainbows*.

The conditions just right to create the imagination for reality.

THIRTY-SIX

ANNUS MIRABILIS

"Away! take heed;
I will abroad.
Call in thy death's head there; tie up thy fears.
He that forbears
To suit and serve his need,
Deserves his load."
But as I raved and grew more fierce and wild
At every word,
Methoughts I heard one calling, Child!
And I replied, My Lord.[1]

—GEORGE HERBERT

Born okay the first time.
The bumper sticker caught my eye on the way to Heathrow Airport. It made me chuckle. Having come from

the other side of the chasm, so to speak, I understood the defense.

But really, I now mused, *how can anyone look at the world as it currently stands and truly think that? And has anyone so self-righteously declared himself perfect enough to absolve himself from any responsibility whatsoever in the mess?* Why not have a bumper sticker instead that just as easily reads, "Am I my brother's keeper?" or "Eve made me eat the fruit," or "Who, *me*?"

If I learned anything as a student of English literature, it was that "re" in front of just about anything makes it better, clearer, and often dearer.

Two books rested boldly on my lap as the plane took off, both gifts to me from Oxford. Soon the Atlantic stretched out below me. I thought of the American writer Nathaniel Hawthorne's words upon leaving England: "The world, surely, has not another place like Oxford: it is a despair to see such a place and ever to leave it." But then I remembered that remembering is the antidote to despair.

My Bible sat on top, its spine now supple as a dancer's, and the bargain sticker gone from its cover. It bulged with mementos from the year. Blake's "Tyger" put to use as a bookmark in the Old Testament, a pamphlet from the Loch Ness monster tour in the New Testament. Airline stubs, theater tickets, several cards from my mom, a picture of me as a chubby toddler on my brother's lap, my poem from Ben, my note from the provost, a folded takeout menu from Jamal's, a church bulletin from St. Ebbe's, a large question mark on rain-dappled paper, the high school newspaper clipping in praise of my father. Some of my favorite things tucked amid prophecies, visions, and miracles. Full of all things lived, memory makes all things living.

When I was packing, my Bible seemed so bulky I feared it would take up all my carry-on space. But then the idea reminded me not to fear.

One last keepsake had slipped from its biblical compression, falling softly from the pages like a feather on my desk. His comments on my senior seminar paper on Donne, written in his graceful hand: my final hard-earned A from Dr. Deveaux.

Is the year only lost to me?

Is this life only lost to us?

I hadn't seen Mrs. Deveaux since the funeral. A former high school Latin teacher, she was a poised elderly lady with a puff of white hair atop a black suit. She wore pearls at the previous college events; she wore the same strand when they buried him. Their eldest son gave an eloquent eulogy, full of the kind of passion only a life truly lived in love can earn. In retrospect, their son reminded me of TDH, both carrying themselves with that same lionlike pride. At the time I had not given a second thought to a marriage of forty years. I did not appreciate four children, raised with purpose and grounded in their faith, now active in local and global communities. I did not feel the groundswell of meaning from the scriptural references. She seemed the perfect partner for someone like him: lively, engaging, full of joy and erudition. At the memorial service, however, she spoke very little. But I do remember the poem she read. Fondly I traced the spine of the second book on my lap, beneath my Bible.

As my first year at Oxford drew to a close, I decided to write Mrs. Deveaux. I wished to share with her what had happened.

I had an inkling she might understand. I owned a desire for her answer.

22 June, 1995

St. Margaret's Road,
Oxford

Dear Mrs. Deveaux,

Upon my arrival at Oxford University in the fall of last year, I had no idea that by spring my worldview would be so radically and irrevocably changed. I never would have believed it. But then again, belief was not yet one of my gifts. That was all before I encountered this set of surprises.

I didn't expect to trade a learning arc for a believing arch. Or a paradox for what is most true. I presumed that somehow having faith would alienate me from the world or doom me to a life of social hypocrisy. I never realized how, instead, it would require me to deal with the real. Or to love more deeply. Even when I wasn't in the mood.

To my great relief, I discovered that, ultimately, grace trumps karma. And I was reminded that a happy ending makes up not only for a lot, but for everything. And then some.

So yes, I came to believe that Jesus was who He said He was.

How to become, as Thomas Merton puts so beautifully, "a brother of God and learn to know the Christ of burnt men"? I would welcome any advice. For now I see that being a thoughtful Christian has never been easy, nor has it been in vogue. I mean "thoughtful" in terms of both owning a compassionate faith that acts in consideration of others, and a faith that has been "examined"—that is, it has been both studied

and tested. Made strong by seeing its wants. Tried and not
found wanting.

The joy is great when the fear doesn't get in its way. And,
well, when push comes to shove (which it must, at the edge of
every precipice for those of us tentative jumpers), as someone
very dear to me says, you just can't make this stuff up.

Yours sincerely,

Carolyn Drake

The day before I left Oxford to go home for the summer, two
special deliveries arrived . . . just in time. The mailman's knock
interrupted my packing. Soon I would be back in the land of fireflies and robust crickets and sea glass. "Where the mighty moose
wanders at will," I hummed, cracking myself up (a little habit I
learned from TDH). Secretly I prayed for roses instead of thorns.

The first was an envelope stuffed with Canadian bills wrapped
in a small, white notepad sheet with a few words scribbled in my
father's distinct artistic hand. He said he loves me and wants to
reimburse me for my airplane tickets home for the summer. I love
the flourish on his Cs, linking our names. With hurting pride, in
the past I rejected such offerings when they did occur, repeating
angrily that I did not need, nor want, his help in any way. But this
time I gently packed the money with the rest of my things. Then
I sat and wrote him a thank-you note to mail on my way to the
airport. I tell him, freely and fully, that I love him, too.

The second parcel was a "brown paper package, tied up with
string."[2] A gift through the mail is one of my favorite things.

As I tore off the paper, a handsome volume of Donne's

poetry appeared. I rolled it over lovingly in my hand, admiring the leather binding. "Much have I traveled in the realms of gold, /And many goodly states and kingdoms seen"; Keats came to mind as I ran my fingers over the gilded pages, his imaginative delight coming to a celebratory peak when reading Homer. The effect so marvelous that he impulsively (or intuitively?) ran to share it with his favorite teacher right away.

A letter slipped out.

5 July, 1995

Dearness Retirement Home
London, Ontario

Dear Caro (if I may),

I am overjoyed at your news, and touched that you would write to share it with me. John indeed spoke very highly of you. He considered you one of his most promising students, which he defined as the "best who are full of passionate intensity." Like any good teacher, my husband liked to learn from his students. He delighted in studying them, and in turn, we delighted together in sharing his experiences. How I miss those conversations. But when a former student takes the pains to get in touch, I feel his presence all over again, and it is even more delicious because of its emanation of influence and legacy. It sustains me, along with the promise of meeting again. There is no sweeter joy, I think, than that of reunion.

"I know God will not give me anything I can't handle. I just wish He didn't trust me so much," Mother Teresa once said. We tend to think of this in light of facing catastrophic events, like the death of a loved one, or being diagnosed with a terminal illness. But as I assume you've also discovered by now, I've found it applies to opportunities too.

Well, Caro, some people come to a relationship with Christ without changing a lot of their basic assumptions. It doesn't seem to upset their applecart too much. But for others, there's a real toppling. Somehow I suspect for you that your apples were not only toppled, but cobbled. But now look at the treat!

Speaking of treats I hope you will enjoy the enclosed gift. I have taken the liberty of marking one particular poem for your future attention. I am sure you are already familiar with it. John and I treasured its language of allusion between us for more than forty years. But you may enjoy reading it with the new eyes you have since acquired at Oxford. Replace human assumptions of love, erotic or otherwise, with God, and, well . . . I'm sure you've become quite adept at this endgame now.

I wish you all Godspeed as you prepare to return to our Tree City. Father Anthony De Mello puts it well: "We sanctify whatever we are grateful for." Ah, Caro, what is the "soul" purpose of education? What does our daily journey teach us? What does it mean, Caro, to be "Home"? Since your note, I think of you often. How do you go off to study literature, only to find that there is no human language that can convey the glory of heaven?

Perhaps the lesson is less about command and more about appreciation.

Yes, Caro, He works in ways that surprise us—in order for us to know Him and choose to live with Him forever. For not only is He a merciful God, a great God, and a personal God, but He is also a serendipitous one, found in places we might never imagine, or rationalize, for that matter.

You ask for my advice. I am flattered, but after three-quarters of a century on this earth, I must now say humbled. The biblical version is simple, really, and I have found it in my own little life to be undeniably tried and true: grace begets grace. Do unto others as you would have done unto you. Forgive others as you yourself have been forgiven. Love one another as you have been loved.

Oh yes, and have patience—with others, with God, and most importantly, with yourself. For it is by degrees that we truly learn that God is with us always. At the end of each question, our Savior stands, reminding us again and again to be of good cheer and to not be afraid. This, I think, is the soundest refrain of all. Ask the questions, and live them, Caro! And in doing so, I pray that you will continue to be surprised by the joy which reminds.

With great affection, your sister in Christ,

Dorothea Deveaux[3]

My stomach dipped with the plane; we would be landing shortly. I looked out the window, admiring the patchwork quilts of farmland, dotted with lakes and, soon, roads humming with tiny cars. Everyone intent on getting to where they had to go, unaware of my gaze. Sometimes when you stop, you do not know where you are. You have been so busy getting to where you are that you don't know where you are trying to go. We are busy looking everywhere, if we bother looking at all.

I opened the dog-eared page to John Donne's "Valediction: Forbidding Mourning" and was reminded. In the margin, a note had been scribbled in Latin: *sit finis libri, non finis quaerendi.*

I recognized it as Thomas Merton's closing line: "Let this be the ending of the book but by no means the end of the searching."

Who knows if complete closure on the process of striving is possible on this side of heaven, but I have learned that there are points of rest, and a center from which to work. An *omphalos*. Everyone has a belly button, except Adam and Eve, as the proverbial joke goes. Belly buttons were not exactly necessary in Eden. One does not need a center to the compass until one is aware of being lost.

"The kingdom of God is within you," Jesus tells us (Luke 17:21). "You know the way to the place where I am going" (John 14:4).

> Thy firmness makes my circle just,
> And makes me end where I begun.[4]

As the plane touched down, I smiled at the memory of TDH's refrain: "*It's all good.*"

The cabin shimmied and groaned as we came to a stop. In the expectant pause before the rush to deplane, I turned, instinctively, to the second book's inside cover.

There, in shaky yet still elegant hand, read the inscription:

Caro,

Dear One,
    A bullshit detector makes a great homing device.
                                    Love, always,
                                    Dorothea

EPILOGUE

BELIEVE WISELY

*Let me make this clear to you . . . nothing that you will
learn in the course of your studies will be of the slightest
possible use to you in after life—save only this—that if
you work hard and intelligently you should be able to
detect when a man is talking rot, and that, in my view,
is the main, if not the sole, purpose of education.*[1]

—J. A. SMITH

Two years have passed since I began living the unanswered
questions with gusto.

It is my birthday.

The height of Southern Ontario heat. After staying in
England to complete my doctoral studies, I am home from
Oxford University for summer break. TDH and I ended up going
our separate ways, staying in touch over the occasional e-mail. He

dated women in Washington, D.C., where he continued to work on Capitol Hill. I entertained various escapades as a new single believing woman in Oxford, trying to navigate my way through such adventures as chaste courtship and interdenominational dating. Less like the Carrie in *Sex and the City*, I would say, and more like Caro in *Sex and the City of God*.

In that rich season of burgeoning and deepening faith, I grew closer to God daily and on my own. In terms of knowing men, however, no one *quite* measured up (literally or figuratively) to TDH.

The deliveryman tries to step over our cat, who had melted into a furry puddle across our front porch. He can't see where he is going over the host of flowers in his arms.

Roses tumble through my door. Mad handfuls, not bouquets.

Their fragrance deepens in the humid air, which hung heavily about the house like a draped curtain. The promise of a storm. The scent of impending rain on roses. Opening.

Happily, I drown.

Surfacing, I read the card. Centered on the blank space sits a single question mark:

Three years after receiving my first Great Valentine, I watch the monarch butterflies drift outside the beach condo window.

It is my honeymoon.

The surf pounds below on Santa Rosa Island, and yet the butterflies float above it, beyond it. Fearless and beautiful. Small and significant. A love letter in motion.

We have traveled together, I marvel, these butterflies and I. Migrating from, and eventually back to, the Great Lakes. Like the butterflies, I have completed a circle too.

The gold ring hugs my finger. Imperceptibly *there*. Through countless surprises after that first year at Oxford, TDH and I were reunited—eventually. So I became engaged to the son of a preacher man. And so it happened that this preacher man married me and his son on a warm October evening a few blocks from the Capitol in Washington, D.C., almost three years to the date of the advent of that first Michaelmas term.

Roses pour over the bedside table; the card, resting nearby, marked by one single (cheeky) punctuation:

!

Fourteen years later. Today.

Academic sabbaticals, like those of farming, both having the same biblical roots in resting on the "seventh." Births and near-births, deaths and near-deaths. Through these I emerge a wife, mother, and professor of literature. The tilling and fallowing of fields, twice-fold. I remember Jacob and Rachel.

Now TDH and I delight in children of our own and the

promise of their discovering this God who loves them, too, in their own surprising ways.

We will tell them our story and the story of how God loves a good story. And how He has authored a good story, for each of us—the best story there was, and is, and ever will be.

In the midst of busy, messy days, filled with demands and delights, I find myself pausing before the picture. The surprise of the gift never ceases to remind.

Early that third cold morning of my first term in Oxford, the incoming class at Oriel College poured onto the front quad for our matriculation portrait. Nervous in our newness and dutifully donning our *subfusc*, we congregated smack in front of the stone-carved *CARO*. The photographer struggled to get us all arranged, and then struggled further to achieve the picture. Since everyone insisted on breathing, vapor hung in the frosty air. This created a dense fog around us, rendering the moment to achieve a clear portrait ever elusive.

One of a handful of women, I sat in the front row, jet-lagged and forlorn. I look miserable in that picture, contemplating how best to inconspicuously leave before term actually started.

Then I heard a strong American voice from a few rows back ring out loud and clear: "Okay, everyone! On the count of three, hold your breath!"

Stunned British silence.

What a brilliant idea, I thought.

The voice counted. "One!"

Everyone stopped breathing.

"Two!"

A dramatic collective inhale. The mist encircling us thinned a little.

"Three!"

The soundlessness of held breath.

The air cleared. The camera clicked.

A communal exhale of astonishment and relief.

Bowing low, the Italian photographer called out, "*Grazie.*"

"*Grazie,*" I murmur back.

That picture now hangs in our living room, proof that the fog can clear as the result of one voice.

From the eternal perspective of grace, I began to see everything with new eyes. Especially my relationships. Especially my relationship with my father. Through grace, I now realized I had so much. Loving him was like giving away pennies when I was rich beyond measure. And somehow my coffers never lessened; in fact, they seemed fuller for the giving. Having my identity in an eternal Father gave me the freedom to explore better how to love best. My father and me . . . and everyone else.

Often, it is messy, but that's okay. Abundance tends to look that way.

Besides, I have discovered that messiness can be close to godliness too. Maybe even closer.

The kingdom of heaven rests within. Home is, indeed, where the heart is. As a result family stands for more than I could ever fathom on my own. Whether by rebirth-right or by adoption, the love is the same.

And *there*.

Absolutely.

Having been surprised by Oxford, coming home now means all of this, no matter where I might be.

Yes.

Acknowledgments

I t takes a village to write a book. And, it would seem, a city to publish it. My heartfelt thanks go out to the following *Surprised by Oxford* supporters:

Homesickness *is* a gift, a reflection of having been loved and cared for dearly, and of great love in return. I am immensely grateful for the amazing family into which I was born, who love me unconditionally (and I know always will): Kelly, my sister and best friend for whom, ultimately, there are no words, nor are they necessary, and her husband, Jason, my dear "other brother," and the promise and delight of their children, Taylor and Spencer; Matt, always my "big brudder" and protector, and his wife, my "big sister" Wendy, and her children, Christopher and Jennifer; my beloved mom, Ann, whose gift of a life of love set the groundwork for a life of faith; my dad, Charles—we are bound by name and so much more; and my "godmother," Margaret Peto, dear link to my roots and ever ardent cheerleader. Then there is my other amazing family—Stu and Linda Weber, preeminent parents of "TDH" and tireless, true servants of Christ, and their godly sons, who have already had much eternal impact on our world: Ryan and his wife, Jessica (and their children, Stuart, Wilson, Sam, and Elizabeth), and Blake and his wife, Jami Lyn (and their children, Rylee and Nathan). Your prayers, support, weathering, and uplifting of us make you, in every sense of the word, true family.

When, so far from my birth sister, I prayed for another sister, who, of course could never replace but at least would be near, God chuckled and gave me several. To swift, smart, and sweet Tabitha Elwood and her dear family (Chris, Avala, and Aza Joy), thank you for immersing yourself in this process with me, of writing and of living, "bird by bird." My appreciation to Lisa Holmlund, pastor and second mom to my kids, who serves like she sings: in perfect pitch to God's glory. You inspire me with your radiant reminder of His love. And my gratitude to Mary-Antoinette Smith, who gave me the courage to start this project, and to trust in God's abundance. I will always draw upon the memory of our walks around Seward Park by Lake Washington.

I extend my love and admiration to my current home church, Montecito Covenant in Santa Barbara and Senior Pastor Don Johnson, who is a good shepherd, indeed, and his lovely wife, Martha. Case in point: thanks for your constant smile even after I threw up by your shoes that night you came to be with me in the ER. Thanks, too, to the magnificent yet down-to-earth Pastor Diana Trautwein, who encourages me to be a woman of God through her own example of spirit, intellect, and genuine care for others. Pastor John Lemmond owns a heart for servitude and a gift for passionately moving others through Christ that inspire me to the ends of the earth and beyond. What a blessing to have all of you, including the wonderful congregation, in our lives. I also wish to thank the Westmont College community, both on campus and in the Las Barrancas neighborhood. You sharpen me and give me rest. You are, indeed, holy ground. Special thanks to the Westmont Neighborhood Women's Bible Study led by the gifted Margaret Chapman, each of whom upheld me in fellowship and prayer through this project: Jean Archer, June Aromatorio, Lora Barnett, Holly Covington, Katherine Farhadian, Elisabeth Gonella, Yeewa Honeyman, Marilyn (Mo) Morrison, Christina Rogers, Kate Vander Laan, Mindy Wolfe, Kim Work, and Ann Scherz. Special thanks to Mandy Abbas for her astute editing, Helene Winter for her graceful wisdom, and Susan Contakes for regularly nourishing my body and spirit.

Warmest thanks to my esteemed colleagues and friends at Seattle University—so many lovely people who supported me through tenure, and then who fed me and loved me through the birth of my children and the genesis of this book. Many of you for various reasons don't consider yourselves beloved children of God, but you have only proven all the more you should. Special thanks to the following and their beautiful families: Father David Leigh, Andrew and Nancy Tadie, Edwin and Noreen Weihe, Jo and Brad Kirchner, Gabriella Guiterriez y Muhs, Victoria Kill, Jennifer Schulz, Charles and Chau Tung, Sean and Andrea McDowell, Paul and Paulette Kidder, Hazel Hahn, and Jacquelyn Miller. From San Francisco, Tracy Seeley, writer, survivor, woman extraordinaire. From London, Ian Underhill and George Donaldson, thanks for helping me out (literally) and for your incredible teaching. To my Oxford friends and professors and college masters, too, especially Andrew and Erica Cuneo, Sam Burrell, and Laura Roman. You all know why.

Eternal gratitude to Randy and Nanci Alcorn, who nurtured this project in its embryonic state and didn't mind at all (in fact rejoiced) when our toddler ground crumbs throughout their home office. Where, indeed, would anyone be if the mighty didn't stoop to help the small? And thank you, Ron and Becky Mulder, for providing us with a place to live (and middle-of-the-night child care) during an emergency at a crucial point in the book's progress, refusing payment of any kind (as they always do). We also hold dear friends who helped immensely with loving care for our children in this process: Janel Collier, Lisa Kissinger, Hayley Crabtree, Cecilia Penrose, Emalie Sundale, Jennifer Goebel, Erin Risher, Kristen Rech, and Shannon Hickey.

I turn back with a grateful heart to Village Green Church in London, Ontario, Canada (Jon Korkidakis, lead pastor). How funny life is that as a young unbeliever, I bicycled madly to your building most summer afternoons, since part of it served as a local library back then. Now, you are our "go-to" church when back to visit family—proof of seeing things with new eyes. Much appreciation to my former pastors, too, who have shaped my faith walk: David Fletcher and Vaughan Roberts (St. Ebbe's Church, Oxford), Mark Dever (Capitol Hill Baptist, Washington, D.C.), Fred Harrell (City Church, San Francisco), John Haralson, Jr. (Grace Church, Seattle), Earl Palmer (University Presbyterian Church, Seattle), and James B. and Renee Notkin (Union Church, Seattle). On those sleepy Sunday mornings, I *was* listening . . .

Finally, I own a deep gratitude and admiration for those who helped get this project even off the ground. First, to Mark Sweeney, my agent, for believing in the project from the very beginning—for his humor and expertise, and for being, well, just plain *good*. To Jennifer McNeil of Thomas Nelson Publishers and many incredibly talented editors who graciously led me on an intense learning curve while making it fun. And to Matt Baugher, vice president at Thomas Nelson Publishers, for his discernment and wit. What a treat to work with you and your team.

Thank you to my three children, Victoria, Byron, and William, for your heart-cracking beauty (inside and out), my little touch-stones of what really matters. Thank you for sharing Mommy with all the demands of the page, and for renewing and restoring me, always, with your deep reminders of joy.

Last and most, thanks be to our God. And to my husband, Kent. For such a story. Yes, for that most of all.

NOTES

Prologue

1. John Donne, "Satire III: Kind Pity Chokes My Spleen," in *John Donne's Poetry*, ed. Arthur L. Clements, 2nd ed. (New York: Norton, 1992), 72–75.

2. Donne, "Sonnet XIV," in *John Donne's Poetry*, 115.

Chapter 1

1. Sophocles, *Oedipus Rex*, in *An Introduction to Literature*, ed. Sylvan Barnet et al., 12th ed. (New York: Longman, 2001), pp. 974–1010, lines 67–76.

Chapter 3

1. Five Man Electrical Band, vocal performance of "Signs," by Les Emmerson, released 1970 on *Good-Byes and Butterflies*, Polydor 2424-020, 33⅓ rpm.

2. Ibid.

Chapter 5

1. William Blake, "The Poison Tree," in *Songs of Experience* (London, 1794).

2. Blake, "London," in *Songs of Experience* (London, 1794).

3. William Butler Yeats, "The Second Coming," in *The Norton*

Anthology of Modern Poetry, ed. Richard Ellmann and Robert O'Clair, 2nd ed. (New York: Norton, 1988), 158.

4. John Milton, *Paradise Lost,* ed. Gordon Teskey (New York: Norton, 2005), bk. 4, lines 216–22.

Chapter 7

1. Dusty Springfield, vocal performance of "Son of a Preacher Man," by John Hurley and Ronnie Wilkins, released 1968 on *Dusty in Memphis,* Atlantic SD 8214, 33⅓ rpm.

Chapter 8

1. Michka Assayas, *Bono: In Conversation with Michka Assayas* (New York: Riverhead Books, 2005), 204–5.

Chapter 9

1. T. S. Eliot, "Journey of the Magi," in *The Norton Anthology of English Literature: The Twentieth Century and After,* ed. John Stallworthy and Jahan Ramazani, 8th ed., vol. F (New York: Norton, 2006), 2312–13.

2. Milton, *Paradise Lost,* bk. 1, lines 1–5.

3. Edna St. Vincent Millay, "Love Is Not All," in *The Norton Anthology of Modern Poetry,* 526.

Chapter 10

1. Thomas Campion, "Laura," in *The Norton Anthology of English Literature,* ed. Barbara Lewalski and M. H. Abrams, 7th ed., vol. 1 (New York: Norton, 2000), 1198.

2. Dodie Smith, *I Capture the Castle* (New York: St. Martin's Griffith, 1948), 113.

3. John Betjeman, "A Subaltern's Love Song," in *The Norton Anthology of Modern Poetry,* 720.

4. "O Holy Night," lyrics by Placide Cappeau, trans. John Sullivan Dwight, music by Adolphe Adam, 1847.

Chapter 11

1. William Shakespeare, *Hamlet*, 1.1.163–70.

Chapter 12

1. W. H. Auden, "September 1, 1939," at Poets.org, accessed May 18, 2011, www.poets.org/viewmedia.php/prmMID/15545.

2. Rita Dove, "Parsley," *The Norton Anthology of Modern Poetry*, 1696–98.

3. Flannery O'Connor to Mr. Alfred Corn, 16 June 1962. Excerpt from THE HABIT OF BEING: LETTERS OF FLANNERY O'CONNOR, edited by Sally Fitzgerald. Copyright © 1979 by Regina O'Connor. Reprinted by permission of Farrar, Straus and Giroux, LLC.

Chapter 13

1. Stevie Smith, "Not Waving But Drowning," in *The Norton Anthology of Modern Poetry*, 654.

2. Pablo Neruda, "Sonnet XVII," trans. Stephen Mitchell, in *Into the Garden: A Wedding Anthology*, ed. Robert Hass and Stephen Mitchell (New York: HarperPerennial, 1994), 10.

Chapter 14

1. The Four Aces, vocal performance of "Three Coins in the Fountain," lyrics by Sammy Cahn, music by Jule Styne, released 1954, Brunswick 45-05308, 33⅓ rpm.

Chapter 15

1. Tony Harrison, "Book Ends," in *The Norton Anthology of English Literature: The Twentieth Century and After*, vol. F, 2532. Reprinted courtesy of Tony Harrison, *Selected and Collected Poems* (New York: Penguin, 1987 and 2007).

Chapter 16

1. Shakespeare, *Romeo and Juliet*, 3.5.42.

Chapter 17

1. Samuel Taylor Coleridge, "Kubla Khan," in *Samuel Taylor Coleridge*, ed. H. J. Jackson (Oxford: Oxford University Press, 1985), 102.

Chapter 18

1. Coleridge, "The Rime of the Ancient Mariner," in *Samuel Taylor Coleridge*, 46–65.

2. C. S. Lewis, *The Screwtape Letters*, rev. ed. (New York: Macmillan, 1982), 39.

Chapter 20

1. Norman McCaig, "Assisi," in *Twelve Modern Scottish Poets*, ed. Charles King (London: Hodder and Stoughton, 1989), 99.

2. J. R. R. Tolkien, *The Lord of the Rings* (Boston: Houghton Mifflin, 2002), 167.

3. Lewis, preface to *The Screwtape Letters*, x.

4. Provost, letter to the author.

5. Tolkien, *The Lord of the Rings*, 167.

Chapter 21

1. Milton, *Paradise Lost*, bk. 1, lines 254–55.

2. Gerard Manley Hopkins, "Pied Beauty," in *The Norton Anthology of Modern Poetry*, 102.

3. Coleridge, "The Rime of the Ancient Mariner."

Chapter 22

1. Christina Rossetti, "A Birthday," in *The Norton Anthology of Literature*, ed. M. H. Abrams and Stephen Greenblatt, 7th ed., vol. 2 (New York: Norton, 2000), 1587.

Chapter 23

1. Donne, "Good-Friday, 1613. Riding Westward," in *John Donne's Poetry*, 123–24.

2. Francis Thompson, "The Hound of Heaven," in *The Norton Anthology of Literature*, vol. 2, 1857–60.

3. Brennan Manning, *The Ragamuffin Gospel* (Colorado Springs, CO: Multnomah Books, 1990), 167.

Chapter 24

1. Rainer Maria Rilke, *Letters to a Young Poet*, trans. M. D. Herter Norton (New York: Norton, 1993), 34–35.

2. Ibid., 69.

Chapter 25

1. Emily Dickinson, "Much Madness is Divinest Sense," in *The Norton Anthology of American Literature*, ed. Nina Baym et al., 3rd ed., vol. 1 (New York: Norton, 1989), 2382.

Chapter 26

1. Blake, "The Tyger," in *Songs of Experience* (London, 1794).

2. Ibid.

3. Ibid.

4. Samuel Beckett, *Waiting for Godot* (New York: Grove Weidenfeld, 1954).

5. Elizabeth Wordsworth, "If Only the Good were Clever," in *Poems and Plays* (London: Oxford University Press, 1931), n.p.

6. "Lord of the Dance," words by Sydney Carter, music adapted by Sydney Carter from a nineteenth-century Shaker tune, 1963.

Chapter 27

1. Philip Larkin, "Church Going," in *The Norton Anthology of English Literature: The Twentieth Century and After*, 2566.

2. Tennessee Ernie Ford, vocal performance of "Sixteen Tons," by Merle Travis or George S. Davis, released 1955, Capitol CL 14500, 78 rpm. "Sixteen Tons" was first recorded by Merle Travis in 1946.

3. Ibid.

Chapter 28

1. Robert Burns, "To a Mouse," in *The New Penguin Book of Romantic Poetry*, ed. Jonathan and Jessica Wordsworth (London: Penguin, 2003), 254–55.

2. Pierre Teilhard de Chardin SJ, "A Bold Request," in *Hearts on Fire: Praying with Jesuits*, ed. Michael Harter SJ (St. Louis: Institute of Jesuit Sources, 1993), 24.

Chapter 29

1. Robert Herrick, "Upon Julia's Clothes," in *The Norton Anthology of English Literature*, vol. 1, 1654.

Chapter 30

1. Yeats, "A Coat," in *The Norton Anthology of Modern Poetry*, 152.

2. Milton, *Paradise Lost*, bk. 4, lines 505–6.

3. John Keats, "*La Belle Dame Sans Mercy*," in *Keats's Poetry and Prose*, ed. Jeffrey Cox (New York: Norton, 2009), 341–3.

4. Keats, "Ode to a Nightingale," in *Keats's Poetry and Prose*, 457–60.

5. Joni Rodgers, *Bald in the Land of Big Hair* (New York: Harper Perennial, 2002), n.p.

6. I am grateful to Pastor Jon Lemmond for this beautiful image.

7. "Do You Hear What I Hear?" lyrics by Noel Regney, music by Gloria Shayne Baker, 1962.

Chapter 31

1. St. John of the Cross, "If You Want." From the Penguin anthology *Love Poems from God*, copyright 2002 Daniel Ladinsky and used with his permission.

2. William Carlos Williams, "This Is Just to Say," in *The Norton Anthology of Modern Poetry*, 320.

3. Aretha Franklin, vocal performance of "A Natural Woman,"

by Carole King and Gerry Coffin, released 1967, Atlantic A-2441, 33⅓ rpm.

Chapter 32

1. Homer, *The Odyssey*, bk. 21, "The Test of the Bow," trans. Robert Fitzgerald (New York: Knopf, 1992), 404.

2. Bellamy Brothers, vocal performance of "If I Said You Had a Beautiful Body, Would You Hold It Against Me?" by David Bellamy, released 1979, Warner Bros. 8790, 45 rpm. The title is taken from a Groucho Marx quotation.

3. Ibid.

4. Nikos Kazantzakis, *Report to Greco* (London: Faber and Faber, 1973), n.p.

Chapter 33

1. Commonly attributed to Johnson.

Chapter 34

1. Hopkins, "God's Grandeur," in *The Norton Anthology of Modern Poetry*, 101.

2. Matthew Arnold, "Dover Beach," in *The Norton Anthology of Literature*, vol. 2, 1492.

3. Arnold, "Thyrsis," in *The Norton Anthology of English Literature: The Victorian Age*, ed. Carol T. Christ, 7th ed., vol. 2B (New York: Norton, 2000), 1498–1504.

4. Milton, *Paradise Lost*, bk 3, lines 1051–53.

Chapter 35

1. Antoine de Saint-Exupéry, *Le Petit Prince* (Hertfordshire, UK: Wordsworth Editions Limited, 1995), 82.

2. Isak Dinesen, *Out of Africa* (New York: Random House, 1972), 261.

3. Alfred Noyes, "The Highwayman," in *Collected Poems of Alfred Noyes*, vol. 1 (n.p.: Obscure Press, 2008), 265–70.

Chapter 36

1. George Herbert, "The Collar," in *The Norton Anthology of English Literature*, vol. 1, 1609.

2. "My Favorite Things," lyrics by Oscar Hammerstein, music by Richard Rogers, from *The Sound of Music*, 1959.

3. Dorothea Deveaux, letter to author.

4. Donne, "Valediction: Forbidding Mourning," *John Donne's Poetry*, 31–32.

Epilogue

1. J. A. Smith, Oxford Professor of Moral Philosophy, from his opening of his course in 1914, as quoted in *The Oxford Book of Oxford*, ed. Jan Morris (Oxford: Oxford University Press, 1978), 330–31.

ABOUT THE AUTHOR

Carolyn Weber holds her BA from the University of Western Ontario and her MPhil and DPhil degrees from Oxford University. She has been Associate Professor of Romantic Literature at Seattle University; she has also taught at Westmont College, University of San Francisco, and Oxford University. Carolyn and her husband share the joy of parenting three spirited children in Santa Barbara, CA, and London, Canada. Find her online at www.pressingsave.com. For photos and more from *Surprised by Oxford*, visit www.surprisedbyoxford.com.